Politics and Public Policy in Indiana

Prospects for Change in State and Local Government

William P. Hojnacki, Editor
Indiana University at South Bend

Contributing Authors

Raymond H. Scheele
Ball State University

James L. McDowell
Indiana State University

Robert T. Perry
Ball State University

Lloyd Rowe
Indiana University Northwest

Mary Louise Baker
Attorney-at-Law

Ralph Baker
Ball State University

C. James Owen
Indiana-Purdue University Fort Wayne

Leonard M. Fleck
Indiana University at South Bend

KENDALL/HUNT
PUBLISHING COMPANY
Dubuque, Iowa

Library of Congress Catalog Card Number: 83–80344

ISBN 0–8403–2974–1

Printed in the United States of America

B 402974 01

Dedication

To those who gave me encouragement to be a participant in and observer of government and politics; Aunt Mary and Uncle Matt, Aunt Boots and Uncle Stanley, and, of course, Mom and Dad.

Contents

Preface

Once begun, this book took a long time to finish. The extended time was not caused by ineptness on the part of the authors nor was it caused by the fact that the field of Indiana government and politics turned out to be more expansive and complicated than we first anticipated; we knew what we were getting into and were confident of our abilities to complete the project. The delay in getting the book from the stage of being simply a good idea to the stage of offering a completed manuscript was caused by the nature of the state itself and by the difficulties we experienced in attempting to account for all of the factors that could influence the political process in Indiana.

Indiana is a dynamic place. The social structure, the economic system and especially the political system are constantly in a state of change. Even the geography of the state is being altered. It took only a superficial investigation to discover that Indiana fails to live up to its often cited reputation as conservative backwater somehow removed from the mainstream of American life. Thus, the extra time spent putting this book together was caused by the difficulties inherent in capturing even a portion of what Indiana is. In short, the project turned out to be larger than we had expected it to be.

Geographically, socially, economically, and politically Indiana is a rich and diverse state. It has had a rich and varied history—a history that has been vital to the growth and development of the United States. Indiana's population is pluralistic and comes very close to being a microcosm of the country as a whole. The state has its own literary, artistic, and cultural traditions. It is a state that has wealth and poverty, is agricultural and industrial, and is both urban and rural. Because Indiana political system reflects this diversity and richness it is in many ways a unique political system.

We have here only been able to capture a portion of the essence of the state. Even our descriptions and analysis of the state's political system is incomplete. The subject area covered is very broad; circumstances change and events move rapidly. It was simply not possible to include everything that should have been included. An understanding of any political system depends in large measure upon an understanding of the history, geography, economics, and the social and cultural relationships within the entity being governed. While we have tried to provide some analysis of these and other factors that contribute to the functioning of the Indiana political system, we recognize that in many ways our treatment is inadequate. In the interest of providing a broad view of Indiana state and local government and politics, we have sacrificed in-depth analysis of particular aspects of the political system.

What we have tried to provide here is a photograph—in writing—of the Indiana political system circa 1982. We tried to provide some breadth and depth to our photograph by providing both an historical perspective and some projections of what the future will hold, but the book remains essentially a still picture of Indiana state and local government and politics taken in the early 1980's. We are not under the illusion that this book represents the final word on Indiana government and politics. We fully realize that the information we present is at best incomplete and will, under any condition, soon be out of date. In spite of these shortcomings, however, we believe the book is timely and useful. We believe that it will serve to achieve the objectives we had in mind when the project was started.

The primary reason for undertaking this project was to provide ourselves with a new textbook for the courses we teach. It is the result of a need expressed by many people. In surveying Indiana colleges and universities, we discovered that almost all offered courses in state and local government and most offered courses that focused on Indiana. We also discovered, however, that there was very little material that could be used in teaching about Indiana government and politics. The lack of adequate teaching materials is serious in its own right, but it also implies some other problems. It implies a lack of scholarly interest in Indiana and a lack of serious research in the field of Indiana government and politics. Beyond the assumption that many social scientists view Indiana as too parochial for serious research, we do not know why Indiana has been neglected by scholars; but whatever the reasons for this neglect, we hope this book will, at least in part, help compensate for it.

In the end, we hope this book will serve three basic purposes. Our basic objective remains undiluted. The book is designed primarily as an undergraduate text for both generalized public affairs and state and local government courses and for specialized courses emphasizing Indiana. A second objective is to serve the general public by providing information and stimulating interest in Indiana state and local government and politics. The hope here is to encourage citizens to become more knowledgeable, to gain deeper understanding about state and local public affairs, and to strengthen their participation in government and politics at all levels. Ultimately, of course, our goal here is to improve the quality of state and local government in Indiana.

A third objective of this book is to, in different ways, advance the frontiers of knowledge of Indiana government and politics and to encourage new research efforts in the field. The individual essays, each in its own way, serve to synthesize knowledge in specific areas; putting them together, we expect to add a dimension to the broad field of Indiana government and politics that is not often presented. In presenting our material we hope that we have identified new questions and new areas in which research could be pursued. Research should be encouraged rather than discouraged by new publications.

We are enthusiastic about this text and hope others will share our enthusiasm. We are indebted to many other people without whose help this manuscript could never have been published. Appreciation also goes to Dr. Joseph Parker of the University of Southern Mississippi who provided the idea for this book and whose early interest helped make the book possible.

Many persons contributed to the production of the individual essays, and each author could compile his own list of persons to thank. Unfortunately, space limitations prohibit the inclusion of such an extensive list. From the perspective of the editor, however, some persons must be mentioned. If it were not for the help provided by the administration, faculty, and staff of Indiana University at South Bend, the book could not have been published. Chancellor Lester M. Wolfson, Dean of Faculties Gerald E. Harriman, and Assistant Dean of Faculties Karen Rasmussen provided encouragement and, through the IUSB Research and Development Committee, a small stipend to help with the publication costs. In particular, Dr. Frank X. Steggert, Director of the Division of Public and Environmental Affairs, along with the Dean of the School of Public and

Environmental Affairs in Bloomington, Charles F. Bonser, and Associate Dean Roy E. Jumper must be thanked for making divisional and school resources available for this project. The tolerance of my colleagues at IUSB-SPEA in allowing us to siphon off these resources at their expense is deeply appreciated.

Special thanks must go to the departmental secretaries, Ms. Lynn Bertman and Ms. Shirley Klein, for all of the extra hours they put in preparing each draft of the manuscript. And finally, thanks must be given to my wife, Sandy, who took the major responsibility for proofreading the final product.

South Bend, Indiana

1
The State of the State

William P. Hojnacki
Indiana University at South Bend

The Indiana State House, Indianapolis
Courtesy of the South Bend Tribune

State and local government is closest to our hearts—and to our pocketbooks. Yet, very often it is farthest from our mind. National events seem to dominate the news media and, as a result, consume much of our political attention. At the same time, state and local governments are the ones that affect us most directly and are the governments with which we most often deal. In terms of our concern for government and politics, we are somewhat out of balance. One reason for our lack of interest in state and local affairs is that we do not know as much about them as we do about national affairs. While there is little we can—or should—do about the attention given to national political events, we can help in dealing with this imbalance by learning more about our own state and community. Thus, a major objective of this book is to help people better understand state and local government in general and Indiana state and local government in particular. The task is not simple. State and local government and politics everywhere, but especially in Indiana, is complicated and difficult to understand.

In order to achieve its purpose, this book proceeds on two assumptions. The first assumption is that the governmental institutions and the political processes of the State of Indiana will need to change if they are to be capable of meeting the challenges they will face in the last two decades of the twentieth century. Challenges will come from many quarters. Virtually every aspect of life in Indiana is experiencing change in one form or another. The composition of the state's population, its social structure and economic base, and even its physical features are being altered. As demographic, social, economic, and physical changes take place, the demands that citizens place on their government also change. In addition to the demands for good services and low taxes, citizens are now concerned with a new range of things. Environmental protection, the cost and availability of energy, and economic development are just a few of the things in which people are now becoming interested. Other issues will arise in the future. Internal changes will be matched by external changes. Indiana is in competition with the other forty-nine states. With the emphasis in the early 1980's on a "New Federalism" that is supposed to give states more power, Indiana's ability to compete with the other states will become more important. Clearly, with all of these changes taking place and with all of the new challenges that will result from them, it is imperative that the system of government and politics also change.[1]

The second assumption is that Indiana will, in fact, attempt to make the changes necessary to meet the challenges it is bound to face. This assumption is not drawn from speculation, but from historical precedent. Indiana has faced challenges in the past and has responded. In the 1960's and 1970's, for instance, Indiana saw the most ambitious constitutional and legislative reform period in the state's history.

Given these two basic assumptions then, the book proceeds, chapter by chapter, to analyze the political institutions and procedures that citizens use to govern Indiana. Each chapter also attempts to focus on public policy. While the chapters have all been contributed by different authors and thus reflect different styles and approaches, there is a common thread that ties them together. Each includes an historical perspective, an attempt to analyze the institutions and processes in terms of the contemporary world, and an attempt to identify the challenges and choices that Indiana government and politics will face in the last two decades of this century. Each chapter then tries to make some assessment of how the institutions and processes—and the public policies they are likely to generate—will change as Indiana approaches the year two thousand.

The Changing Nature of Government and Politics

The process of government and politics in Indiana may not be totally unique, but it does function somewhat differently than in most other states. One of these differences comes from who participates and why. John Fenton, a noted political scientist, once referred to Indiana as a state that holds two things more important than anything else—basketball and politics—and that at any given time it is difficult to tell which is more important.[2] Whether Professor Fenton's characterization is true or not, there can be little doubt that Hoosiers take their politics (and their basketball) more seriously than most people. Indiana has a high level of citizen participation in public affairs. In the 1970 "off year" elections, for instance, 87% of the voting age residents turned up at the polls; the fifth highest percentage of all states.[3] Voting, of course, is only one form of political participation, and for many Indiana residents it is not the most important. Thousands of Hoosiers participate directly in government service, and thousands of others participate indirectly through the mechanisms of the state's political party system. In addition to Indiana's 92 counties, 565 municipalities, and 1,008 townships, there are hundreds of other special purpose units of government, authorities, boards, commissions, and advisory bodies of all descriptions. Indiana has more than 4,500 "voting precincts," that serve as a base of the state's major political parties. All of these entities, plus state government itself, provide a multitude of opportunities for citizens to participate in the affairs of the state.[4]

At the state level alone, citizen participation is encouraged in several ways. First, Indiana is one of the few remaining industrial states that operates with a part-time, non-professional legislature. It is considered to be a citizen legislature. Second, Indiana, from an organizational perspective, has a weak executive branch. The executive branch is weak in the sense that power is divided among many offices and individuals, and many of the state's administrative and regulatory agencies are controlled by multi-member bipartisan boards or commissions.[5] This arrangement allows many individuals, who would otherwise not be able to do so, to exercise some measure of power at the state level. Third, political parties have encouraged participation in state government by serving as brokers between the government and citizens. Parties have traditionally been able to exercise considerable influence in state-level government, particularly in terms of finding people jobs and dispensing favors.[6]

Over the years, the system of citizen participation in state government seems to have worked reasonably well. The decentralized nature of the executive branch and the informality of the legislature were counterbalanced by a relatively strong party system. It was the party system that gave the power to the governor's office that it lacked constitutionally and statutorally, and that provided some degree of discipline to an otherwise nondisciplined state legislature.

This traditional relationship between the state's party system on one hand and the executive and legislative branches on the other hand is, however, breaking down. Beginning in the late 1960's and extending into the 1980's, both the state government and the party system experienced a number of changes. These changes have had and will continue to have an impact on citizen participation at the state level. The legislature has become more professionalized, and the executive branch has become more centralized. Parties have lost much of their ability to influence the outcome of state government actions, and thus, are themselves weakened. In general, the ability of citizens to participate in state level public affairs has been reduced. In the 1976 presidential election, only 61% of the voting age population turned out at the polls, the sixteenth highest in the country.[7]

Participation in local government remains high, but it too is changing. In the 1960's many local school districts were consolidated, and in the 1970's Indiana attempted, in different ways, to reform local governments and make them more professional. These changes were compounded, as was the case at the state level, by a weakening of the political party system in cities and counties. The primary cause for the reduced power of political parties is a reduction in political patronage available to parties. Pressure from the federal government, the growing power of public employee unions, and a general concern for merit and civil service personnel systems have combined to make patronage, and thus role of political parties, far less important than once was the case.

Clearly then, the Indiana system of government and politics is changing, and the changes are likely to continue for some time to come. These changes, however, are not occurring in isolation. Political change most often follows, rather than precedes, other social and economic changes. Thus, in order to understand political change, it is necessary to understand the changes that are taking place in other aspects of life in Indiana.

The Setting

Indiana is seen by both residents and non-residents alike as being typical of middle America. Indiana does come close to being a microcosm of the country as a whole. Although there are no mountains or oceans, the geography is varied, the population is diverse, and the economic base is multi-dimensional. Indeed, one city—Muncie—has been singled out at the archtypical "Middletown" of America.[8]

Indiana stretches 265 miles from the southern tip of Lake Michigan to the Ohio River. Encompassing some 36,000 square miles, it ranks in area as the thirty-eighth largest state in the nation. Geographically, from north to south, Indiana can be divided into three fairly distinct and roughly equal areas. The northern third of the state has varied physical characteristics. Prior to the coming of European and English settlers, there were gently rolling hills, marshes (now mostly drained), and an abundance of natural lakes. The eastern section of this third of the state was part of a large hardwood forest, while the western portion was part of a great prairie region. Much of the land in both the east and the west portions have subsequently been turned over to agricultural or industrial use, the northern third bears little resemblance to the way it looked in the late 17th Century.

The middle third of the state is very flat and is bisected by the Wabash river system, the largest river system in the state. Once heavily forested, this third of the state now contains some of the most fertile, agricultural land in the world. It is this area that contributes to Indiana's ranking as the third largest producer of soybeans and the fourth largest producer of corn in the country.

The southern third of the state is the least densely populated, quite hilly and remains heavily forested. This portion of the state looks much like it did two hundred years ago. It contains large deposits of coal, limestone, and other minerals and features many caves and underground streams.[9]

Demographically, Indiana is a study in contrasts. About 90% of the land is given over to agricultural uses, but about 65% of the population lives in urban places. Indiana's 1980 population is listed as 5,334,300, making it the twelfth largest state. Indianapolis, the state capital, with a 1980 population of over 750,000, is considered to be one of the largest cities in the country; and there are five cities with populations in excess of 100,000. At the same time, there are over 450 small towns and rural communities.[10]

Indiana's population is diverse. From its beginning as an outpost for French traders, the state has experienced several shifts in the character of its population. The French never attempted to colonize the area. The early settlers were primarily English, and Anglo-Saxon descendants are still the dominant population group in most areas. Many of the early settlers, however, did not come directly from England or even from the Eastern part of the United States. Rather, they came from Tennessee, Kentucky, and other parts of the American South. The influence of these imigrants and their descendants can still be seen in several parts on the state, especially in the lower third. Southern influence in the state was actually increased during the First and Second World Wars when many residents of the rural South moved to Indiana to fill industrial jobs.[11]

Contrasting the influence of the American South in southern Indiana is the European influence in the northern fringe of the state. In the early years of the state, immigrants came from northern and western European countries (Ireland, Germany, Scandinavia, etc.), while in later years they came from southern and eastern European countries (Italy, Poland, etc.). Thus, today the areas from South Bend to the Calumet region (Gary, Hammond) reflect a heavy ethnic population. In addition to these general concentrations, different communities around the state feature

Figure 1.1. Map of Indiana
Source: Indiana Fact Book 1979. State Planning Services Agency Indianapolis, page 14.

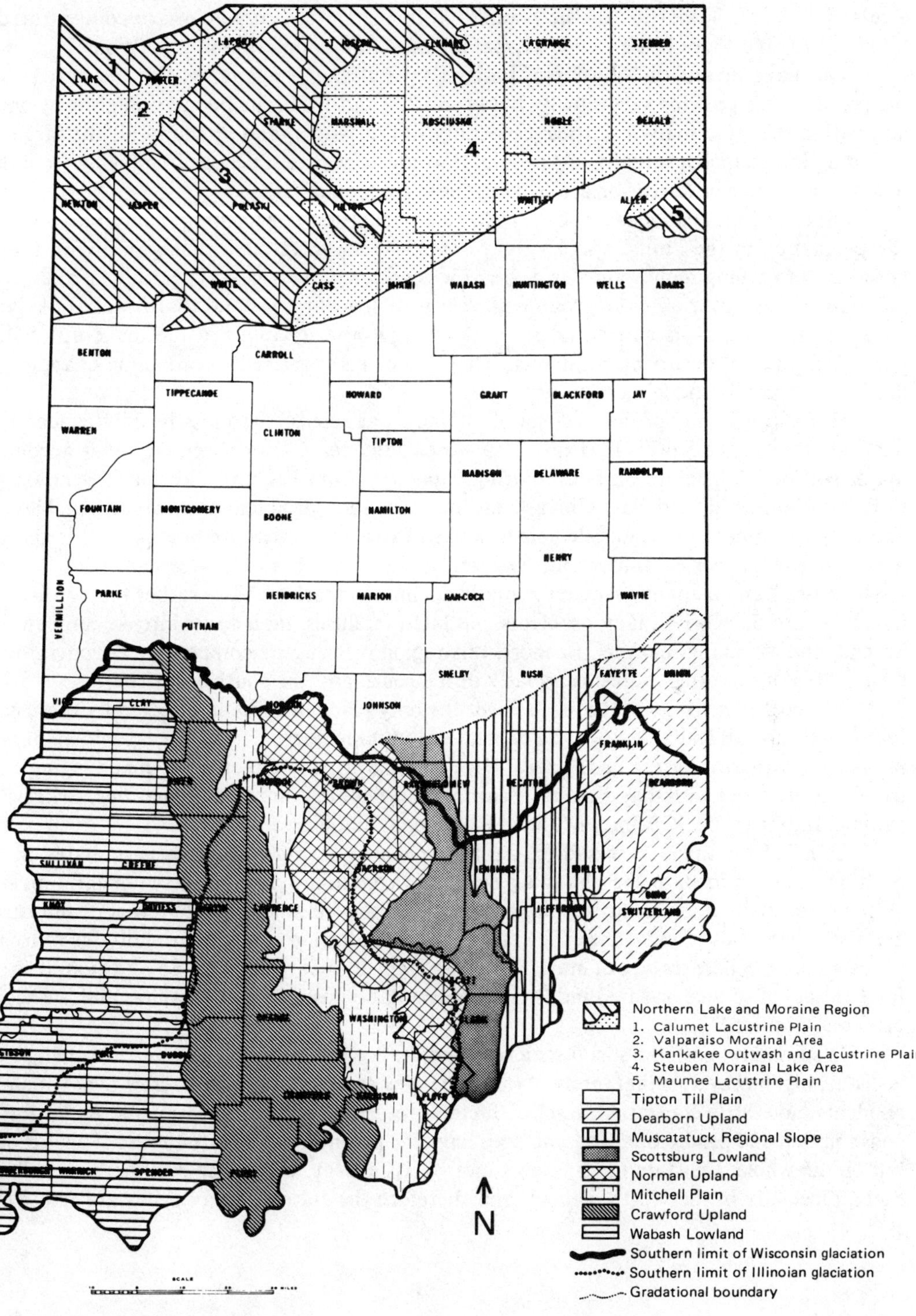

distinct concentrations of populations. For instance, German descendants are important in Jasper; Swiss descendants are important in Bearn; and Amish are important around Nappanee. Each section of the state seems to have its unique population characteristics. Blacks, which account for a relatively small proportion of the population in the state as a whole, are concentrated in the larger cities, and there is a growing Hispanic and Asian population in all regions.

The make-up and distribution of Indiana's population is changing. For the state as a whole, the population is growing very slowly. Between 1970 and 1980, the population grew by only 5.7%; and within the state many counties, especially in the North, and virtually all the largest cities, including Indianapolis, actually lost people. It would appear that people are moving from the cities to suburban and rural areas or are leaving the state altogether.[12]

Other changes can also be seen. Indiana's population is becoming older. The proportion of the population in the "middle age" groups of 35 to 55 years old—that group with the highest potential for earning money and for paying for government services—is getting smaller, while the population group over 60—the group with relatively low earnings and that which is likely to need government services—is getting larger.[13] These and other changes in the make-up of Indiana's population are not occurring randomly. They are directly related to economic changes, and Indiana's economy is changing rapidly.

Historically, the northern fringe of Indiana was one of the most heavily concentrated industrial areas of the world. It is this area—especially the Calumet region—that accounts for a major portion of the state's manufacturing capacity. From Elkhart and South Bend on the east to Gary, Hammond, and East Chicago on the west, such products as steel, automobile, aircraft and farm implement parts, mobile homes, and railroad equipment are produced. It is also a region with major oil refineries. Important, however, is the fact that the largest industries in the region are "mature," and in many cases are actually declining in terms of jobs rather than growing. These industries are beset with many problems: outdated facilities, high costs, intense competition from abroad, and shrinking markets. In short, this region is losing its competitive edge with newer industrial regions in other states, especially in the south and the southwest.[14]

The northern fringe of the state is not the only place in Indiana affected by these economic factors. Almost all Indiana cities are dependent, to some degree at least, on basic manufacturing industries. Almost all areas of the state have been negatively affected by the changing economic trends. Other cities with major manufacturing facilities are Anderson, Columbus, Evansville, Fort Wayne, Indianapolis, Kokomo, Muncie, Richmond, and Terre Haute.[15]

Of all of the areas in the state, the Indianapolis metropolitan area is probably in the best position to accommodate the changing economic conditions. It is an economically diverse city. While it has many manufacturing plants, especially ones related to the automobile industry, there are also other kinds of industries. The city is a transportation center, especially for railroads, and it has a major concentration of state and federal government facilities. In addition, it is a center for a variety of service oriented industries, most notably insurance companies, and is a major food processing center.[16]

In summary, both the social structure and the economic base of Indiana are changing. What is disturbing, however, is that many of these changes are resulting from factors over which Indiana residents have little control. One set of factors, for instance, is the worldwide pattern of energy consumption and production. Indiana does have the potential for greater levels of coal production, but on the whole, the state must import most of its energy, especially oil. Further, Indiana's climate, especially in the North, is cold, and therefore the state's energy needs are relatively high.

Indiana, thus, is at an energy disadvantage to such energy producing states as Louisiana and Texas. A second set of factors is the development of new industrial technologies. Industries such as computers or electronics are, for a variety of reasons, developing elsewhere, and automation is reducing the number of jobs available in Indiana's traditional industries. A third set of factors stems from the relative position the American economy holds compared to the economies of other countries in the world. In particular, such industries as automobiles and steel are facing stiff competition from abroad and, as a result, are seeking to increase their competitive ability. In many cases the companies engaged in these industries are closing their Indiana plants to relocate in modern facilities with lower attendant costs in other states.[17]

If Indiana's economy is to remain viable in the future, and if Indiana's government is to be able to provide the kinds of services that residents want, then the government must be in a position to respond to the economic and social changes that the state is experiencing. Whether or not the state will be able to respond remains to be seen; but if history can be used as a guide, the state will be able to successfully meet these new challenges. The state has had similar challenges in the past and has met them successfully.

Indiana in History

Indiana was carved out of the old Northwest Territory, the first area annexed by the United States following the American revolution. This huge land mass was later divided into the Great Lakes states of Ohio, Indiana, Illinois, Michigan, Wisconsin, and part of Minnesota. Indiana was established as a separate territory in 1801, although its territory was much larger than is encompassed by the current state boundaries. Indiana, with its current boundaries, was admitted to the Union in 1816.[18]

In 1801 there were only about 2,000 white settlers in the area that is now the state, most of whom were located along the Ohio River. While the territory that is now Indiana was visited by French explorers, trappers, and traders as early as 1670, no permanent communities were established the major influx of new residents did not occur until the early part of the 19th century. The first community settled was at Vincennes, which became the first territorial capitol.[19] William Henry Harrison of Ohio was appointed as the Territory's first Governor by President Jefferson in 1801 and served in that capacity until 1809. Harrison, after gaining a reputation as a military leader, went on in 1840 to be elected President. The Indiana General Assembly first convened in 1805. In 1813, the capitol was moved from Vincennes to Corydon, making it the first state capitol. The State Capitol was moved to Indianapolis in 1821.[20]

The years 1800 to 1850 were the pioneer period in Indiana history. The state grew rapidly during this period, especially in the south, and it met and overcame its first series of challenges. The original movement of settlers was from the Ohio River north. Settlement of the northern part of the state did not occur until the latter part of the pioneer period, and rapid growth did not take place until after the Civil War.

During the pioneer period, the major issue facing Indiana was interior development. Growth in the middle third of the state lagged behind growth at northern and southern regions. While the Ohio River provided good transportation access in the south, and the Great Lakes provided transportation routes in the north, central Indiana had only the Wabash River as a water transportation system. The extending of the "National Road" (now U.S. 40) east to Indianapolis in 1840 and the building of the "Michigan Road" (now U.S. 31 and U.S. 421) from the Ohio River to Lake Michigan helped, but the lack of a comprehensive inland water transportation system was thought to be retarding the development of commerce and industry in the state. In response to this perceived need, the state embarked on a massive internal development program based on building a series of canals that were supposed to link the Great Lakes with the Ohio River via the Wabash River system. These projects, undertaken in the 1830's and 40's, were financed by state issued bonds.[21]

In the mid-1840's, with the coming of the railroads, this system began to collapse, and ultimately, the state was forced into bankruptcy. The demise of these projects had a profound impact on state government. Not only did the state choose to write a new state constitution (1851), the one that is still with us today; but the character of state politics was altered until the Civil War.

From 1800 to 1825 almost all Hoosiers were Jeffersonian Republicans, and the first state constitution was a liberal Jeffersonian document. There can be little doubt that if the original constitution had survived the crisis of the 1840's, government and politics in Indiana would have been considerably different from what they turned out to be. After 1825, and coinciding with the period of intense internal development, Indiana residents began to divide their political loyalties. Indeed, between 1830 and the mid-1840's, allegiance was almost equally divided between the Jacksonian Democrats and the National Democrats (later the Whigs) under John Quincy Adams. The state voted for Jackson in 1824, 1828, and 1832 but supported the National Democratic and Whig candidates in 1836, 1840, 1844, and 1848. Between 1830 and 1840 there was a clear movement of the state from the Democrats to the Whigs. One reason that William Henry Harrison was the Whig nominee in 1840 was to insure that Indiana would remain a solid Whig state. The coming internal development crisis, however, gave the Democrats the advantage. The state house was controlled by the Democrats from 1843 to 1860, and the Democrats controlled the writing of the 1851 Constitution which was based on Jacksonian principles.[22]

With the Civil War, the Republican party became the dominant party in the state and remained as the majority party until 1932. During the Civil War, while the vast majority of the residents identified with the North (Indiana was never a slave state), there were a number of areas, particularly along the Ohio River, where sympathy for the Southern cause existed. It was the existence of these areas of Southern sympathy that gave an excuse to Governor Oliver P. Morton to establish a repressive and autocratic regime that also served to strengthen the hand of the Republicans. In effect, he promoted the position that being a Democrat was tantamount to being a Southern sympathizer.[23]

In the period following the Civil War, Indiana went through a second period of rapid growth and development, but this time it was concentrated in the central and northern regions. Indianapolis became a major rail center and could claim the title of being the largest city in the country not on a navigable waterway. In the Southern region the Ohio River continued to provide cheap transportation for coal and limestone, and Lake Michigan facilitated industrial development in the Northern part of the state. The city of Gary, which was eventually to become the state's second largest city, was not founded until after 1900 and was created precisely because of a decision by the U.S. Steel Corporation to build a massive mill on the shores of Lake Michigan. This decision was made because of the opportunity the Great Lakes provided to bring in iron ore and ship out finished products. It was, of course, this period of economic growth and development that laid the foundation of the present day economic difficulties.[24]

The Indiana system of government and politics changed little from 1860 to 1890. As long as the state (and the country) was enjoying peace and prosperity, there was little sentiment to change what was apparently working quite well.[25] As the turn of the century approached, however, new social, economic, and political concerns began to emerge, and Indiana, like the rest of the country, eventually felt the impact of a new populist reform movement. Indeed, in some ways Indiana became a leader of these turn of the century reform efforts. A major reason Indiana was able to assume a leadership role in this populist reform movement was because of the work of Albert Beveridge, a Republican U.S. Senator from 1899 to 1911. As a progressive Republican who backed President Theodore Roosevelt, Beveridge supported progressive legislation for both Indiana and the country as a whole. Indiana was one of the first states to create a Railroad Commission, (that ultimately became the Public Service Commission), an important regulatory body, and in 1915 Indiana established a direct primary for local elections. Indiana also supported the income tax, women's suffrage, direct election of senators, and prohibition amendments to the U.S. Constitution.[26]

The First World War was an economic asset to Indiana. Basic industries continued to grow, and there was a ready market for Indiana agricultural products. After the war, although there was a reduction in the demand for farm products, Indiana became the nation's second largest producer of automobiles. The prosperity generated by the war continued throughout the 1920's, and with it came continued dominance of the Republican Party in state governmental affairs.

The Republican Party of the 1920's, however, lost the progressive flavor it had had earlier in the century under Beveridge's tutelege. As the decade of the Twenties proceeded, the party and the institutions it controlled moved further away from the political center and became increasingly conservative. It was during this period that the Republican Party and, consequently, both Indianapolis city government and state government came under the influence of the Ku Klux Klan. So influential was the Klan that at one point they could even claim control of the Governor's office.[27]

The stock market crash of 1929 and the Great Depression of the early 1930's presented Indiana with a new set of challenges and profoundly affected the course of Indiana government and politics. Nothing since the Civil War affected Indiana as deeply as the Great Depression. In 1930 the Democrats took control of the state house, and in 1932 they won the governorship, an office they held until 1944. In office, the Democrats, especially under Governor Paul V. McNutt (1933–37), not only took steps to implement the "New Deal" programs of the Franklin D. Roosevelt administration, but also took steps to improve their own party position. In an economic sense, Governor McNutt proved to be as effective an advocate of the Democrats as Governor Morton was for the Republicans during the Civil War. A number of changes, both substantive and procedural, were made in the process of state and local government. One effect of these changes was to strengthen the position of political parties by resolidifying the job oriented and patronage politics system that was traditional to Indiana.[28]

During the 1940's Indiana, like other states, diverted many of its resources to the effort of winning the Second World War. This war, however, like the First World War, proved to be economically beneficial to the state. Indiana business, industry, and agriculture prospered. With this prosperity came a return of Republican Party influence, if not dominance, in state government and politics.

While it was the conservative wing of the Republican Party that became dominant in the late 1940's and early 1950's, there was no attempt at a wholesale repeal of the New Deal era legislation. The major impact of this period was that there was little new progressive legislation passed. In particular, there were no serious attempts to alter or reform the make-up of state and local government.[29]

In the 1960's the Democrats, following the election of President John F. Kennedy (1960) and Lyndon B. Johnson (1964), reasserted themselves. The result of this Democratic resurgence was a rebalancing of the two major parties. The state throughout the 1960's and 1970's became essentially a highly competitive two-party state. During this period, in any given election, either the Democratic or Republican Party had an equal chance to win the state. Elections during this period were decided on the basis of either national issues and trends or as a result of the personalities of the candidates involved. In the late 1970's, however, and especially as a result of the 1980 election, it appeared that the Republicans were once again gaining the advantage over the Democrats.

The 1960's and 1970's also saw the start of a new wave of reformism in the state. These reforms were initiated under Democratic administrations but were continued under Republican administrations. The first impetus for these reform efforts came from United States Supreme Court decisions affecting Congressional redistricting and state legislative reapportionment. The basic thrust of these reforms was to reorder and modernize state government. Although there was also an interest in modernizing local government, the first concern at the state level was with the General Assembly. The legislature moved from biannual to annual sessions, salaries were increased, and individual legislators were given increased resources with which to work.

The state Constitution, during this period, was altered with the objective of creating a strengthened executive branch. Amendments were passed to permit the Governor to succeed himself and to have the Governor and Lieutenant Governor of the same party to run as a team. The terms of offices for the minor elected officials (Treasurer, Auditor, etc.) were lengthened from two to four years, and a state primary election system for the nomination of Governor, Lieutenant Governor, and United States Senators was introduced.

The state judicial system was also reformed. The major reform was the adaptation of a Missouri plan for selecting judges at all three levels: trial, appellate, and supreme courts. Other reforms were also implemented on a piecemeal basis in the organization of trial courts.[30]

Local government, too, although in a more limited way, felt the impact of the new wave of reformism. The most dramatic, if not the most significant, reforms at the local level came with the legislatively imposed consolidation of the city of Indianapolis and Marion County government. The resulting "Unigov" has been touted as one of the most progressive urban government reforms in the United States. This reform was followed by less comprehensive changes in local government structure in St. Joseph County and South Bend, and Lake County and Gary.[31]

The state legislature, during this period, also took steps toward loosening the very tight control that state government held over local government. Limited municipal home rule legislation was passed in 1971, and limited county home rule was passed in 1973. Further, in the late 1970's the legislature went a step further and created a Local Government Study Commission that had as its primary goal developing new recommendations concerning local government reform. The work of the Local Government Study Commission finally had an impact with the 1981 session of the General Assembly. This session of the legislature passed a series of bills that extended and further defined the concept of local government home rule and gave local units of government the power, in some limited ways, to reorganize themselves.[32]

The 1960's and 70's also saw some changes in the way that the state level administrative agencies operated. Paralleling the reduced influence of patronage politics was an increase in emphasis on merit employment and new interest on the part of many state employees in collective bargaining. Increasing numbers of state (and local) government workers joined public employee labor organizations.

Changes in all the major policy areas with which the state has an interest could also be seen. With the advent in the late 1960's of a new wave of federally funded programs—especially in the social and human service areas—the state began delivering a wider range of services than had ever been the case before. New programs were developed in environmental protection and in community and economic development. Innovations were made in the state planning and budgetary processes. The state university systems were expanded, and a variety of quality improvement efforts were made in the elementary, secondary, and various specialized educational programs. The state park and recreation systems were expanded, and hundreds of miles of new interstate highways were built. To be sure many program areas such as mental health, corrections, welfare, and others were seen by many observers to be deficient, but even in most of these areas some steps were taken to improve the effectiveness, if not the scope, of the programs involved.

A major policy change occurred in the early 1970's under the administration of Republican Governor Otis Bowen when the state legislature, in anticipation of the national "taxpayer's revolt" of the late 1970's, passed a comprehensive property tax replacement program. This tax package altered the entire state revenue raising procedure. It decreased, then froze, property taxes and increased the state sales tax. The tax program proved to be politically very popular, and it gave the state government additional revenue with which to work. It also, however, severely restricted the ability of local units of government to raise revenue and may well have contributed to an increasing array of local government problems.[33]

Indiana entered the 1980's with the forces of social, economic, and political change hard at work. The full impact of these changes has yet to be determined. What is known is that government did respond to the changing social and economic conditions, but these responses were at best moderate. Whether or not the constitutional, institutional, and procedural changes that were made will prove adequate to meet the new challenges that the state will face is an important question—it is the major question that this book seeks to answer.

Toward the Year 2000

Indiana in the 1980's and 1990's will be a different place than it was in the 1960's and 1970's. A whole new set of challenges will develop. There is growing concern over the cost and availability of energy and a new interest in preserving the environment. Transportation is likely to once again be an import issue, and new, yet to be determined issues are likely to arise out of the fundamental changes that are taking place in the state's economic base and social structure.

Further challenges will arise from the new concern over state-federal relations that emerged from the administration of President Reagan. The "new federalism," as this concept has been called, has as its primary thrust a return of power to the states. The cost of this return of authority from the federal government to the states, however, is that financial support for many programs will be significantly reduced. An important question here is the extent to which state governments in general and Indiana state government in particular are able and willing to take over new and different responsibilities.[34]

Looking toward the year 2000, especially in light of its new responsibilities, it is apparent that Indiana has both assets and liabilities. The state's natural resources remain as a major asset. How we use these resources, however, could be a liability. Those factors that served to make Indiana an attractive place to settle two hundred years ago are still attractive. Coal is in abundant supply, and the land devoted to agriculture is still fertile and productive. Difficulties stem from the fact that coal, considered "dirty," is no longer a primary source of energy, and from the urban sprawl that the state is experiencing. One manifestation of urban sprawl is that prime agricultural land is being turned into shopping centers and housing developments.

Probably Indiana's most important asset is its water supply. In addition to access to the Great Lakes and the existence of many natural lakes and streams, Indiana has created thousands of acres of reservoirs and has a very high average rainfall. There is a danger, however, that this very important resource will be abused. Pollution has been and will continue to be a problem; marshes have been unwisely drained, and the natural drainage patterns of many rivers and streams have been irreversibly altered. Whether or not water remains an asset or becomes a liability depends on how it is used. As other areas of the country face increasingly severe water shortages, this resource in Indiana, if it is managed correctly, could become even more important in the future than it has been in the past. If, on the other hand, it is mismanaged, its availability could become one of the state's major problems.[35]

Indiana has a stable population. For the most part, Indiana residents are well educated and skilled in their various occupational pursuits. To be sure, Indiana has both wealth and poverty, and Indiana cities are facing the same types of urban problems that exist in other parts of the country; but many of the problems in Indiana are not as severe as they are in some other states. Indiana's current population must be considered a relative asset. Capital is available for individual and corporate entrepreneurship. Indiana communities have economic resources, skilled workers, and the facilities to increase economic productivity. If current demographic trends are not altered, however, this asset too could turn into a liability. If the trend that is drawing workers in prime age categories from Indiana and other "frost belt" states to the "sun belt" states continues, then in the future Indiana's aging population may be seen as a liability. This demographic trend can be reversed only if the state's economic liabilities are turned into assets.

In many areas, existing manufacturing facilities are antiquated and underutilized. Many of the industries to which they belong are no longer growing, and many are seeking to relocate their operations in other states. Clearly, Indiana must take the initiative to find new industries and revitalize older ones. Certainly, Indiana has the economic and political intrastructure to accomplish this task.

Indiana's major health care, educational, and social service institutions—both public and private—must be considered as an asset to the state. Indiana's system of higher education, vocational and technical schools, public and private colleges and universities, and even the state's medical, dental, and law schools are recognized for their quality. Indiana has a good health care system and an outstanding state park and recreation area program. The difficulty in viewing these state institutions as an important asset is that they are not as static as the term "institution" must connote. Both institutions and the environments in which they function are continually changing. Unwise budget cuts or unacceptable interference in their operation by government could turn these assets into liabilities.

The major question Indiana faces as it approaches the year 2000 is not one of measuring its advantages against its disadvantages or somehow attempting to see if its assets outweigh its liabilities. The question is how does the state seek to preserve and exploit, for society's benefit, its assets while overcoming its liabilities? The country and the world are changing, and Indiana must change with them.

The state of the State of Indiana is thus one of change, and this change is pervasive. While the old problems are not automatically disappearing, new and different problems of governance are constantly emerging, and all must somehow be dealt with. These challenges are not insurmountable. The precedent has been set, the population is willing, and the institutions are capable. The basis for instituting the needed changes has been established. Thus, the question is not *if* Indiana will institute change but how the change will be instituted. It is this question then that is the subject of the chapters that follow.

Notes

1. *A National Agenda for the Eighties: A Report of the President's Commission for a National Agenda for the Eighties*. Washington, D.C.: U.S. Government Printing Office, (1980) pp 1–10.
2. Fenton, John. *Midwest Politics*. New York: Holt, Rinehart and Winston, (1966). See the section on Indiana politics.
3. 1973, *Information Please Almanac*. New York: World Telegraph and Sun, (1972). Ahead of Indiana Were Utah 95.8%, South Dakota 91.3%, Idaho 88.4%, Maine 87.7%, New Hampshire was the lowest in the country at 58.4%.
4. *Here Is Your Indiana Government*, (18th Ed.), Indianapolis, Indiana: Indiana State Chamber of Commerce, (1977) pp 61–99.
5. Indiana in many cases requires bipartisan participation; e.g., mandated participation of Democrats and Republicans rather than nonpartisan participation where no party affiliation is noted.
6. See Fenton, John. *Midwest Politics, op. cit.* The author describes Indiana as having a "job oriented" political party system.
7. See *The World Almanac and Book of Facts, 1978*. New York: Newspaper Enterprise Association, (1977). Part of the reduced proportion of the voting age population actually voting can be accounted for because of lowering the voting age from 21 to 18.
8. Lynd, Robert S. and Lynd, Helen Merrel. *Middle Town in Transition: A Study in Cultural Conflicts*. New York: Harcourt Brace and World, Inc., (1937). This study was a follow-up study on one done ten years earlier by the same authors.
9. See Packard, Leonard O., Overton, Bruce, and Wood, Ben D. *Geography of the World*. New York: The MacMillan Company, (1956) pp 155–180.
10. "Advance Reports of the 1980 Census of Population and Housing: Indiana," Washington, D.C., U.S. Department of Commerce, (1981).
11. See Fenton, John. *Midwest Politics, op. cit.*, and Barnhart, John D. and Carmony, Donald F. *Indiana from Frontier to Industrial Commonwealth*, vol. I, New York: Lewis Historical Publishing Company, (1954).
12. "Advance Reports of the 1980 Census of Population and Housing: Indiana," *op. cit.*
13. *Ibid.*
14. *A National Agenda for the Eighties: A Report of the President's Commission for a National Agenda for the Eighties, op. cit.*
15. *World Almanac and Book of Facts*, (1978), *op. cit.*
16. *Ibid.*
17. *A National Agenda for the Eighties: A Report of the President's Commission for a National Agenda for the Eighties, op. cit.*
18. The "Northwest" territories were ceded to the United States in the Treaty of Paris in 1783, the treaty that officially ended the American Revolutionary War.
19. Barnhart and Carmony, *Indiana from Frontier and Commwealth*, vol. I, *op. cit.*, p 84.
20. *Ibid.*, pp 97–109.
21. *Ibid.*, pp 161–180.

22. *Ibid.*, pp 182–199, 276–298, and 388–407.
23. Barnhart, John D. and Carmony, Donald F. *Indiana from Frontier to Commonwealth,* vol. II New York: Lewis Publishing Co., (1954), pp 1–16.
24. *Ibid.*, p 129–157, 201–252.
25. *Ibid.*, pp 308–326.
26. *Ibid.*, pp 308–400.
27. *Ibid.*, pp 389–400.
28. *Ibid.*, p. 475–488.
29. *Ibid.*, pp 489–504.
30. See Peirece, Neal R. and Keefe, John. *The Great Lake States of America.* New York: W. W. Norton, and Co., (1980).
31. See Bollens, John C. and Schmandt, Genry G. *The Metropolis,* (4th ed). New York: Harper and Row, (1982), pp 320–322.
32. "Understanding the New Local Government Law." Indianapolis, Indiana: Local Government Study Commission, (1981).
33. Owen, C. James and Hall, Dean R. "Financing Local Government in Indiana," Fort Wayne, Indiana: Taxpayers Research Association, (1980).
34. Kailo, Andrea. "Reforming the Federal System: Agenda from the States," *State Legislature.* (February, 1981), pp 5–9.
35. *A National Agenda for the Eighties: A Report of the President's Commission for a National Agenda for the Eighties, op. cit.*

2
Political Parties in Indiana

Raymond H. Scheele
Ball State University

Voters at a party rally
Courtesy of the South Bend Tribune

If one were to choose as a proud grouping those American states whose politics are probably the most decent and worthy of respect, one would group Wisconsin, certainly, with Minnesota, California, and Connecticut. And if one were to choose those states whose politics (excluding the baroque courthouse states of the South) are the most squalid, corrupt, and despicable, then one would add West Virginia, to that Jukes family of American politics that include Indiana, Massachusetts, and Texas.

Theodore H. White, The Making of the President, 1960

The unique quality of Indiana politics was the extent to which 'corrupt practices' were institutionalized and accepted as a normal part of the political game by the press and citizenry of the state.

John H. Fenton, Midwest Politics

Political scientists and journalists long have marvelled at the unique character of Indiana politics, where political practices that were condemned by reformers at the end of the last century still flourish in the 1980's. Yet, while reports of "corrupt" practices are common to Indiana's political system, the state also has produced several political leaders of national recognition. Indiana has had two Democratic National Chairmen, Frank McKinney, Sr. (1952) and Paul M. Butler (1954–60). In the past twenty years Indiana has seen one serious but unsuccessful campaign for a Presidential nomination conducted by one of its U.S. Senators (Birch Bayh). In this same time, in Indiana's congressional delegation there has been a Minority Leader of the House of Representatives (Charles Halleck), a Majority Whip in the House (John Brademas) and a Chairman of the House Rules Committee (Ray Madden). In 1981 the two national women's groups of the Democratic and Republican Parties were headed by Hoosiers (Patty Evans and Betty Rendel, respectively). The President of the National League of Cities was the Mayor of Indianapolis (William Hudnut). Mayor Richard G. Hatcher of Gary, Indiana, served as the President of the U.S. Conference of Mayors.

Outside observers may leave Indiana with an impression of people laced together with political corruption and venality, but another measure of a system is the caliber of leaders emerging from it. On this latter measure, Indiana's political system ranks high.

The combination of "corruption" and leadership in Indiana is captured in a comment by two recent observers of Indiana politics: "In reality, Indiana is a place of incongruous contrasts."[1] Understanding these contrasts requires a knowledge of the structure of Indiana's political parties, an insight into the way they finance their operations and nominate their candidates, and a view of the behavior of Hoosiers as they cast their ballots on election day.

The Party Organization

The purpose of a political party is to win office. To accomplish this purpose several functions must be performed, including the nomination of candidates, the orchestration and financing of campaigns, and the mobilization of voters for selected candidates. These functions have been performed traditionally by the political party organization, which is an elaborate structure established and regulated by state law.[2] Both parties operate with the same legal structure, with state law specifying the various levels of organization and the manner in which people are selected to serve as party officials.

The precinct organization is the base of the party structure. The number of precincts in Indiana is determined by the 92 counties, in which elected county commissioners draw precinct lines. This process has resulted in nearly 5,000 precincts in Indiana. On the first Tuesday after the first Monday in May in even-numbered years, Indiana's statewide primary election is held.

On the ballot in each precinct are the candidates for precinct committeeman. Indiana state law provides for a loose form of the "closed primary." Voters must publicly declare to the election judges whether they are voting in the Democratic or the Republican primary. The winner of the precinct committeeman's job is the person receiving the plurality of ballots from those self-declared members of his or her party in the precinct. After the primary election the precinct committeeman appoints a vice-committeeman of the opposite sex. This selection process results in nearly 10,000 precinct officials statewide for each party.

After the primary election the precinct committeemen and vice-committeemen from each county meet in their county convention to elect a chairman, vice-chairman, secretary and treasurer for the county committee. The county chairman and vice-chairman must be members of the opposite sex.[3]

The county chairmen and vice-chairmen in each of Indiana's ten congressional districts subsequently meet to elect a district chairman and vice-chairman, who are also members of the opposite sex. These two district officials automatically become members of the state central committee. Throughout the 1960's and 1970's Indiana had eleven congressional districts. The 1980 census of population resulted in the loss of one congressional seat, bringing the total number of congressional districts down to ten. Consequently, beginning with the 1982 primary, the state central committee of each party will have twenty voting members. These twenty people (ten men and ten women) elect a state chairman and vice-chairman who are members of the opposite sex. The state chairman is a powerful figure within the party, acting as a key political advisor and "patronage dispenser" when the party controls the governorship, and serving as the chief party spokesman when the party is out of power. The ways in which Indiana's two political parties are structured ranks the parties among the highest in terms of party organization authority of all the states.[4]

The organizational structure of the political parties in Indiana is illustrated in Figure 2.1.

The pyramid-shaped structure of Indiana's parties has certain consequences for the way in which the organizations function on a day-to-day basis. The higher one goes on the pyramid the fewer people there are to select leaders and invoke accountability. For example, a state chairman in the 1980's can be elected with a majority of only 11 votes in the state central committee. This fact makes for a highly personalized system of party governance. It also means that it is extremely difficult to mount a successful factional campaign to depose an incumbent chairman.[5] The persistence of the precinct, county, district, and state party officials helps explain why certain patterns of party activity continue from year to year in Indiana.

The persistence of these patterns of party activity provide the major reason why Indiana is considered one of the last bastions of political "machines" in America. According to the authors of one of the most widely consulted political almanacs:

> "The most powerful political machines still functioning in the United States are not to be found in the big cities of the East Coast, but rather in the heart of Middle America: in the city of Chicago, of course, and in the state of Indiana. The machine headed for so many years by Mayor Daley is more famous, but the Indiana machines, if less well known, are probably in better shape, as they hum away in Indianapolis, the state's other big cities, and practically all of Indiana's 92 county courthouses."[6]

Political machines must provide incentives to people to work for the "organization" and vote for the candidates of the party. Traditionally, the most important incentive is a job. Hence, in states where patronage is abundant one is more likely to find political organizations that are well organized and have developed regularized methods of "getting out the vote" on election day. Unfortunately, there are few accurate studies on the extent of political patronage in the states.[7] One

Figure 2.1. Party organization chart
Adapted from *Here Is Your Indiana Government*, Indianapolis: Indiana State Chamber of Commerce, 18th Ed. 1977, page 144.

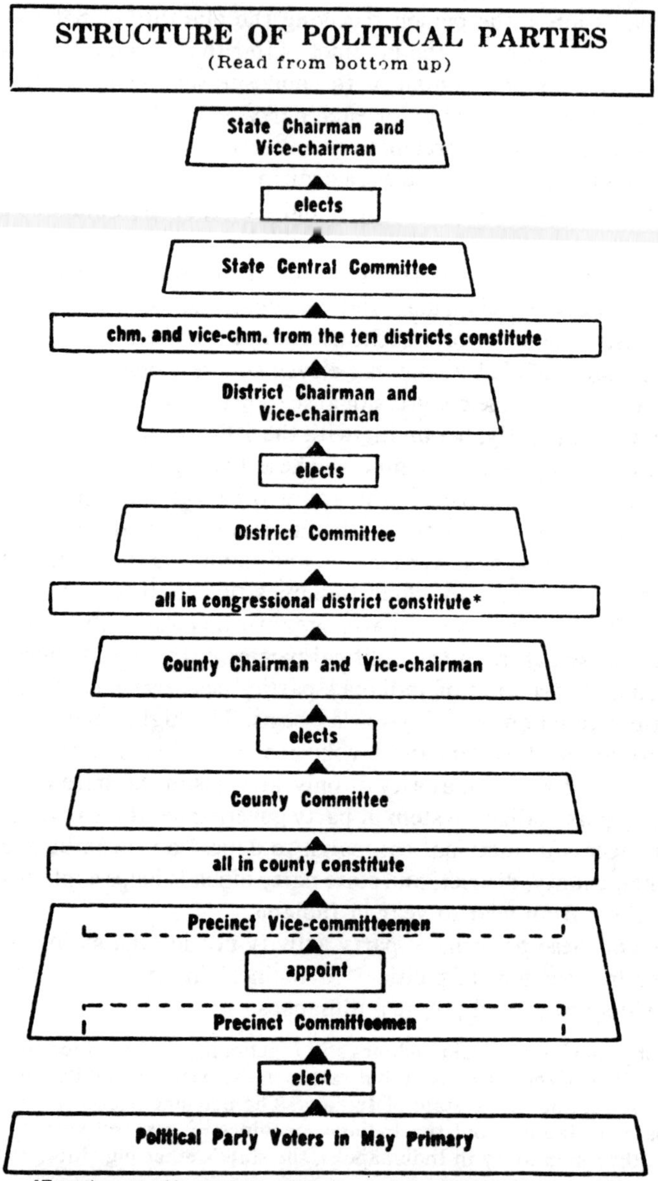

*Exceptions to this provision occur in counties which contain one district wholly within their boundaries, plus part of one or more additional districts also within their borders (Lake and Marion counties). Each political party may establish its own rules governing the naming of county representatives on the committee of a district which is only partly within the county. . . . The county chairman in these counties may serve as, or appoint, the committee members to represent the county on the committee of the district wholly within the county.

of the reasons for this is that state and local personnel systems, including those in Indiana, have not kept pace with modern administrative practices that allow accurate classification of public employees. Moreover, there are certain customs and legal provisions in the states that allow public functions to be performed by people who will not appear on any personal listing of public employees. Contracts for services, such as for consultants and lawyers, are examples of this new form of political patronage. But whatever the problems are in terms of measuring the extent of patronage, Indiana's reliance on it appears to be diminishing, much to the chagrin of many public officials and party leaders.[8] Federal court decisions have severely restricted the power of elected officials to dismiss employees for partisan reasons. Coupled with federal guidelines on employee hiring and retention in those positions funded with federal dollars, these decisions have undermined the strength of the patronage system. But this system permeated Indiana politics for generations, and in its latter days the incentive of jobs remains as a major undergirding of the state party system.

Financing Indiana's Political Parties

Patronage, in its many forms, serves as a major source of money for the two political parties. The most famous (or infamous) method of raising money for the political parties is the "2 percent club," originally started in the 1930's under Democratic Governor Paul V. McNutt, one of Indiana's more progressive governors. The "2 percent club" refers to the fact that all patronage employees should donate 2 percent of their gross salary to the political party in power. It is expected that these donations will be made in cash or personal check to the party's central committee. Both the Democratic and Republican parties employ this method, although the pressure of recent court decisions has undermined the blatent solicitation of 2 percent donations and party officials and office holders alike now contend the practice is totally "voluntary" and no threats of dismissal are made when a public employee refuses to contribute.

It is impossible to trace the amount of money that actually pours into party coffers from the voluntary contributions from patronage workers, although it is generally believed the practice raises several hundreds of thousands of dollars each year. At the state level such contributions are made to the state central committee of the party controlling the governor's office. At the county level the donations are received by the county central committee of the party controlling the office in which the employee works. Local officials occasionally refuse to turn their 2 percent money over to the county central committee, choosing instead to use it for their own campaigns or to spend it in support of a friend's candidacy for another office. When this happens without the blessing of the county chairman, it is a clear signal of a factional dispute within the county organization.

The persistence of the 2 percent club can be attributed to the elaborate political clearance system used by both parties in obtaining public jobs for individuals. Although the exact nature of the system varies from term to term, an applicant for a patronage job is expected to obtain political clearance from his or her precinct committeeman, county chairman and, if it is a state job, from the state chairman. These party officials can exercise "veto" power over the hiring of a person they believe will not support the party organization or the party official.

In recent years, the political fund-raising dinner has replaced the direct donations from the 2 percent club in many cities and counties. Most party central committees sponsor an annual dinner (Jefferson-Jackson Day for the Democrats, Lincoln Day for the Republicans) in which patronage workers are expected to buy and sell tickets. The fund-raising dinner has the advantage of expanding the base of contributors to the party by soliciting contributions from non-party people, businesses, political action committees and labor unions.

Another major source of funds for the two parties is the revenue produced from the sale of automobile licenses in the state. The party controlling the governor's chair is awarded the "concession" for license branches in all 92 counties. The county outlets are operated by private firms formed by the county chairman and other local party officials. The extra service fees paid by motorists when they obtain their licenses actually go into the coffers of the private firm which, in turn, makes direct contributions to the party committee and various campaign committees. On a statewide basis, it is estimated that approximately ten million dollars are raised from these extra service fees, out of which the branch operators must pay the costs of doing business (e.g., rent, utilities, salaries).[9] From the money that pours into the county committees from these fees, the state central committee of the party controlling the governor's office assesses each license branch a certain fee for every license sold. This money is used to help finance the operations of the state central committee and the various statewide campaigns. In 1980 the Republican State Central Committee realized almost $200,000 from this assessment against the license branches.[10]

The county chairmen controlling the license branches have formalized a reward system for contributors to the local party by reserving low license plate numbers for individuals and firms that donate to the party. The issuance of county license plate numbers to motorists is totally within the control of the local license branch. Low numbers are assigned on a sliding scale depending on the amount contributed to the party. In Marion County (Indianapolis) a number "1" license plate goes to contributors of $1,000 or more. Number "2" goes to those contributing $300; number "3" to those giving $150, and so on.[11] The local political leaders and the party contributors therefore receive a visible token for their support of the county organization.

In 1977 the Indiana General Assembly, with bipartisan support, expanded the license branch funding system to both parties by authorizing the purchase by motorists of personalized license plates. A motorist must pay an extra charge of $40 for the plate. Part of the money is retained by the license branch and some goes to the state bureau of motor vehicles. The remaining amount ($30) is divided equally between the two state central committees. Each state committee, in turn, divides its share equally with the county central committee in the county in which the plate was purchased. This system of license plate funding assures the party that is not in power that some revenue will be derived from the operations of the license branches.

The political control of license branches is coming under increasing attack. No other state permits such open control of license branches by a political party, and critics contend that the fee system forces individuals to make political contributions against their will. Some Democratic state legislators filed a law suit in 1981 to end the patronage-based license branch system and it appears that there is growing sentiment in the Democratic Party to abolish the practice. Of course, aside from the money derived from the personalized license plates, the Democratic Party has not received license branch revenue since 1968, the last year they controlled the governor's office. Even without a court verdict against the license branch operations, it is likely that certain reforms will come. One of these reforms is likely to be an open accounting of all funds received by the license branches. Currently, a license branch is audited only on the funds remitted to the state bureau of motor vehicles. Another result may be that the general assembly will have to confront directly the issue of public financing of statewide elections. This issue has been avoided in Indiana in spite of the increasing costs of campaigns.

Campaign costs in Indiana are high. On a per vote basis, Indiana is near the top among all states on the amount of money spent in statewide election contests.[12] In the 1980 race for the U.S.

Senate, between incumbent Democrat Birch Bayh and U.S. Representative Dan Quayle, $4,516,016.09 was spent.[13] With 2,198,376 Hoosiers voting in the general election, the cost of that race per vote was slightly more than $2.05.[14]

Several factors other than inflation are contributing to the increased costs of campaigns. Over the past twenty years, television advertising has become the dominant form of political communication, and the expense of producing and purchasing television time has driven up campaign costs in all states. Indiana is particularly affected by this reliance on television because of the numerous TV "markets" in the state. The dominant market is Indianapolis, where the TV signals cover approximately one-half of all households in Indiana. Fort Wayne, South Bend, Evansville and Terre Haute also cover significant numbers of homes. But commercials in all these markets still leave significant portions of the state uncovered. Much of Southern Indiana receives television coverage from Louisville, Kentucky or Cincinnati, Ohio. The heavily populated Northwest portion of Indiana is in the Chicago television market. Consequently, for a campaign to saturate the state with political commercials, it is necessary to buy time in eight different markets, three of which are out-of-state, and some of which are large markets where costs are high.[15]

Another reason for escalating campaign costs is the use of primary elections for nominating U.S. Senators and the Governor. Indiana moved to the direct primary for these offices in the mid-1970's, and it is estimated that primary elections increase campaign costs by about one-third.[16] A final factor affecting the cost of campaigning is Indiana's reliance on the patronage system. Most of the attention directed to patronage politics focuses on the political clearance needed to obtain a job and the amount of money that is raised through donations made by workers on the public payroll. But the other side of "job oriented politics" is the amount of money required to pay political workers in the counties. Party organizations in the larger counties are expected to reimburse precinct committeemen and volunteers for expenses incurred in election activities. Such payments amount to several thousands of dollars. The patronage worker is therefore involved in a two-way flow of political money. He or she may contribute to the campaign but is likely to receive at least a portion of the money back for election day "expenses." The patronage system in Indiana locks the parties into a financing mechanism out of which it is difficult to escape.

Nominations and Elections

Three out of every four years there are elections in Indiana. There is the normal cycle of presidential and "off-year" elections. Sandwiched between these, preceding the presidential election year, is the year in which city and town elections are held. Figure 2.2 shows the offices which are up for election in each of these years.

The party elections, or primaries, are held the first Tuesday after the first Monday in May. The general election coincides with the national date, the first Tuesday after the first Monday in November.

Indiana has moved only recently to the direct primary for the nomination of statewide officials. 1976 was the first year in over a generation in which the U.S. Senate and the Governor were nominated by primary election voters instead of the respective state political party conventions.

The two state political conventions play an important role in the party system. Whereas they no longer nominate candidates for the U.S. Senate or for Governor, they retain this power for all other statewide offices.[17] This nominating power makes the Indiana state political party conventions among the most powerful in all 50 states. Delegates to the state conventions are chosen in their respective party primaries, where they appear on the ballot seeking the office of "Delegate

Figure 2.2. Four-year election cycle of Indiana offices

Presidential Election Year (Every 4 even-numbered years, 1984, 1988, 1992, etc.)	**City and Town Elections** (Every 4 odd-numbered years preceding presidential election, 1983, 1987, 1991, etc.)	**Off-Year Elections** (Every 4 even-numbered years between presidential elections, 1986, 1990, etc.)
President/Vice-President of the United States	Mayor	Secretary of State
Governor/Lt. Governor	City Council	Treasurer of State
State Attorney General	City Clerk	Auditor of State
State Superintendent of Public Instruction	Town Board	Recorder of Supreme and Appellate Courts
Reporter of Supreme and Appellate Courts	Town Clerk-Treasurer	U.S. House of Representatives (10 districts)
U.S. House of Representatives (10 districts)		One-half of the State Senate (25 of 50 seats)
One-half of the State Senate (25 of 50 seats)		State House of Representatives (100 seats)
State House of Representatives (100 seats)		Selected County Officials
Selected County Officials		Township Officials

to the State Convention." The sole function of the delegate is to attend the state convention, for which he is not paid, and vote for nominees, the party rules and the party platform.

The movement to primary election nominations for the U.S. Senate and Governor has undoubtedly weakened the power of the state conventions. But this move away from the state convention enjoyed the support of Hoosiers. In a statewide public opinion survey conducted in 1980, 46.3 percent of all respondents stated they favored the direct primary as the method for nominating candidates for Governor. Only 5.7 percent stated they preferred the state conventions to name the nominees. A sizeable proportion of the sample, however, (39.6%) stated they wanted some type of combination between the direct primary and the state convention.[18] There is significant support among Hoosiers to fashion a combination between the direct primary form of nomination and the convention system. Other states use such a combination system, usually involving state convention endorsements of candidates, in which the delegates control which candidates will appear on the primary election ballot. For example, in Colorado any candidate receiving at least 20 percent of the convention vote gets on the primary ballot; New York specifies a 25 percent convention vote.[19] For Indiana to change its nomination process in this fashion would require a change of dates for the meeting of the conventions and a change in the way convention delegates are selected, since they are currently elected in the primary. Such massive structural changes are unlikely to occur in a state noted for the persistence of existing procedures.

It is too early to tell what impact the expansion of the direct primary will have on Indiana's party system. In both 1976 and 1980 the Republican Party enjoyed uncontested races for the gubernatorial nomination whereas the Democrats had contests both years. There is some data suggesting that state convention nominations for important offices help make a political party more united or "cohesive" by bringing together all factions to wage battle against the opposition in November.[20] But the success of the Indiana Republican Party in avoiding hotly contested primaries for Governor suggests that a cohesive party depends on factors other than the method of nomination.[21]

Competition between the Democratic and Republican Parties in the general election, while always spirited in Indiana, has been declining in recent years. The Republican Party has won every gubernatorial election since 1964, with victories exceeding 55 percent of the vote in 1972, 1976 and 1980. Throughout the 1970's the Republicans maintained control of the state legislature, losing the House of Representatives for two years in the 1974 elections and losing control of the State Senate for two years following the 1976 election.

The degree of inter-party competition has been measured in the 50 states in various ways. In the most widely used measure, Indiana has always been ranked as a two-party competitive state.[22] The measuring scale is based on four factors: (1) the average percent of the popular vote won by Democratic gubernatorial candidates; (2) the average percent of the seats in the State Senate held by the Democrats; (3) the average percent of the seats in the State House of Representatives held by the Democrats; and (4) the percent of all terms for Governor, State Senate, and House in which Democrats had control.[23] This scale fails to incorporate measures for election contests or results involving federal offices (U.S. Senate, Congress) or lower level state offices.[24] The scale results in a figure carried to four decimal places that indicates the extent to which a state party system is purely competitive. When the figure is .5000 the parties are evenly divided; when the figure exceeds .5000 the partisan advantage is with the Democrats; when the figure is below .5000 the advantage is with the Republicans.

Austin Ranney, in previous calculations of scale scores for all states, ranked Indiana as a two-party competitive state with a score of .3545 for the years 1946–1963.[25] In a later version covering the years 1956–1970 Indiana's score increased to .4450, thereby indicating an increased level of two-party competition, with the advantage remaining with the Republicans.[26] In recomputing Indiana's score for the years 1970–1980, however, the score drops back to .3550, virtually the same competitiveness score that Indiana earned for the years 1946–1963.

These figures suggest that the success of the Democratic Party in the 1960's was only a temporary surge in party fortunes which soon receded. The Republican victories have not converted Indiana into a one-party state, but the extent of their success has led prominent Democrats to question whether or not their Party can successfully compete without external help. Their thoughts are characterized by Neal Peirce and John Keefe as follows:

> ". . . Democrats win statewide office in Indiana only when a fluke occurs. The most telltale signs of an approaching 'fluke,' or Democratic victory, they said, are a split among the Republicans, a public trend toward a new face or a new style of politics, or a strong (for Indiana) presidential candidate at the top of the ticket."[27]

But the "fluke theory" of Democratic success fails to explain Democratic domination of Indiana's congressional delegation. Since the 1974 election, Democrats have maintained a majority of Indiana's 11 congressional seats. The redistricting of congressional seats on the basis of the 1980 census places this Democratic majority in jeopardy, but the advantages enjoyed by incumbents make it likely that several incumbent Democrats will win reelection from their new districts.

The Democratic defeats at the state level have not been repeated at the local level. Mayors and city councils in Indiana are elected in years in which no other offices are on the ballot. In these years Democrats have maintained the majority of the mayors in Indiana's larger cities.[28]

Finally, a point that is overlooked by the "fluke theory" of Democratic success is the fact that more Hoosiers consider themselves to be Democrats than Republicans. The Republicans have managed to fashion recent statewide victories in spite of the fact that more voters indentify themselves with the opposing party. Explaining this incongruity in Indiana's electoral process requires a close look at the way Hoosiers vote on election day.

Table 2.1. Partisan Identification in Indiana, 1980

Strong Demo	Not-Very Strong Demo	Independent Demo	Independent	Independent Republican	Not-Very Strong Rep.	Strong Rep.	D/K N/A	Total
15.1 (15.0%)	169 (16.7%)	141 (14.0%)	118 (11.7%)	128 (12.7%)	138 (13.7%)	122 (12.1%)	41 (4.1%)	1008 100.0%

Source: John D. Cranor, Gary Crawley, R. T. Perry, Thomas Sargent and Raymond H. Scheele, *A Summary Report: A 1980 Survey on Voting and Citizen Attitudes in Indiana,* 1980. Bureau of Government Research, Ball State University.

Voting Behavior in Indiana

In a May 1980 survey of adult Hoosiers, respondents were asked to classify themselves according to the political party with which they identified. The question was: "Generally speaking, do you consider yourself to be a Democrat, a Republican, or an Independent?" If the respondent identified as a Democrat or a Republican, a follow-up question was asked: "Do you consider yourself to be a strong Democrat (Republican), or a not-very-strong Democrat (Republican)?" If the respondent replied "Independent" to the initial question, he or she was then asked "Which of the two parties do you lean toward?" This sequence of questions permits a seven-fold classification of partisan identification. These data are reported in Table 2.1.

As the responses clearly show, Democrats enjoy an "edge" in the electorate of nearly six percentage points. Those classifying themselves as strong Democrats or not-very-strong Democrats total 31.7 percent, while those in the two Republican categories total 25.8 percent of the electorate. But the partisan identifiers within each party are outnumbered by the independents. By classifying those who respond "Independent" to the initial question, the data show that 38.4 percent of the electorate consider themselves independents, although only 11.7 percent profess not to even "lean" toward one of the two parties.

While the Democrats hold an advantage in the electorate in terms of party identification, the built-in-edge is not so large as to preclude Republican victories if the GOP finds the right formula to appeal to Hoosier voters. The various elements in such a formula include holding the Republican identifiers and carrying the vast majority of the independent vote; appealing to disenchanted Democrats; and making every effort to turn out Republican voters on election day while relying on the Democrats to have lower participation rates. Throughout the 1970's the Republican party has managed to weld these elements into a formula that has produced victory in most statewide races.

The Democrats are the "majority-party-in-the-electorate" in Indiana, but their lead is not massive and their failure in recent years to win statewide elections suggests that Indiana may be in the throes of realignment—converting from a Democratic to a Republican majority in terms of the self-identification of voters.

The last realignment of the party system on the national level occurred from 1928 to 1936. In this realigning era the New Deal Coalition was formed and the Democrats emerged as the national majority party-in-the-electorate. This national realignment had its Indiana counterpart.

As described by Hyneman, Hofsttter and O'Conner, the elections of 1930, 1932 and 1936 were particularly important ones, redistributing the electoral strength within the party system. The Indiana realignment is summarized in the following way:

> The critical changes were accomplished in two sequences of elections: first, the downward plunge of Republican support and ascendency of the Democratic party in the 1930's, and second, the recovery of support that the Republican party enjoyed as the New Deal took shape and reaction to it set in. Since the state leaned heavily to the Republican side throughout the 1920's, it will be appropriate as well as convenient to refer to the shifts and readjustments of party strength as changes in the fortunes of the Republican party.[29]

The decline of Republican fortunes in the 1930's, as measured by actual votes cast in elections, reveals that there was a remarkable conversion taking place. Urban voters moved massively to the Democratic party (this movement was most pronounced in Lake County), but in many rural counties of the state there appears to have been a countermovement toward the Republicans. In fact, the net partisan shift favored the Republican party in two-thirds of Indiana's counties (60 of 92).[30] But while many Hoosiers were actually changing their party identification during the 1930's, much of the realignment was a product of new voters deciding to cast their ballots. "It appears that the induction of previously nonvoting citizens into the political arena significantly changed the composition of the electorate, to the special advantage of the Democratic party."[31] The surge in turnout was more pronounced in the urban counties than in the rural counties, and this fact helps explain the inability of the Democratic party to sustain its New Deal gains in Indiana. In Indiana urbanites do not turn out at the polls in the same proportion as rural dwellers.[32] It appears that this fact, in the 1980's, will work to the disadvantage of the Democratic party. The psychological edge they have in the minds of voters cannot be translated into electoral victories unless the voters go to the polls.[33] There has been no appreciable surge in voting turnout in recent elections, which suggests that Indiana is not on the threshold of a partisan realignment. Rather, the Republicans through an imaginative mixture of various elements into a statewide formula, have managed to win statewide elections and dominate the state political system.

Statewide political victory depends a great deal on political geography. Indiana's population displays certain characteristics of the nation. Rural counties have been growing at a faster rate than urban counties throughout the 1970's and urban sprawl continues with sparsely populated counties adjacent to the urban areas experiencing tremendous growth as people move from the larger cities and counties. Table 2.2 reports population data on the 15 most populous counties according to the 1980 census. These counties grew at a rate of only 1.44 percent over the decade, compared to the statewide average of 5.67 percent. Their share of the statewide population declined somewhat in the 1970's, from 59.456 percent in 1970 to 59.075 percent in 1980. Obviously, the fact that nearly 60 percent of the population resides in 15 of the 92 counties colors the political forces at work in elections. Statewide candidates must run well in these counties if they are to stand a realistic chance of winning. The Republicans have been markedly successful in carrying the populous counties for the statewide ticket. In the 1980 gubernatorial race the Democratic nominee (John Hillenbrand) carried only two of the 15 largest counties. Statewide, Hillenbrand carried only 17 of the 92 counties, with the majority of these being in Southern Indiana, which contains most of the dominant Democratic counties. The Democrats have been clearly outmaneuvered by the Republicans, and their weak position is documented by their inability to carry the more populous counties of the state, where their built-in-edge gives them an advantage they have been unable to exploit.

Table 2.2. Population of Indiana's Largest Counties, 1970 and 1980

County and Principal City	1970 Population	1970 Rank	1980 Population	1980 Rank	Percent Change
Statewide	5,195,382		5,490,179		5.67
Marion (Indianapolis)	793,769	1	765,233	1	−3.6
Lake (Gary)	546,253	2	522,965	2	−4.3
Allen (Ft. Wayne)	280,455	3	294,335	3	4.9
St. Joseph (South Bend)	244,827	4	241,617	4	−1.3
Vanderburgh (Evansville)	168,772	5	167,515	5	−0.7
Madison (Anderson)	138,522	6	139,336	6	0.6
Elkhart (Elkhart)	126,529	8	137,330	7	8.5
Delaware (Muncie)	129,219	7	128,587	8	−0.5
Tippecanoe (Lafayette)	109,378	10	121,702	9	11.3
Porter (Valparaiso)	87,114	12	119,816	10	37.5
Vigo (Terre Haute)	114,528	9	112,385	11	−1.9
La Porte (Michigan City)	105,342	11	108,632	12	3.1
Monroe (Bloomington)	85,221	13	98,387	13	15.4
Clark (Jeffersonville)	75,876	16	88,838	14	17.1
Howard (Kokomo)	83,198	15	86,896	15	4.4
Totals	3,089,003		3,133,574		

Source: U.S. Census Bureau.

Just as the national party system is a function of the 50 state party systems, Indiana's party system can be said to be a product of the 92 county systems. The decentralized nature of American political parties has been eroded in the last three decades by statewide and national communications, but the precincts remain as the common denominators for political parties. And in Indiana, the precincts are created by the counties. The significance of this fact has been pinpointed by Hyneman and his co-authors.

> **". . . Cumulation of association of a population within a county stamps certain attitudes upon that population and seduces them into certain practices. In this view the different turnout levels and party preferences of adjoining counties are not wholly accidental; they are in good part an expression of a county and a part of it.[34]**

Voting statistics reveal precincts and counties that have remarkably similar vote totals for party nominees from one election to the next. The consistency of these vote totals, when understood within the context of other political, social and economic forces such as party organization finances and activities, population shifts, communication networks, and income and employment trends, suggests that partisan change in Indiana will likely follow the patterns of the past: it will be gradual and incremental. In this regard, political parties in Indiana will likely remain as confusing institutions to outside observers who fail to make the effort to understand the unique ways in which they reflect the political culture of Hoosiers.

Conclusion

The incongruous contrasts that mark Indiana's political party system are evident in the way the parties are structured, the way political operations are financed and in the way Hoosiers vote. Safely located in America's heartland, Hoosiers have developed strong political traditions that are oftentimes written into law and are likely to change only incrementally. Old practices die hard in such a system. This fact makes outsiders marvel at the peculiar practices that continue in Indiana long after they have been abandoned in other states.

But one of the strongest Hoosier traditions is competition, and the party system in Indiana reflects this. The leaders that have emerged on the national scene are products of a political party system of intense competition where skills are rapidly developed and fresh ideas and new techniques are quickly accepted—and then adapted to the customs and practices of Indiana.

Notes

1. Peirce, Neal R. and Keefe, John. *The Great Lake States of America.* New York: W. W. Norton and Company, (1980) p. 238.
2. The only references to political parties in the Indiana Constitution are found in the sections referring to the judiciary and are intended to separate judges from partisan politics.
3. Although an equal number of men as against women is assured in the top two positions of the county organizations, men overwhelmingly control the more powerful post of county chairman. Following the 1980 county conventions, 9 women were elected as Republican county chairs while the Democrats elected only 8 in Indiana's 92 counties.
4. In a study by Ronald E. Weber, "Competitive and Organizational Dimensions of American State Party Systems," paper prepared for the Northeastern Political Science Association, 1969, on factors of party organization authority, quoted in Malcolm E. Jewell and David M. Olson, *American State Political Parties and Elections,* The Dorsey Press, Homewood, Illinois, 1978, pp. 61–62, Indiana, and 7 other states are ranked the highest in terms of party organization authority. The other 7 states are: Connecticut, Delaware, Michigan, Minnesota, New Jersey, New York and South Dakota.
5. At the county level the control of the county chairman is enhanced by his power to appoint vacancies in the offices of precinct committeeman and vice-committeeman. These precinct officials are the ones after the primary election who elect the county chairman. At any time there will be some vacancies in the posts of precinct committeeman and vice-committeeman in virtually all counties.
6. Barone, Michael, Ujifusa, Grant, and Mathews, Douglas. *The Almanac of American Politics, 1978.* New York: E. P. Dutton, p 262.
7. For an excellent discussion of patronage in state political party organizations see Malcolm E. Jewell and David M. Olson, *op. cit.,* pp 78–83.

8. In an October, 1981 conference three former Governors of Indiana and the incumbent Governor were agreed in lamenting the passing away of political patronage in Indiana. *The Muncie Star,* October 7, 1981, p 21.
9. *The Indianapolis Star,* September 20, 1981, p 1.
10. *Ibid.*
11. *The Indianapolis News,* October 8, 1981, p 17.
12. In a listing of campaign costs per vote cast in selected statewide races between 1962–68, Indiana ranked as the most expensive state at 96 cents per vote. The data were derived from reports from the Citizen's Research Foundation at Princeton, New Jersey and are cited in Austin Ranney, "Parties in State Politics" in Herbert Jacob and Kenneth Vines, eds., *Politics in the American States,* 2nd ed. Boston: Little, Brown, (1971), p 102.
13. This figure was derived from the Federal Election Commission "Report of Receipts and Disbursements" through December 31, 1980 for the Birch Bayh for Senator Committee and the Quayle for Senate Committee. Bayh's committee had net operating expenditures of $2,432,007.35 while Quayle's committee reported $2,084,008.74.
14. Even in non-election years party politics are expensive in Indiana. In 1981, a year in which no elections were held, the budgets for the two state central committees together totaled over $2,000,000. Of this the Republicans, who held all statewide offices and both U.S. Senate seats, budgeted $1,800,000 while the Democratic State Central Committee limped along on a budget of $250,000. See "Democratic Comeback?" by Ed Ziegner, *The Indianapolis News,* October 31, 1981, p 13.
15. Two other TV markets exist in Indiana: Lafayette, Indiana, which has one station, and Dayton Ohio, which penetrates the far eastern edge of the state.
16. Ranney, Austin, in Jacob and Vines, eds., 2nd ed., *op. cit.,* p 102.
17. In 1976 and 1980 the Lt. Governor also was nominated in the direct primary. The 1981 General Assembly moved this nomination back to the state convention.
18. Cranor, John D., Crawley, Gary, Perry, R. T., Sargent, Thomas A., and Scheele, Raymond H. *A Summary Report: A 1980 Survey on Voting and Citizen Attitudes in Indiana.* Bureau of Government Research, Ball State University, (1980) pp. 43–44.
19. Jewell, Malcolm E. and Olson, David. *op. cit.,* p 96.
20. *Ibid.,* p 115.
21. Jewell and Olson, *Ibid.,* p 114 describe Indiana's Republican Party as a "bifactional" party in a two-party competitive state. They define a bifactional party as one "dominated by two main opposing groups" (p 116). Curiously, the Indiana Democratic Party is categorized as being "cohesive." Their categories are based on data for the 1960–1976 period. Indiana's two parties may well have switched places since this time.
22. The measure was first developed by Richard E. Dawson and James A. Robinson in "Inter-Party Competition, Economic Variables, and Welfare Policies in the American States," *Journal of Politics.* (1962) pp 265–289. Austin Ranney adapted the measure to focus exclusively on state offices and reported his findings in the first edition of Herbert Jacob and Kenneth Vines, eds., *Politics in the American States.* Boston: Little, Brown, (1965) p 65.
23. Ranney, Austin in Jacob and Vines, 1st ed., *op. cit.,* p 64.
24. Ranney's index has been criticized for failing to account for electoral competition within state legislative districts. See David Ray and John Havick, "A Longitudinal Analysis of Party Competition in State Legislative Elections," *American Journal of Political Science.* (February 1981) pp 119–128
25. Ranney, Austin in Jacob and Vines, 1st ed., *op. cit.,* p 65.
26. Ranney, Austin in Jacob and Vines, 2nd ed., *op. cit.,* p 87.
27. Peirce, Neal R. and Keefe, John, *op. cit.,* pp 260–261.
28. Hyneman, Charles S., Hofstetter, E. Richard, and O'Conner, Patrick F. *Voting in Indiana: A Century of Persistence and Change.* (1979) Bloomington: Indiana University Press, pp 128–129.

29. *Ibid.*, pp 112–113.
30. *Ibid.*, p 115.
31. *Ibid.*, p. 117.
32. *Ibid.*, p. 121. Historically, Hoosiers have an excellent record among the states in voting turnout. Recently, however, voting participation in the state has been slipping as compared to other states.
33. There are many possible explanations for nonvoting. Hyneman, *et. al.*, *Ibid.*, p. 182 suggest with respect to Indiana that socially and economically "developed" counties contain social forces that induce electoral volatility and affect turnout. The literature on urban political machines suggests that political leaders may have a vested interest in keeping turnout low, thereby increasing their chances for control, especially in primaries. One factor that is directly related with increased turnout is the presence of closely fought contests. The gubernatorial races of the 1970's in Indiana have not been hotly contested.
34. *Ibid.*, pp. 135–136.

3

The Indiana General Assembly

James L. McDowell
Indiana State University

The Indiana State House of Representatives in session
Courtesy of the South Bend Tribune

The legislative authority of the state is vested in the Indiana General Assembly. This branch of the state government, therefore, has as its principal responsibility the enacting, revising, or repealing the thousands of laws which daily affect the lives of some or all of the more than five million persons who live in the Hoosier State.

The General Assembly is a "citizen legislature," that is, its members do not serve on a full-time basis as in many states but go to Indianapolis for a few weeks each year to consider major—and minor—issues of public policy. Thus, Indiana's legislators can devote a substantial amount of time and energy to devising a state budget of more than $11 billion for the 1981–83 biennium, an action which will affect all taxpayers and every person who receives some state or local government service. On the other hand, the members of the assembly can allot a couple of hours from a crowded schedule to consider adoption of a state insect in order to demonstrate to school children how the legislative process functions.

For all of its apparent willingness to serve the people, the General Assembly has not always been highly regarded. Kin Hubbard's legendary homespun philosopher once remarked sardonically, "The legislature has come and gone, causing much comment." Others have joined in the attack. When Indiana was considering changing its legislative schedule from the traditional 61 days every two years, an anonymous sage opined, "The state would be better off if the legislature met two days every 61 years."

Indiana, of course, is not the only state whose legislature has been criticized. Many persons have attacked state legislatures as a group, citing them as America's most extreme form of institutional lag or faulting them for attempting to solve jet-age problems with horse-and-buggy methods. But one set of criticisms specifically directed at the Indiana General Assembly came from the Citizens Conference on State Legislatures in 1971.[1] Briefly, the CCSL study examined legislative rules, procedures and operations, and resolved the legislature was generally incapable of resolving effectively the problems confronting Indiana citizens. The group ranked the Indiana General Assembly 40th among the nation's state assemblies and suggested a long list of needed reforms.

Responding not necessarily to the CCSL recommendations but more likely to the urgings of the Indiana Constitutional Revision Commission,[2] a body the legislature itself had created in 1967, the General Assembly altered substantially its method of operation in the next decade through amending the Constitution, enacting legislation, and amending chamber rules. The reforms of the 1970's appeared to alter significantly the manner in which the General Assembly could consider the public policy concerns of the citizens of Indiana.

This chapter considers the Indiana General Assembly within the framework of the state government. It examines the men and women who serve as state legislators and how they transfer public concerns into public policy. It is also concerned with the impact of procedural reforms on the operation of the legislature. Finally, this chapter takes a look ahead, attempting to assess the future of the legislative institution in the decade ahead.

The Legislative Environment

The Indiana General Assembly appears to be a typical example of the American legislative institution. It is a bicameral (two-house) legislature, made up of a 50-member Senate and a 100-member House of Representatives. Except, Nebraska, which has operated under a unicameral (one-house) system since 1937, every other state has a two-chamber legislature. Senators serve four-year terms as the case in 37 other states, with one-half of the membership is elected every two years. House members serve two-year terms like those in 46 other states, and the entire membership is selected at each biennial election.

The General Assembly meets in annual sessions for up to 61 days ending no later than April 30 in odd-numbered years, and for up to 30 days ending no later than March 15 in even-numbered years. The legislatures of 42 other states also meet yearly. Its members are elected and the chambers are organized on a political basis, the situation in all other states except Nebraska, which has the nation's only nonpartisan legislature. The Assembly's two houses, as do all other legislative chambers in the United States, organize themselves into standing committees to facilitate the consideration of bills dealing with particular topics and to recommend which bills should be considered by the total membership of either house. Finally, most of Indiana's legislators run for office from single-member districts; that is, with the exception of some House districts in the most populous counties, an Indiana voter selects one Senator and one Representative to serve in Indianapolis. This is the manner in which the voters of the country choose the overwhelming majority of the nation's some 7,500 state legislators.

Distinguishing Features

However, while the Indiana General Assembly has characteristics similar to those of other state legislatures, there are certain distinctions which set it apart from other legislatures. One feature is the size of the membership. The 100-member House is about average—25 states have more members in their lower chambers, the biggest being New Hampshire with 400 representatives. But the 50-member Senate is among the larger upper houses—only seven states have upper chambers with more members. Although the relatively large membership of the Indiana Senate is occasionally considered an impediment to the smooth functioning of the chamber, it does offer one major benefit. On the basis of the 1980 census, each Hoosier Senator represents about 55,000 residents. For the same degree of representation, Illinois would require about 103 senators instead of its 59 members, and California would have 200 senators, not 40.

In terms of meeting in annual sessions, Indiana is a relative latecomer, especially among the major industrial states. Prior to 1971, the General Assembly convened only in odd-numbered years in sessions limited by the Constitution to 61 calendar days (including weekends). Legislators proved generally unwilling to conduct state business on Saturday or Sunday, so the biennial session in reality was no more than 45 to 48 working days in most years—or a month-and-one-half out of every 24 months. This enforced brevity necessitated the legislators using the time-honored practice of stopping the clock prior to midnight on the final session day in all but three of the 18 sessions between 1935 and 1969. It also led to the need for several special sessions during this period in order to complete work on the state budget.

With this evidence at hand, many observers, especially the Constitution Revision Commission, believed the issues confronting the state toward the close of the 1960's were too extensive and varied to be dealt with sufficiently in such a brief period of time as 61 calendar days every other year. Accordingly, a number of organizations supported a proposed amendment permitting the Assembly to decide how often and for how long it should meet. The electorate ratified this amendment in 1970, and the legislature established in 1971 the meeting schedule in effect ten years later.

Further, the Indiana legislature is noticeably different from those of other states in the matter of its political balance. Democrats dominated American state legislatures in the 1970's, electing approximately two-thirds of all members and controlling 77 of the nation's 99 legislative chambers in the 1977 sessions and 68 houses in 1979.[3] Indiana offers a sharp contrast to this trend: Republicans controlled both houses of the General Assembly in five of the seven sessions from 1967 to 1981; each party controlled one house in the 1975–76 and 1977–78 sessions. Indeed, this Republican prevalence in the 1970's is nothing unusual—for Indiana this party dominated either the House or the Senate in 21 of the 29 sessions between 1925 and 1981. Democrats controlled both chambers at the same time on only four occasions over the same period, the last coming in 1965. At least one observer suggests the districting system in effect for much of this century was a contributing factor to much of the Republican success.[4]

Districts and Representation

The General Assembly is the "people's branch" of the state government. Accordingly, there must be some method devised to represent Indiana residents in the state legislature. On the surface, this would not seem to be such a formidable task. The Constitution requires that legislators shall be chosen by the voters from districts alloted among the counties on the basis of a special census every six years of male inhabitants 21 years and older.[5] But the constitutional directive notwithstanding, Indiana lawmakers proved exceedingly unwilling to comply with that mandate in most of the twentieth century.[6]

The process of redrawing legislative districts involves two steps. First, there is the largely automatic stage of apportionment, the allocating of districts among political subdivisions on the basis of some factor, usually population or county units, or some combination of these. For Indiana, as mentioned above, the factor was the six-year enumeration of males 21 years and older. Then, there is the highly politicized chore of districting, that is, actually drawing the boundaries of the districts from which House and Senate members will be elected. Decisions made at this stage not only affect the political makeup of the legislative body but also largely determine which sets of groups will influence and benefit from state policies and programs.

Indiana legislators joined their counterparts in all but a few states in refusing to redistrict for more than 40 years. Over these four decades, moreover, no state or federal court would compel the General Assembly—or the legislature of any other state for that matter—to act, usually citing the separation of powers doctrine or claiming that redistricting was a political matter. The districts enacted by the 1921 legislature were still in effect in 1963 and obviously were no longer representative of either the male residents of voting age or the total population of the state.[7] The theoretical minimum of the population which could select a majority to the Indiana House in the 1962 elections was 34.8 percent and a majority to the Indiana Senate 40.4 percent.[8]

The legislature proved to have considerable difficulty in the 1960's in satisfying the United States Supreme Court decision that both chambers of a state legislature must represent the principle of "one man, one vote" as nearly as practicable.[9] The legislature passed six different proposals for each house before finally satisfying the federal justices. In 1971 and 1972, however, the General Assembly fared better. The legislature in the first session created single-member districts for each chamber, but it altered House constituencies in the second session to provide for a combination of single- and multi-member districts. This action followed a federal court ruling that multimember districts did not necessarily discriminate against minorities living in urban areas.[10] The plan provided 53 single-member districts, 13 districts electing two members, and 7 districts choosing three members to the House. On the basis of the 1970 census, these districts were among the most representative in the nation. The population of Senate districts varied by less than 2 percent from the statewide average, and the population of House seats was calculated at ±1.0 percent of the mean.

The task of redrawing legislative district lines confronted the General Assembly again in 1981. On the basis of a modest increase in the number of Hoosier residents indicated by the 1980 federal census and the redistribution of the population throughout the state, the legislature produced a substantially different set of House and Senate districts in most sections of Indiana. To be sure, the minority Democrats complained bitterly that the majority Republicans (in control in the House by a 63-to-37 margin and in the Senate by a 35-15 edge) had engaged in blatant "gerrymandering," that is, drawing districts purely for partisan advantage. For example, they pointed out that Vigo County was divided among five House districts, where it had been split between two in the 1971–72 remapping. Nevertheless, the 1981 legislative maps (with minor revisions made in 1982) fulfilled the judicial mandate that districts be as equitable as possible in reflecting the "one man, one vote" standard. In fact, the Indiana districts designed for use through the elections of 1990 do not reflect the total population but the voting-age population of the state—as of 1980. The legislature continued the practice of single-member districts for the Senate and a combination of single- and multi-member districts in the House. In the lower chamber during the 1980's, voters will elect members from 61 single-member districts (an increase of eight), nine two-member districts (a decrease of four), and seven three-member districts. All multi-member districts are located in the most populous counties of Indiana.

Providing proper representation by reallocating districts according to population growth or loss in the various areas of the state is, of course, a periodic problem facing the General Assembly. The legislators must devise new districts following each decennial federal census. In Indiana, the only agency authorized to redistrict is the General Assembly. There is no redistricting commission as exists in other states. If the legislature fails to act, the only alternative is reapportionment under federal judicial supervision.

The Legislators of Indiana

The individuals who serve in the Indiana General Assembly must meet certain requirements. On the one hand, these requirements are constitutional and legal; on the other, they are practical and political. Many persons in the state qualify to serve in constitutional and legal terms, but only a relative few can reasonably seek a legislative office and fewer still can logically hope to win. This section examines some of the characteristics of the Hoosier legislators.

Qualifications

Constitutional requirements for membership in the legislature include those of United States citizenship, minimum age, and two periods of residence. Members of the House must be at least 21, while Senators must be at least 25. Candidates must have been inhabitants of Indiana for at least two years prior to election and residents of their districts for at least one year.[11] This latter residency provision became noteworthy in 1981 when the House expelled two persons who had been elected on the grounds they had not lived in their districts the necessary length of time. Candidates must also meet certain legal requirements, including being a registered voter. A conflict of interest law enacted in 1974 provides that candidates, including incumbent legislators seeking re-election, must file statements of economic disclosure in addition to their declarations of candidacy. These statements of economic interest must include any dealings a candidate has had with a registered lobbyist and the receipt of any gifts of more than $100 value. Failure to file the economic statement results in a candidate being ruled off the primary election ballot.

The preceding constitutional and legal requirements are relatively modest and in themselves, do not prevent many would-be assemblymen from seeking office. However, there are practical and political considerations which sharply reduce the number of those on the primary election ballot.

The General Assembly is a part-time or "citizen legislature," one of those which, in spite of its change to yearly sessions, has resisted the move to full-time or "professional" status. This effectively limits legislative candidacies to those who may be considered "self-employed"—such as lawyers, businessmen or farmers, or retired persons and housewives. These individuals can afford to devote the time necessary to deal with the state's affairs in return for the compensation they receive. Legislative compensation will be discussed in greater detail below.

Two additional economic factors serve to restrict legislative candidacies. First, it has become extremely expensive to seek public office. It is not uncommon for candidates to spend upwards of $3,500–$5,000 to seek nomination to the General Assembly in a contested primary race, particularly in an urban district. Especially in the case of first-time candidates, these efforts are largely self-financed. Second, because of a relatively high turnover rate in Indiana, would-be legislators cannot depend upon this salary as the principal source of income.

The most important non-legal consideration, however, is political. Not only do many persons live in parts of Indiana where party organizations still influence nominations, but many individuals who might hope to serve in the General Assembly simply do not fit the racial, ethnic, or religious cast of the district in which they reside. White candidates have little chance in black-dominated inner-city districts, and black candidates have little hope of winning in white suburban constituencies. Likewise, Protestant candidates generally do not fare well in heavily Catholic districts, and the reverse is also true. One's partisan preference is also a factor. Many persons reside in areas where their party is usually the minority. In Indiana, it is generally advantageous for a person to be a Democrat if he lives in most areas of the state south of the Old National Road (U.S. Route 40, now Interstate 70), and a Republican if he lives in most areas north of this line. The National Road is said to bisect the state both culturally and politically.[12]

However, this is not a hard and fast rule. Voters in Lake and St. Joseph counties in the northern part of the state regularly send Democrats to the legislature, while residents of Vanderburgh County frequently elect Republican legislators.

Tenure and Turnover

An extremely high rate of turnover of membership, which results in a substantial loss of legislative experience, is a common feature of American state legislatures—particularly in the lower chamber with its shorter term and lesser prestige. The Indiana legislature has been no exception to this situation.

It is generally believed that lengthy, continuous service contributes to legislative competence or, conversely, that a newly-elected legislator lacks the tools to be an effective lawmaker. Whether or not this is true, a series of studies indicates that the Indiana General Assembly has long had an exceptionally high rate of first-term members. Moreover, only a small percentage of legislators serve as many as three sessions. An examination of six sessions from 1925 through 1935 indicated that the average length of service of House members over this period was 1.7 sessions, for Senators three sessions; that only 7.6 percent of House members served as many as four terms; that 58 percent of Senators left office after one term; and that over this period, 60 percent of House members and 29 percent of Senators were serving in their first session.[13]

More recent studies confirm these statistics and indicate that turnover of the legislative membership, especially in the House of Representatives, continued to be constantly high through the 1960's. From 1925 through 1957 (17 sessions), only 31 percent of all House members who served were elected to as many as three terms, and the turnover rate was exceedingly great among members from urban areas: 62 percent served only one term, 84 percent only two terms during this period.[14] In 19 of the 23 sessions from 1923 through 1967, more than 40 percent of House members were in their initial terms. In the 1967 session, in fact, 46 percent of the membership of both chambers were newcomers.[15] This figure was somewhat affected, however, by the 1967 session being the first following reapportionment.

However, there is evidence to suggest that the turnover rate in Indiana may be lessening. There was a 42 percent turnover in the membership for the 1973–74 session, but that session was also the first after a redistricting. Otherwise, Indiana's turnover in the balance of the 1970's was well below national estimates of between one-third and one-half of the state legislators being novices at each session. From 1975–76 through 1981–82, Indiana's turnover averaged only 26 percent, reaching a low point of 21 percent in 1979–80.[16] Moreover, legislators were staying in office longer. By the end of the 1970's, more than two-thirds of House members had served at least three sessions, and about half the Senators had similar tenure.

Compensation

Inadequate compensation has frequently been cited as a cause for high rates of legislative turnover. This may have been the case in Indiana in 1927 when members received $10 per day and no expenses (up from a $6 per diem in 1925), or even as late as 1969 when legislators were paid $1,800 per year (including the year when the legislature did not meet) and only a limited mileage allowance.

This is not the case in Indiana at present. Since the changeover to annual sessions in 1971, the salary and expense allowances of the Hoosier assemblymen have increased steadily—as the turnover rate has decreased. The Council of State Governments estimated the biennial compensation of Indiana lawmakers for 1977–78 at $23,903, ranking Indiana 20th among the states.[17] This ranking was based on a legislative salary of $6,000 per year, $35 per day expenses while in session, $75 per week between session, and mileage. The compensation was greatly improved by the 1981–82 session when legislators were making $9,600 per year in salary plus $50 per session day in expenses, in addition to the between-session and mileage allowances. In addition, the Speaker of the House and President Pro Tempore of the Senate each receives an additional $3,000 per year, and the majority and minority floor leaders of each chamber and the chairmen of the legislative budget committees are paid an extra $1,500 per year.

The higher compensation, along with improved facilities and increased staff support, probably has contributed to the reduced level of turnover in Indiana. But it proved an insufficient inducement to retain the services of more than a few legislators toward the end of the 1970's. Included among those who retired voluntarily rather than seek to continue in office were several veteran members—not merely long-time assemblymen but leaders of the two chambers: two Senate Presidents Pro Tempore, a Senate majority leader, a Speaker of the House, and a chairman of an important House committee. They returned to private life of their own accord, concluding that increased benefits did not make up for the longer periods spent away from their families and principal occupations.[18]

Social Characteristics

There has been continuing interest exhibited in the backgrounds of Indiana legislators, apparently in expectation that knowledge of the personal, educational, and occupational characteristics of members of the General Assembly may provide clues to their legislative behavior. This conjecture may well be spurious, but the efforts to determine who makes the laws in the Hoosier State do provide an overview of the General Assembly which suggests three things: Indiana legislators have been and are similar to legislators in other states; Indiana legislators have not been and are not a cross-section of the state's population; and Indiana legislators of the present are not particularly different—in terms of their backgrounds—from their predecessors of the 1920's and 1930's.

The General Assembly has the atmosphere of a white, middle-aged men's club as, indeed, do practically all American political institutions. In the session which convened in 1981, the legislature was composed of 138 men and 12 women, of 143 white and seven black members. Both sets of figures are obviously far out of line with each group's proportion of the state's population. At that, these figures did indicate a slight improvement for women and blacks over their situation in the 1970's when there was an average of 141 men and 144 white legislators in the sessions of that decade. And the membership levels of both women and blacks was markedly higher than in earlier decades of this century. In terms of age, about 60 percent of the legislators serving in the 1970's were from 40 to 49 years of age. In the 21 sessions from 1923 through 1963, some 26 percent of the members were between 30 and 39, and 51 percent were between 40 and 59.

As to religious affiliation, the legislature remains heavily populated by Protestant denominations, although not nearly so overwhelmingly as in the 1923–1963 period when 89 percent of the members were Protestant. As in that earlier period, most of the Catholic members are Democrats, who largely represent urban areas. Finally, the level of formal education completed by members has increased throughout the century. More than 60 percent of the legislators serving in the 1970's had completed college, many having done post-graduate work, and no member reported less than a high school diploma. This is an improvement over the 52 percent who were college graduates in the 1961 session, and the overall figure of 33 percent with college degrees in the 1923–1963 period. The greater percentage of college graduates in the 1970's is to be expected, of course, as this reflects the growing importance placed on formal education in the United States. Otherwise, given the gentle thawing in the attitudes toward public service by women and blacks, the personal characteristics of legislators over more than half a century indicate no significant changes in the composition of the General Assembly.[19]

The same is true in terms of the legislators' occupational characteristics. Those professions most prominent in the 1920's and 1930's are yet the most conspicuous. They are the occupations in which, as mentioned earlier, the participants could be considered "self-employed": lawyers, business executives and merchants, insurance and real estate salesmen, and farmers. Not only can persons in these categories arrange their work schedules to allow them time to serve in the legislature, they also are in jobs that invite the personal contacts necessary to a political career.

These groups have dominated the membership of the General Assembly for nearly 60 years. That in itself is not surprising for the reasons noted above. What is also not surprising but is quite interesting is that these groups have continued to populate the legislature in approximately the same proportions over these six decades.

Whether lawyers run for legislative office because of a real desire to help shape the laws of the state or because, until recently, they could not bring attention to themselves through advertising is unknown. However, the lawyer is in an occupation long present in the legislature in both considerable and consistent numbers. About 27 percent of the legislators were lawyers in the period 1925–1935; about 25 percent from 1923–1963, with 24 percent of the membership in the 1961 session; and some 23 percent in the 1970's.[20]

Businessmen, including small merchants and insurance and real estate salesmen, have also long been prominent in the legislature. Generally, it is believed they have sought office in hopes of keeping taxes low and government regulation of their endeavor minimal. From 1923 through 1963, this group constituted about 25 percent of the Indiana legislators, although it ranked as high as 29 percent in 1961. This category dropped to about 20 percent of the membership in the late 1970's as representatives from other groups began to appear in the Assembly.

As the number of persons engaged in agriculture in Indiana has declined during the twentieth century, so has the number of farmers in the legislature. From a high of 21 percent of the membership from 1923 through 1963, including 19 percent as late as 1961, this group has dropped to the point where it constituted only 9 percent of the legislators in the 1970's. Another reason for this change was the reapportionments of the legislature that took place in the 1960's. These reapportionments reduced the influence of agricultural interests and increased the influence of urban and suburban interests. One occupational group which partially supplanted farmers in the legislature of the 1970's is that composed of teachers and administrators in Indiana's public schools and universities. This category filled about 13 percent of the legislative seats at the end of the decade.

In concluding this brief look at the legislators of Indiana, it is important to point out that these individuals do not now, nor have they ever, represented a cross-section of the state. They are better educated, from more prestigious occupations, and generally more well-to-do than most Hoosiers. They are products of the backgrounds of their constituencies in that only persons who reflect the ethnic, religious and political complexion of a district are likely to become members of the General Assembly. This is the way it has been and the way it is likely to continue.

The Legislative Organization

The Indiana General Assembly, as are all other legislatures in the nation, is a highly structured and formally organized body. It follows the traditional two-tiered framework. Each chamber elects a set of officers, who are responsible for running the legislative and political affairs of that house. Each chamber also creates a set of standing committees, which have the duty of reviewing proposed legislation on particular subjects and deciding whether to recommend bills to the full membership for further consideration. This section discusses the organization of the Indiana legislature, indicating similarities between the two chambers and pointing out distinctions which cause the two houses to function differently.

Leadership Positions

Certain individuals in a state legislature, as in any organization, are most influential than others. Particularly in a two-party state like Indiana, the influential individuals tend to be those who hold formal positions of authority in the General Assembly: the Speaker of the House of Representatives; the President Pro Tempore of the Senate; the floor leader of each party; and, occasionally, the chairmen of important committees. In Indiana, as in most states, the Speaker enjoys extensive formal authority. The President Pro Tempore enjoys somewhat less power due to differences in the rules of the two houses and constitutional duties assigned to the Lieutenant Governor.

The Speaker of the House is the presiding officer of that chamber. Elected formally by the entire membership, he is actually the choice of a pre-session caucus of the majority party. Occasionally, factional or personal contests for the position occur, and these may result in some dissension among the ranks. But once the caucus selects its candidate, all members are expected to support the party's choice when the legislature organizes at the opening of each session. A failure to support the caucus selection by any member of the majority usually results in that member being assigned to relatively unimportant committees and having little hope of getting any of his bills passed.

Figure 3.1. Organization of the Indiana General Assembly

House of Representatives (100 members)		**Senate (50 members) President (Lieutenant Governor)**	
Majority Party	**Minority Party**	**Majority Party**	**Minority Party**
Speaker		President Pro Tem	
Speaker Pro Tem		Asst. President Pro Tem	
Majority Floor Leader	Minority Floor Leader	Majority Floor Leader	Minority Floor Leader
Asst. Majority Floor Leader	Asst. Minority Floor Leader	Asst. Majority Floor Leader	Asst. Minority Floor Leader
Majority Caucus Chair	Minority Caucus Chair	Majority Caucus Chair	Minority Caucus Chair
Asst. Majority Caucus Chair	Asst. Minority Caucus Chair	Asst. Majority Caucus Chair	Asst. Minority Caucus Chair
Majority Whip	Minority Whip	Majority Whip	
Asst. Majority Whip			

House Standing Committees* (Chair) (Ranking Minority Member)

1. Age and Aging
2. Agricultural
3. Cities and Towns
4. Counties and Townships
5. Courts and Criminal Code
6. Education
7. Elections and Apportionment
8. Energy and Environmental Affairs
9. Financial Institutions
10. Governmental Reorganization
11. Human Affairs
12. Insurance Corporations
13. Interstate Cooperation
14. Judiciary
15. Labor
16. Natural Resources
17. Public Health
18. Public Policy and Veteran Affairs
19. Public Safety
20. Roads and Transportation
21. Rules and Legislative Procedure
22. Urban Affairs
23. Ways and Means

Senate Standing Committees* (Chair) (Ranking Minority Member)

1. Appointment and Claims
2. Commerce
3. Elementary and Secondary Education
4. Energy and Environmental Affairs
5. Finance
6. Government Affairs
7. Health, Welfare and Aging
8. Higher Education
9. Insurance and Financial Institutions
10. Interstate Cooperation
11. Judiciary
12. Labor and Pensions
13. Legislative Apportionments and Elections
14. Metropolitan Affairs
15. Natural Resources
16. Public Policy
17. Roads and Transportation
18. Rules and Legislative Procedure

*The number and names of the standing committees are subject to change

Because of the extensive formal powers granted him by the House rules, the Speaker is regarded as the second most influential public official in Indiana, next after the Governor. His influence and prestige stem not only from the manner in which he exercises his ability to determine the destiny of legislation but also from the high degree of visibility he can gain throughout the state from his position as leader of the House. Thus, the position of Speaker is important politically as well. In other words, becoming Speaker of the House can be a significant stepping stone toward higher office as evidenced by former Speakers Birch Bayh (U.S. Senator, 1963–1981) and Otis Bowen (Governor, 1973–1981).

The formal authority conferred on the Speaker includes the power to select the chairman and all members of each standing committee, to assign all bills to committee, to recognize members wishing to speak on some issue, and to hand down bills for amendment or final vote. With each of these formal duties, however, the Speaker has informal power which gives him considerable license to determine the manner in which the House shall function.

In appointing the membership of each committee, the Speaker ordinarily accepts the advice of the minority leader as to his party's members on each committee, but he is not required to do so by House rules. The Speaker could, therefore, frustrate the desires of the minority to place certain individuals on the more important committees. In naming committee chairmen, the Speaker can use these positions as a form of patronage, rewarding legislators who supported him in the pre-session caucus and ignoring those who opposed his nomination. Having persons loyal to him directing the more important committees can aid the Speaker in maintaining control of the House.

In assigning bills to committee, the Speaker may exercise considerable discretion and place a bill where it will receive a favorable reception or bury it in a committee whose chairman will never hold a hearing. The Speaker is directed by House rules to refer bills to committee, but he may assign a bill not to the subject-matter committee one might logically expect but rather to one of several "catch-all" committees, the principal duty of which is to kill legislation not wanted by the leadership.

The power to recognize members for the purpose of speaking on some bill or other legislative concern gives the Speaker the opportunity to control the order and length of discussion or to ignore some member altogether. No Representative may take the floor without gaining the permission of the Speaker.

For all the importance of the preceding powers of the Speaker, they are relatively insignificant in comparison to his authority to hand down bills for amendment or final consideration. Once a bill is reported out of committee, it is placed in the possession of the Speaker. He is charged with making up a daily calendar of all bills ready for action, but it is entirely up to the Speaker whether he calls any bill for House action. This is his most effective device for preventing the adoption of any legislation he, his faction, or his party happens to oppose. The House rules provide no means for removing a bill from the control of the Speaker.

This discussion of the informal powers of the Speaker of the House has emphasized the potential negative aspects of his authority and the possible abuses of the governmental process at his command. It was done so in order to stress the extent of the formal powers available to him. Without such far-reaching authority in the hands of the presiding officer, the 100-member House of Representatives might never be able to come to collective decisions on the several hundreds of items which come before the chamber each session. But no politician astute enough to achieve the position is likely to misuse his authority—especially if he wishes to return as Speaker.

The President Pro Tempore of the Senate is neither so powerful nor so influential as the Speaker. For one thing, the President Pro Tem, as he is informally known, is not the presiding officer of the Senate. That duty lies with the Lieutenant Governor by constitutional provision.[21] It is the Lieutenant Governor who has the power to recognize members for the purpose of speaking to a matter of legislative concern; to join in debate whenever the Senate is sitting as a committee of the whole; and to cast the tie-breaking vote whenever the Senate is equally divided. Prior to the 1971 session, the Lieutenant Governor had the authority to appoint committee members and refer bills to committee. The Senate in that session, however, removed these powers, leaving the Lieutenant Governor with only his constitutional duties.

The President Pro Tem is elected by the vote of the entire Senate but is, in reality, the choice of the majority party in a pre-session caucus. As in the House, all party members are expected to support the caucus choice when the Senate formally organizes. Those who do not provide their support cannot expect to receive favorable committee positions.

The powers of the President Pro Tem include the authority to choose the chairman and all members of each standing committee, and to assign bills to committee. He ordinarily accedes to the wishes of the minority leader as to his party's members on each committee but, as is the case with the Speaker, he does not have to accept these recommendations. He also has considerable discretion as to which of several committees he may assign many bills and, like the Speaker, the President Pro Tem may effectively kill a bill by this action.

The principal reason the President Pro Tem lacks the power and influence of the Speaker within the General Assembly is that he has no official control over the fate of a bill after he refers it to a committee. In the Senate, the author of a Senate bill or sponsor of a House bill is the only person who may move a bill toward amendment or final consideration. The President Pro Tem may be able to use his personal persuasion to delay or defeat a measure, but individual Senators retain control over their bills after they leave committee. This, incidentally, is authority House members frequently seek when they are in the minority but rarely ask for when their party gains control of that chamber.

The lesser formal powers of the President Pro Tem do not prevent him from being an effective leader. Indeed, in Indiana, where the majority party usually runs either legislative chamber as it pleases, the President Pro Tem has ordinarily been able to operate as he sees fit, employing an iron fist or the velvet glove as he believes necessary. The failure to grant the President Pro Tem the same extensive authority as given the Speaker of the House stems from two convictions: first, that the Senate is a more mature, experienced and deliberative body; and second, that the smaller of the two legislative chambers does not require rigid rules in order to function efficiently.

Other influential leaders in the two chambers are not elected by the entire membership but are appointed by the party caucuses. In each house, the majority party names a floor leader responsible for directing his party's legislative program on the floor and a caucus chairman who leads the discussion of party positions in off-the-floor meetings. In the House, the majority also names a whip who has the duty of lining up votes for his party's position on pending legislation and a speaker pro tempore who presides when the Speaker is absent. The minority party in each house also names a floor leader—its candidate for Speaker or President Pro Tem as the case may be—and a caucus chairman. Their duties are the same as the corresponding positions in the majority party, but they have no official status under the rules adopted by the General Assembly.

The Committee System

It would be impossible for either house of the General Assembly as a collective body to examine each piece of legislation introduced, consider it on its merits, and pass or reject it. There is too little time—remember, the legislature has limited the number of days it will meet each year; and there are too many bills for such deliberation—1,628 in the 1981 session, and that figure was far below the record of 1,770 bill introductions established in the 1977 session.[22] In order to make the best use of the time available and, hopefully, to deal only with those measures worthy of the entire chamber's attention, each house has established a system of standing committees. Each committee deals with a particular subject, as agriculture, education, or labor; or at the most with a few related topics, as insurance and corporations, or public health and environmental affairs.

The committee system has two purposes: to expedite the progress of legislation by permitting the simultaneous consideration of many measures by small groups of legislators and to bring some degree of expertise to the first important stage of the legislative process. The committees in each house concentrate on bills dealing with their particular subject matters and decide which of these measures should be recommended for action by the entire chamber. This frees each individual member from the necessity of dealing with every measure introduced and, in the early days of a session, allows each member to focus on only those bills referred to the committees on which he serves. Further, because a committee is supposed to be composed of members interested in and knowledgeable about a subject, the committee system can eliminate undesirable or unneeded legislation early in the session.

There is no question that permitting simultaneous consideration by the various committees of the hundreds of bills confronting each chamber is beneficial to the function of the General Assembly. There is some question, however, whether Indiana's committees really bring a great deal of expertise or specialization to the process. Due to the frequent turnover, even though it appears to have been reduced to something under 30 percent, many members of a committee may not have developed any great competence on a particular subject. On the other side of the coin, there is also the possibility that specialization could result in some conflict of interest: lawyers may bring expertise to the judiciary committee and teachers bring knowledge to the education committee, for example, but both groups may have vested interests in the outcome of their deliberations.

As pointed out earlier, the Speaker appoints members and the chairmen of all House standing committees, and the President Pro Tem names the members and chairmen of all Senate standing committees. Politics is usually a factor in the choices made by the leadership, as is the knowledge of and interest of a member in the subject area. However, "seniority" is ordinarily not a factor in the making of committee assignments—not only because there is relatively little seniority in either chamber, given the frequent turnover, but also the members with the longer tenure often change committee assignments, moving to more prestigious committees.

The number of committees in the Indiana legislature has declined substantially since the 1931 session when there were 60 committees in the House and 52 in the Senate. As late as 1971, the House had 28 committees and the Senate 26. When the General Assembly convened in 1981, these numbers had been further reduced to 25 committees in the House of Representatives and 18 in the Senate. However, this reduction in numbers is somewhat misleading, for the cutback in the number of committees was accompanied by an increase in the number of subcommittees in each chamber.

The standing committee can play an important role in the legislative process by advancing worthwhile bills to the floor for further consideration and consigning the remainder to the dustbin—in effect, separating the wheat from the chaff. In Indiana, however, the standing committees frequently do not function in this manner. Any author or sponsor of a bill who requests a committee hearing will ordinarily receive one, and his presence at the committee session virtually guarantees his bill will be reported to the floor with a favorable recommendation. There is a legitimate question as to how effectively the committee system in the Indiana General Assembly functions.

The Legislative Function

The Indiana General Assembly has the potential to be the most powerful branch of the state government. Under the Tenth Amendment to the United States Constitution, the states are the repository of all governmental powers not delegated to the national government nor prohibited to the states or to the people. The Indiana Constitution had delegated some of these residual, or reserved, powers to the executive and judicial branches of the state government, but the General Assembly may constitutionally exercise any power by demonstrating that a power has not been denied it nor delegated exclusively to some other unit of government.

By employing this reservoir of reserved powers, the Indiana legislature can be an agency of considerable consequence. But while there exists the potential of very broad authority, there also exists the reality of specific restraints on the use of these powers. Some of these restraints are imposed by the national government: in no uncertain terms, for example, such as forbidding states to enter into treaties, coin money, pass ex post facto laws, or grant titles of nobility; and in more general terms, such as prohibiting states from abridging privileges and immunities or denying persons due process of law and equal protection of the laws. Many of the restraints, however, are imposed by the state itself, in the Indiana Constitution. This section reviews certain categories of power which the General Assembly possesses and examines restrictions placed upon their use.

Powers and Restraints

The primary power of the General Assembly is, of course, its authority to make public policy by enacting new statutes or by amending or repealing existing laws. But in addition to its "lawmaking" power, the Indiana legislature has the authority to perform certain functions of a "nonlawmaking" nature.

The General Assembly has powers of an "executive" character, relating to its possible participation in the appointment and removal of state executive officials. In actuality, however, neither house of the legislature participates in the executive appointment process. In most states, appointment by the Governor of at least some officials requires the approval of at least the Senate. This is not the case in Indiana where, over the years, the legislature has granted the Governor statutory authority to appoint the principal officials of about 400 agencies without requiring legislative confirmation. Periodic efforts to amend the Constitution to require certain appointments to be subject to review by the Senate have been unsuccessful. However, while the General Assembly has largely abandoned its opportunity to participate in the appointment process, it remains one of few state legislatures in the nation which may remove executive officials without the necessity of going through the impeachment process. The Constitution specifies that the legislature may remove all state officials "for crime, incapacity, or negligence" by a two-thirds vote of the members elected to each house on a joint resolution for that purpose.[23] The legislature has never invoked this power.

Impeachment is the "judicial power" of the General Assembly. This process involves two steps, impeachment—in effect, indictment, as by a grand jury on the county level—by the house, and trial by the Senate. A vote of two-thirds of the members elected to the House (67) is required by the Constitution to impeach a state official, and a two-thirds vote of members elected to the Senate (34) is required for conviction. The legislature also has never employed this power to remove a state official, although it was considering doing so in the 1920's until the incumbent Governor resigned from office.

The General Assembly also has powers of "investigation." This activity, of course, occurs whenever a legislative standing committee holds a hearing to determine the need for a particular piece of legislation. Its more appropriate application applies to the function of the legislature in overseeing the activities of an administrative agency, that is, determining whether the agency is applying the law in the manner the legislature intended, or similar instances. In most cases, the General Assembly will establish a select committee, composed of members of both chambers, to investigate a situation. The Indiana legislature makes extensive use of this power in establishing interim (between sessions) study committees, which are directed to determine the need for new or additional legislation on a particular topic and report the findings to the next session.

Finally, the General Assembly has "intergovernmental" powers in that it deals with both the national government and its state and local units in various ways. As part of the state's participation in the federal system, the legislature decides whether to ratify a proposed amendment to the United States Constitution. Indiana has ratified all 14 proposed amendments submitted since it became a state in 1816 and, as of 1981, was the last (in 1977) of 35 states to approve the proposed Equal Rights Amendment. The legislature may petition the Congress to call a new constitutional convention, and it has done so either on its own or in conjunction with other states. The legislature may join with other states in interstate compacts, and it has concluded several such agreements with neighboring states. And the legislature may decide whether to participate in the numerous federal programs. It has accepted some and rejected others. The General Assembly also employs its intergovernmental powers in determining the relationship between the state and the local units of government, largely deciding for municipalities and counties of the state their structure, functions, and revenue-raising capabilities.

The principal restraints on the Indiana General Assembly are on its principal power—to make laws. These restraints are found in the state's own Constitution, a reaction by the framers of the 1851 document to various abuses committed by the legislature under the first Constitution of 1816, and in the rules which each chamber adopts on its own. Thus, the Constitution prohibits the legislature from enacting special or local laws, as it tended to do prior to 1851, and requires the General Assembly to pass legislation of general and uniform application throughout Indiana.[24] In addition to the prohibition on special legislation, the Constitution limits the power of the legislature to incur indebtedness, a definite reaction to the Assembly's actions in the 1840's, and prescribes certain procedures the legislature must follow in enacting laws. Each house also adopts its own rules at the beginning of each session, and these also affect the legislative process.

The Legislative Council and more recently the Legislative Service Agency have become important parts of the legislative process in Indiana. Since the Legislative Council was created in 1967, replacing both the Legislative Advisory Commission and the Legislative Bureau, it has provided members of both the House and the Senate with resources that would otherwise be unavailable to them.

The Legislative Council is a bipartisan group of House and Senate leaders. This group is composed of eight members from each body and includes the Speaker of the House and the President Pro Tem of the Senate. The Lieutenant Governor, as the President of the Senate, serves ex officio as a non-voting member. The primary purposes of this body are to oversee the operation of the legislature, including making recommendations on both procedural and organizational matters, and to coordinate the work of the various committees in each House. It has the power to hold hearings and undertake investigations. The Council also has the responsibility for administering the staff of the Legislative Service Agency.

The Legislative Service Agency was spun off of the Legislative Council in 1978 to allow the Council to concentrate on policy matters. The Legislative Service Agency employs a large permanent staff and provides a number of services for both committees and individual legislators. Its primary responsibilities are in the area of doing research and drafting bills. Like the Legislative Council, the Legislative Services Agency is strictly bipartisan and works for both Houses.[25]

The Council, along with the Legislative Services Agency, has helped the legislature in becoming a more professional body. These units make the individual legislators less dependent upon outside sources for research and other information. These units provide the legislators with nonpartisan—and insofar as it is possible—unbiased analyses and assessments. Thus, legislators now have to rely less on the executive branch and outside lobbyists for information.

Rules and Procedures

The Constitution and the rules each chamber establishes attempt to bring order and fairness to the legislative process in Indiana, to prevent one group or party from abridging the rights of another group or party or the rights of the citizens of Indiana. The Constitution actually limits the legislature in only three ways: revenue measures must originate in the House of Representatives, a bill must relate to only one subject, and a bill must be read "by sections" on each of three separate days.[26] The legislature had to cope with each of these requirements in the 1970's. In its continuing battle with the Governor from 1975 to 1977 over the issue of parimutuel wagering, the legislature passed one bill (1976) which would have distributed a portion of the state's horse-betting income to the state's common school fund. The Governor vetoed the bill on the grounds it was a revenue-raising measure and should not have originated in the Senate. In 1971 the General Assembly attempted to codify all state statutes. The bill was approved but the state Supreme Court held it unconstitutional because the bill related to more than one subject. This necessitated the passage of a constitutional amendment in 1974 to permit the codification of state law. And in 1977, the legislature adjourned without passing a budget, and a special session, which could have extended to 40 days, was necessary. The General Assembly, however, invoked the "case of emergency" provision of the Constitution and passed the budget for the 1977–79 biennium and 13 other bills in a one-day session lasting only 12 hours—after failing to cope with these issues in the four-month regular session.[27]

The point here is twofold: rules are necessary for orderly and fair procedure in the General Assembly; but rules can also be manipulated, either to delay or prevent consideration of legislation, or to bypass certain steps in the legislative process. Legislators can find a variety of ways to thwart the progress of a bill in the step-by-step process toward which a bill may become a law (which, in practice, is somewhat more complex than the basic procedure outlined below) by using technical objections and parliamentary tactics.

Indiana legislators employ two devices which occasionally result in potential laws appearing almost out of nowhere. One device is the "vehicle bill"—known in other states as a "skeleton bill." It is literally a "bare-bones" piece of legislation, for it is a measure introduced without any content at all but applicable to a certain subject area. Usually these vehicle bills are assigned to the Rules and Legislative Procedures Committee in either house where they are in the control of the leadership. If, after the bill introduction deadline has passed, some legislation on a particular topic seems necessary, the leadership can insert content and report the bill to the floor. Thus, legislation can suddenly appear on some topic, ready for the amendment stage.

Legislation can also reappear, after it has apparently been defeated, through use of a device known as "bill stripping." This involves replacing the provisions of a bill which has passed one house with the contents of another measure which has been delayed or defeated. For example, a House member may introduce a bill to require all cats to wear a bell so they will not be able to sneak up on birds. A House committee kills the bill, or the House defeats it on final consideration. However, a Senator is also interested in protecting wild birds in this manner, so he takes a House bill which is at the amendment stage in the Senate and substitutes the "belling the cat" provisions for the original content of the bill. If the Senate passes this amended ("stripped") bill and the House accepts the Senate amendments, then the bill would become law—if not vetoed by the Governor. Thus, it is possible to bypass floor action in one chamber entirely and yet enact some measure into law. This procedure is ordinarily reserved for more controversial issues than the example used here. Also, House and Senate rules require that a bill may be stripped only with the written consent of the original author.

The General Assembly has established a series of deadlines to aid in the consideration of legislation. Thus, there is a certain period of time for members to introduce bills, a period for committees to consider the bills assigned, and a period for each chamber to pass or reject its own bills. This deadline is normally the 40th day of the long session and the 18th day of the short session, but these deadlines may be suspended by a majority vote in either house. The remainder of the session is devoted to a period of time for committee consideration of bills which have passed the other chamber, a period to pass or reject bills from the other house, and, finally, a period for considering and adopting or rejecting conference committee reports. The entire procedure is as follows: See Figure 3.2.

1. Introduction (first reading). After the Public Law Department of the Legislative Services Agency checks a bill for format and technical errors, a member files the bill with the appropriate officer, either the Clerk of the House or the Secretary of the Senate. This individual then assigns the bill a number (House bills begin with 1,001, Senate bills with 1) and delivers it to either the Speaker of the House or the President Pro Tem of the Senate, who refers the bill to a committee.
2. Committee action. This is the stage at which most bills fail. If the committee chairman decides to hold a hearing on a bill, the committee will take testimony and decide whether or not to report a bill out to the floor for further consideration. In practice, many bills are not given a hearing because the author does not seek one. However, if a committee does hold hearings on a bill, it ordinarily reports the bill to the floor with a favorable or "do pass" recommendation. The committee may report the bill out as written, as amended in committee in the light of the testimony it heard, or with substitute provisions for the original content. What happens most frequently, however, is that bills are "pigeonholed," that is, they are never given a hearing and are buried for the duration of the session.

Figure 3.2. How a bill becomes a law in Indiana

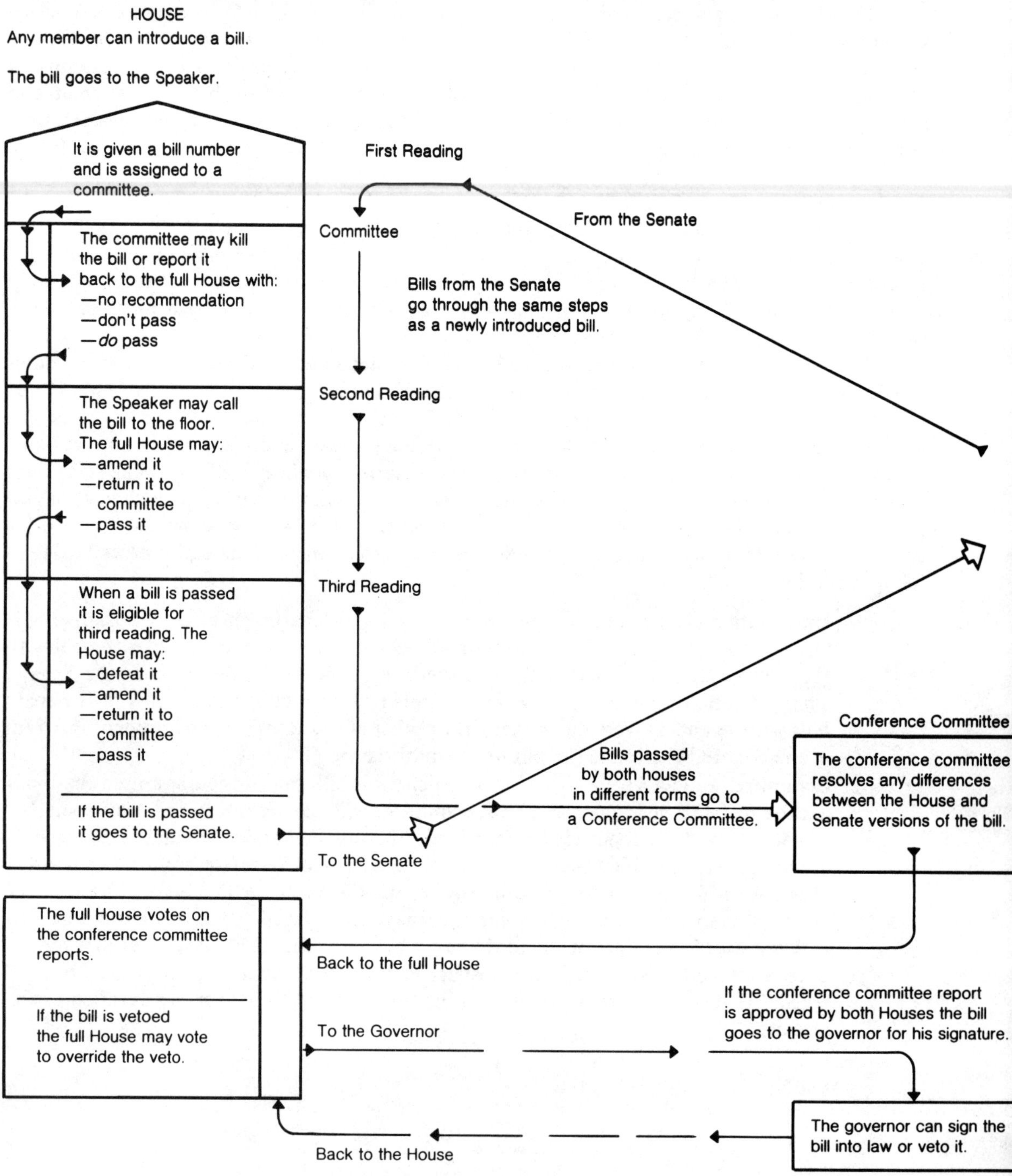

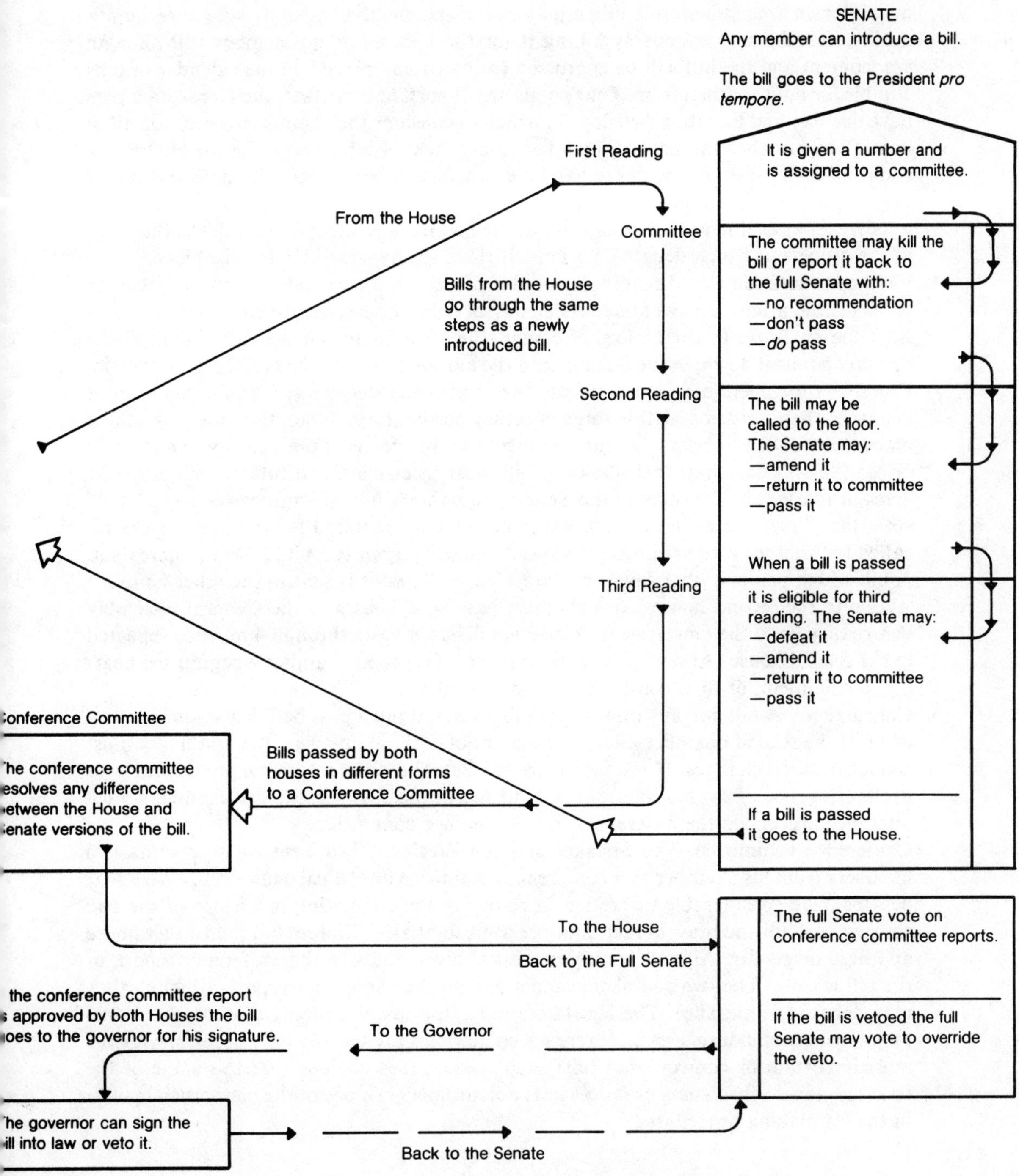
SENATE
Any member can introduce a bill.
The bill goes to the President *pro tempore*.
It is given a number and is assigned to a committee.
First Reading
From the House
Committee
The committee may kill the bill or report it back to the full Senate with:
—no recommendation
—don't pass
—*do* pass
Bills from the House go through the same steps as a newly introduced bill.
Second Reading
The bill may be called to the floor. The Senate may:
—amend it
—return it to committee
—pass it
When a bill is passed
Third Reading
it is eligible for third reading. The Senate may:
—defeat it
—amend it
—return it to committee
—pass it
Conference Committee
The conference committee resolves any differences between the House and Senate versions of the bill.
Bills passed by both houses in different forms to a Conference Committee
If a bill is passed it goes to the House.
The full Senate vote on conference committee reports.
To the House
Back to the Full Senate
the conference committee report is approved by both Houses the bill goes to the governor for his signature.
To the Governor
If the bill is vetoed the full Senate may vote to override the veto.
The governor can sign the bill into law or veto it.
Back to the Senate

3. Amendment and debate (second reading). When a committee reports a bill to the floor, the Speaker or President Pro Tem places it on a calendar of bills eligible for "amendment, recommitment or engrossment." That is, this is the point at which any member may offer an amendment to a bill; a majority of the membership may vote to recommit a bill to committee, effectively killing it for the session; or no member will offer an amendment and the bill will be engrossed (printed) and placed on the calendar of bills eligible for final consideration. Four points are important here: first, the House members have one day and Senators two days in which to consider the committee report on a bill before any member can propose an amendment; next, a bill remains on the House calendar until the Speaker decides to hand it down, on the Senate calendar until the author calls it for consideration, third, it requires only a majority of the members present to approve an amendment, not a majority of the members elected; finally, this is the stage in the process at which debate on a bill—if there is any—is likely to take place.
4. Final consideration (third reading). A bill is placed on the calendar of bills eligible for passage and, after a delay of one session day in either house, the membership may consider the measure. In the House, of course, the bill remains on the calendar until the Speaker hands it down; in the Senate until the author calls it for a vote. On controversial issues, the members may again debate the merits and demerits of a bill, but in most instances the discussion at this stage is rather perfunctory. When the presiding officer places the bill "on its passage," the members vote by means of pressing a green ("aye") or red ("nay") button at their desks. A bill must receive a Constitutional majority (51 votes in the House, 26 votes in the Senate) to pass. A bill which receives more "aye" votes than "nay" votes but not the minimum number required for passage may be recalled for another vote within three days. A majority against a bill, however, defeats it. A bill which passes a chamber is an "enrolled bill" and it is sent to the other house.
5. Action in the second house. All bills must pass both houses of the General Assembly before they go to the Governor for his action. Thus, steps 1 through 4 must be repeated in the second house. At any of several points in the second chamber—committee hearing, amendment, or final consideration—a bill can fail.
6. Concurrence. A bill not only must pass both houses, it must pass both houses in identical form. If the second chamber alters the content of a bill in any way, the first house must concur in these changes. If the first house accepts the different language, the bill goes to the Governor. If the first house refuses to accept the changes, the two chambers must attempt to reconcile the differences in a conference committee.
7. Conference committee. The Speaker and the President Pro Tem each appoints two members from his chamber to a conference committee on the particular bill. These four persons have considerable discretion in resolving the conflicting provisions of the two versions of a bill and may, in fact, produce a substantially different bill than either house approved originally. All four members must approve and sign the conference report, or the bill is dead. The two chambers cannot amend the conference report, although they may debate the measure. The legislators must approve the report by a constitutional majority in each house. Since conference committees are usually only necessary for the most important or controversial bills each session, it is obvious that this stage of the process—especially coming as it does near adjournment—is one of the most crucial points in the lawmaking procedure.

8. Governor's action. A bill which has passed both houses of the General Assembly is presented to the Governor for his consideration. By practice, although not required by either the state Constitution or statute, the Attorney General usually reviews all bills before they reach the Governor's desk and offers an opinion as to the constitutionality of each measure. The Governor has seven days after receiving an "enrolled act" of the legislature in which to take one of three steps: sign the bill into law; hold the bill without signing it, allowing the bill to become law without his signature on the eighth day after it is presented to him; or veto the bill and return it to the chamber of origin together with his objections. The Constitution requires the Governor to take one of these three steps on every bill which passes the General Assembly. In other words, the Governor does not have a "pocket veto" by which he could kill a bill after the legislature adjourned by refusing to act on it. This authority is available to the President of the United States and some governors, but it is forbidden the Indiana chief executive.
9. Override. If the Governor vetoes a bill, the legislature—even the next session—has an opportunity to override the Governor's action. If the house of origin passes the bill over the Governor's objections, the bill is sent to the second chamber where a majority vote to override enacts the bill into law in spite of the Governor's disapproval. The vote necessary to override a veto in Indiana is the same as that required to pass a bill originally—a Constitutional majority of 51 votes in the House and 26 votes in the Senate.

The rules of procedure discussed above and the formal organization detailed in the preceding section of this chapter combine to make the Indiana General Assembly a highly structured institution. In one respect, this is absolutely essential because of the hundreds of measures which confront the legislators in each session. In another, however, this has become one of the bigger hurdles to overcome in making public policy. Members who wish to delay or defeat certain measures are able to employ both the organizational framework and the procedural methods to accomplish their purpose. As in every state legislature, it is frequently easier to prevent action in the Hoosier assembly than it is to enact a bill into law.

The Legislature and Public Policy

The average citizen of Indiana is not greatly interested in the equity of his legislative districts. Nor does he care much about turnover rates or the socio-economic characteristics of those who make the laws. He is not particularly concerned with the organizational structure of the legislature or with the process by which a bill does or does not become a law. In short, only a very few residents of the Hoosier State care very much about the make-up of their General Assembly or the processes it employs.

However, the average citizen of Indiana does care about the final product of each session of the legislature and its impact upon him. Will it cost him more to support the various units of government of the state; that is, will the legislature increase the state income tax or sales tax rates, or will it permit local governments to raise additional revenue through increased property tax rates? Will the state provide sufficient money for road maintenance and repair? Can he legally drive on the highways of the state at speeds greater than 55 miles per hour? In short, the average citizen is concerned about the public policy made by the General Assembly.

Such factors as the equality of representation, the types of persons serving in the legislature and their degree of experience in government, and the methods by which the legislature operates do have an impact on what the General Assembly accomplishes or fails to do each year. Redistricting, at best, is an indirect influence on legislative performance. It affects only the manner in which lawmakers are chosen, not what issues the General Assembly considers nor the way in which legislators approach their duties. However, the redistricting in 1971–72 did bring to the Indiana legislature a number of members who advanced proposals and expressed attitudes either previously understated or not voiced at all. Procedural reforms enacted in the 1970's permitted the General Assembly to approach the needs and concerns of Indiana residents in a more orderly and rational manner. Yet, for all the changes adopted during that decade, the Indiana General Assembly remains subject to a number of outside influences—from the Governor and other administration officials, from the host of lobbyists who populate the halls of the State House each session—and these have a substantial impact on the types of public policy issues the legislature considers each time it meets.

This section surveys the impact of procedural reforms upon the ability of the Indiana legislature to function effectively, and the effect of outside influences on the actions of the General Assembly. Further, it considers the types of public policy issues the legislature considers and enacts or rejects.

Procedural Reforms

As late as the close of the 1960's, the Indiana General Assembly was not considered to be a very effective legislative body. It met only briefly every other year. Each chamber contained nearly 30 standing committees and permitted bill introductions beyond the midpoint of the session. Thus, there was little efficient committee review of potential laws, and most bills reached the floor without receiving careful study. In 1969, for example, the last session meeting under the 61-calendar-day restriction, the legislature attempted to deal with nearly 1,600 bills in a two-month period. The fact the General Assembly passed 31 percent (497) of the bills introduced serves not so much as testimony to the legislators' prowess in that year as it does as an indictment of the legislative procedure in effect at that time. Only a few could dispute the 40th place ranking among the nation's state legislatures the CCSL study had assigned the Indiana General Assembly.

In the 1970's, however, the legislature adopted many procedural reforms designed to permit the General Assembly to consider public policy concerns more effectively. Although a mid-1970's study suggested that the Indiana legislature seemed to be wearing the trappings of legislative reform but was actually dressed in the "emperor's new clothes,"[28] the General Assembly by the end of the decade had substantially improved its operating efficiency. The change to annual sessions, the establishment of permanent office space for members away from the floor, and modifications in the rules permitted the legislature to function more effectively. The reduction in the number of committees, the abolishing of proxy voting in committees, the opening of conference committee meetings to the public, and the establishing of deadlines for various phases of the lawmaking process made the legislature more accountable to Indiana citizens. An increase in the size and utilization of professional staff, both for legal and fiscal research and for committee work, permitted the legislature to gather and use information more proficiently. The increase in the representative quality of the legislative districts enabled the General Assembly to reflect more ably the diverse interests of the Hoosier State.

The adoption of procedural reforms such as these did improve the ability of the legislature to function more effectively. However, the existence of new methods and approaches toward the legislative process did not necessarily result in the enactment of different types of public policies. One of the principal reasons was the legislature's reluctance, or inability, to avoid outside influences, particularly from the Governor and other administration officials and from the representatives of various interest groups.

Outside Influences

The Indiana General Assembly, as most state legislatures, is rarely an initiator of public policy. Rather, it responds and reacts to the suggestions of others, principally the Governor, who annually establishes the agenda for the General Assembly in his "state of the State" address; the several hundred department heads who as full-time administrators tend to be more aware of what is necessary than are the part-time legislators; and the one thousand or more lobbyists who crowd the halls outside the legislative chambers each session to seek beneficial legislation for their clients.

Although the formal powers of the Indiana Governor have been rated among the weakest of the nation's 50 chief executives,[29] this does not give a true picture of the potential he has to be the most important external influence on the legislative product. He establishes in broad terms in his address to the General Assembly and in other public statements what the policy of the state should be. He suggests a level of state taxing and spending, allocating fiscal resources among the state programs through a budget prepared by an agency whose directors he appoints. It is true that his veto is the weakest in the country, but his use, or threatened use, of the veto has been extremely formidable in Indiana: in the 1970's, the Governor found it necessary to veto only 6 percent of all the bills passed by the General Assembly—and the legislature was able to override fewer than 10 percent of these vetoes. Clearly, the legislature enacts few statutes of which the Governor does not approve.

The heads of the many and varied administrative agencies, boards, commissions and departments in Indiana also influence the legislators' consideration of public policy issues. These department heads, however, rarely operate independently of the Governor for, under Indiana law, they are solely responsible to him. Thus, it is unlikely a department head will seek a budget increase or enactment of some policy without the prior approval of the chief executive. On the other hand, these agency directors operate on a daily basis and are much more knowledgeable about the needs of their operations than are Indiana's part-time lawmakers. They frequently make a persuasive case for their particular concerns before the General Assembly.

The lobbyists provide another outside influence on the legislature. These professional representatives of hundreds of interest groups from within, and occasionally outside, Indiana far outnumber the 150 elected assemblymen. More than 1,000 persons usually register as lobbyists each year. The number of persons who ignore the registration requirement may be as great. Leaving aside the occasional instances of cash bribes which have occurred and the frequent use of campaign contributions and hospitality rooms, the question becomes one of how much influence lobbyists have in Indiana. The answer is, a considerable amount.

Any proposed legislation that would benefit some group at the expense of others will find lobbyists attempting to promote and derail that proposed law. The lobbyists—representing business and labor, teachers and truckers, contractors and doctors, public utilities and the liquor industry, local governments and the state's public universities—are employed to see that the General Assembly either "improves" existing law as it affects their group or, at the very least, does not disadvantage them in relation to some competing group. Apart from providing free meals and drinks, the principal function of the lobbyist is to provide legislators with information—facts and figures which the part-time Hoosier lawmaker with only modest (albeit improved) staff assistance cannot always get for himself. Lobbyists in Indiana rarely deliberately mislead legislators, for a group's representative is effective only so long as he has access to the lawmakers and retains his credibility. To emphasize the importance of the lobbyist, remember that the individual legislator, with limited staff assistance, must be aware of and keep track of upwards of 400 bills at the passage state. The lobbyist and the interest group he represents, with sufficient personnel at their disposal, watch the progress of only the relatively few pieces of legislation important to their group.

Policy Considerations

The end result of each session of the General Assembly is the passage of several hundred new statutes. These laws may repeal or revise existing legislation, or they may add new regulations to the lawbooks. But while every law is of interest to someone, few of the legislature's acts have an impact on most Indiana residents. Indeed, even with the improved procedural arrangements and the more progressive outlook of many Indiana legislators toward the end of the 1970's, the General Assembly proceeds much as it did a decade or two before: the bulk of the items facing each session are relatively minor in scope, and the few major issues are usually not new but have been postponed from previous years. In fact, through the 1980 session, the Indiana legislature provided a classic example of the "Dillon's Rule" concept, that is local governments were "creatures of the state." About one-third of the bills considered each session by the General Assembly dealt with some aspect of local government.[30] In contrast, the legislature could defer action on such issues as public employee collective bargaining, strengthened lobbyist regulation, or adequate funding to repair and maintain the state's highways.

This is not to indicate that the Indiana General Assembly ignored all significant concerns during the 1970's. A lack of space prevents a detailed examination at this point of the public policy issues considered in each of these sessions. However, the legislature did take action in several important areas, enacting a revised criminal code, expanding the open meetings requirements for governmental bodies, and passing "sunset" legislation to provide for periodic review of the need for the continued existence of the numerous state administrative agencies, to cite only three examples.

Probably the legislature's most notable actions came in the areas of tax relief and "home rule" legislation. Well before the adoption in California in 1978 of "Proposition 13," a state constitutional amendment designed to reduce local property tax payments, Indiana passed in 1973 its own version of property tax relief. Funded by an increased sales tax (from 2 to 4 percent) and exempting prescriptions and most food, the state's Property Tax Replacement Fund pays up to 20 percent of each local taxpayer's real estate tax bill each year. In addition, the legislature limited the amount of money a local unit of government could raise through taxing real estate. The General Assembly in the latter portion of the 1970's found it necessary to permit several modest "thaws" in the property tax "freeze," but the legislature continued to provide Hoosier taxpayers with some of the more reasonable tax bills in the nation.

In its 1980 and 1981 sessions, the General Assembly also took action which could have far-reaching consequences for local governments—and relieve the legislature of having to deal with so many local concerns each year. It enacted a set of "home rule" laws which would permit every city of more than 2,000 population (except Indianapolis) and every county except Marion County the option of restructing its government as it pleased. If a local government did not wish to change its organization, it could continue to operate under provisions established by the General Assembly. However, if a local government wished to adopt a home-rule charter, perhaps establish a council-manager form of government, it could do so if the change were approved in a local referendum. Ironically, Indiana permitted this optional form of government from 1921–29, but—aside from Hawaii—was the only state to mandate particular local government organization through 1981.

The Legislature in the 1980's

As the Indiana General Assembly entered the decade of the 1980's, it remained a legislative body in transition.

The experience of ten years of meeting in annual sessions still had not determined for the members the role of the short session. For example, the legislature continued to enact biennial budgets although the need for an annual review of state spending was one of the justifications for yearly meetings established by the Constitutional Revision Commission in 1969. The legislature also refused to take advantage of all the time available to it, preferring to adjourn well in advance of its constitutional deadline in all but one (1977) of the first 12 sessions under the annual session concept. Further, until the 1981 session, the General Assembly did not schedule periodic recesses during the first portion of a session in order to permit the standing committees an uninterrupted term in which they could advance bills to the floor, a prospect also envisioned by the Constitutional Revision Commission and the framers of the 1970 amendment. Consequently, the legislature continued to meet a number of its limited session days each year with practically nothing to do because the committees had not had sufficient opportunity to advance bills to the amendment stage. Also, the General Assembly remained generally subservient to outside influences, especially that of the Governor. The legislature's independence during the 1970's existed primarily because Indiana's chief executives during that period chose not to attempt to dominate the General Assembly.

The legislature as it entered the 1980's, therefore, continued to be a significant force in the daily lives of Hoosiers, but it seems to yet realize its potential.

Notes

1. Citizens Conference on State Legislatures, *The Sometime Governments: A Critical Study of the 50 American Legislatures.* New York: Bantam Books, (1979) pp 210–213.
2. Indiana Legislative Council, *Report of Constitutional Revision Commission.* Vol. 1 of *Biennial Report to the Indiana General Assembly: 1969.* Indianapolis: State of Indiana, (1969).
3. Pound, William. "The State Legislatures," *Book of the States: 1980–1981.* Lexington, Ky.: Council of State Governments, (1980) p 79.
4. McCall, Charles H. "The Indiana Legislature and Politics" in James B. Kessler (ed.), *Empirical Studies of Indiana Politics.* Bloomington: Indiana University Press, (1970), p 17.
5. Indiana, *Constitution of 1851,* Art. IV, sec. 2, 4 and 5. These provisions, while remaining in the document, have been superceded by the United States Supreme Court's decision in *Reynolds v. Sims,* 377 U.S. 533 (1964).
6. The following discussion of Indiana's reapportionment problems is drawn from James L. McDowell, "Indiana" in Leroy Hardy et. al. (eds.) *Reapportionment Politics: The History of Redistricting in the 50 States.* Berkeley, Ca.: Sage Publications (1981), pp 110–115. See also, Leon H. Wallace, "Legislative Apportionment in Indiana: A Case History," *Indiana Law Journal,* Vol. 42, No. 1 (Fall 1966) pp 6–76.

7. If the General Assembly had wanted to redistrict during the 1940's and 1950's, it would have had difficulty. The last statewide census of male voters was taken in 1931. The 1933 session is the last which could have reapportioned on Indiana's constitutional basis.
8. *Book of the States: 1967–1968.* Chicago: Council of State Governments, (1968), pp 66–67.
9. *Reynolds v. Sims,* 377 U.S. 533, (1964).
10. *Whitcomb v. Chavis,* 403 U.S. 124, (1971).
11. Indiana, *Constitution of 1851,* Art. IV, sec. 7.
12. Fenton, John H. *Midwest Politics.* New York: Holt, Rinehart and Winston, (1966), pp 155–157.
13. Hyneman, Charles S. "Tenure and Turnover of the Indiana General Assembly," *American Political Science Review,* Vol. 32, No. 1, (February 1938), pp 55–57.
14. Carey, George W. "A Comparison of Rural and Urban State Legislators in Iowa and Indiana," in Kessler, *op. cit.,* p 88.
15. McCall, p 14.
16. Figure calculated by the author.
17. *Book of the States: 1978–1979.* Lexington, Ky.: Council of State Governments, (1978), p 31.
18. McDowell, James L. "The Decline of the Citizen Legislator," *APS Review.* Georgetown University, Vol. 1, No. 2, (Autumn 1978), p 21.
19. McCall, pp 13–14 (1923–1963); Janda, Kenneth, et al., "Legislative Politics in Indiana" in Kessler, *op. cit.,* pp 25–26, (1961); McDowell, James L. and Perry, Robert T. *Indiana State Government,* 2nd ed. Indianapolis: Indiana Academy in the Public Service (1982), pp 93–94 (1971–1980).
20. These statistics and those in the following paragraphs relating to occupational characteristics are from Hyneman, pp 55–57 (1925–1935); McCall, pp 13–14 (1923–1963); Janda, et. al., pp 25–26 (1961); and McDowell and Perry, pp 93–94 (1971–1980).
21. Indiana, *Constitution of 1851,* Art. V, sec. 21.
22. Indiana State Chamber of Commerce, *Legislative Report.* Indianapolis: published annually.
23. Indiana, *Constitution of 1851,* Art. VI, sec. 7.
24. Indiana, *Constitution of 1851,* Art. IV, secs. 22 and 23.
25. *Here Is Your Indiana Government, 1981–82* (20th ed.) Indianapolis, Indiana: The Indiana State Chamber of Commerce, (1981) pp 7–8.
26. Indiana, *Constitution of 1851,* Art. IV, secs. 17, 18 and 19.
27. McDowell, James L. "Well Conducted Encore Ends Legislative Disharmony," *Spectator.* Terre Haute, Vol. 143, No. 23, (June 4, 1977), p 13.
28. McDowell, "Legislative Reform in Indiana: The Promise and the Product" in Welch, Susan, and Peters, John G. (eds.). *Legislative Reform and Public Policy.* New York: Praeger, (1977), p 169.
29. Schlesinger, Joseph A. "The Politics of the Executive" in Jacobs, Herbert and Vines, Kenneth N (eds.). *Politics in the American States,* 2nd ed. Boston: Little, Brown and Co. (1971), p. 232.
30. Indiana Association of Cities and Towns, *Legislative Bulletin No. 6,* (February 9, 1979). The passage of a package of "home rule" legislation in the 1980 and 1981 sessions may have alleviated this situation somewhat.

4
The Executive Branch in Indiana

Robert T. Perry
Ball State University

Indiana Governor, Robert Orr signing a bill into law.
Courtesy of the South Bend Tribune

From the days of the first Governor of the state, Jonathan Jennings, to the present, citizens of Indiana have expected the state's chief executive to provide leadership for the solutions to administrative problems. As the top government official of the state, the Governor can direct, manage, coerce or do whatever is necessary to achieve desired actions. At least, that is what is often perceived and expected. The Governor, however, often finds himself in a complex web of structures and circumstances for which he has no "real" authority. As the "Head of State" by title, the Governor assumes the real or perceived responsibility and must find methods for maximizing his control over the substantial number of authorities and agencies. Unlike the President of the United States, who can appoint the top administration personnel, the Governor in most states, including Indiana, finds himself at the apex of an organization which is largely directed by forces beyond his control. Yet, among his duties, responsibilities, and roles the Governor serves as an administrator, a legislator, the head of the state military, his political party's spokesman, the leader of public opinion, and the ultimate judge on special occasions. In the following pages we will examine the executive system in Indiana and how the Governor manages to influence the direction of the state.

The Executive Branch and the Indiana Constitution

The executive branch of Indiana state government is one of three co-equal and independent branches or departments according to the State Constitution. The intent of the constitution framers is clear as they devoted one article (Article 3) to a brief statement on the distribution of government power. This statement, "the powers of government are divided into three separate departments; the Legislative, the Executive including the Administration, and the Judicial. . . ."[1] precedes any discussion of the specific functions, duties and responsibilities of any of these departments. Indiana, like the other forty-nine states, follows the American creation and tradition of government power distribution by utilizing the "separation of powers" doctrine.

Whereas the national constitution does not make distinct and separate references to executive and administrative branches of government, the 1851 Constitution of Indiana separately discusses these elements of government: Article 5, Executive and Article 6, Administrative. A review of titles of Articles in the Indiana Constitution—Bill of Rights; Sufferage and Election; and Distribution of Powers, Legislative, Executive, Administrative, Judicial. . . .—could quickly lead one to identify the administrative branch of government as a co-equal partner within the "separation of powers" doctrine. The distinction between policy making and the day-to-day operation of government business, however, is limited within the context of the Constitution. In the Distribution of Power Article, the executive branch is said to include the administrative; thus, the use of separate articles in the Constitution becomes somewhat inconsequential. The Executive Article vests the executive power of the state in the Governor. The Administrative Article outlines the several state and county offices which shall be filled by the electorate. Although elected, these offices hold ministerial responsibilities for specific government functions without possessing executive powers. Besides the executive personnel of the Governor and Lieutenant Governor, the Constitution provides that the voters will elect a Secretary of State, an Auditor and a Treasurer. In addition, the Superintendent of Public Instruction, an office created by the Constitution, is filled by election. Prior to an amendment adopted in 1972, the office was mandated by the Constitution to be elective. Since then, the General Assembly has statutorily retained it as an elective office. Statutory provisions rather than constitutional requirements have also created the office of Attorney General and provided that it be filled by election.

The sharing of executive and/or administrative authority with other elected officials in Indiana places the Governor in a situation which is comparable to his counterparts in other states.

Besides the Lieutenant Governor, the Governor shares executive/administrative power with the above mentioned five elected officials, three by constitutional mandate and two by legislative action. In addition to these officials, Indiana citizens also elect a Clerk of the Supreme and Appellate Court and a Reporter of the Supreme and Appellate Court. These are not included in the administrative listing of offices due to their specific judicial functions.

The number of Indiana elected executive and administrative officials, seven, ranks the State in the middle among states for the number of elected officials.[2] Nineteen states elect fewer executive and administrative officers, with two states, Maine and New Jersey, only electing the Governor. Twenty-seven states elect more executive officials than do Hoosiers. Leading the big ballot states are Michigan with 36, Texas with 34, and Ohio with 29 elected state officials.

Likewise, Indiana is in the middle among the states in number of agencies which are headed by elected officials.[3] Indiana has seven agencies headed by an elected executive or administrator. Twenty-one states have fewer agencies headed by elected officials, and eighteen states have more agencies which are presided over by elected leaders. North Dakota and Mississippi head the list for the most agencies with elected leadership, each having twelve.

Exempting the governorship, when comparing Indiana offices to those in other states, Indiana is very much a part of the traditional and common pattern for organizing and selecting state officers.[4] Forty-one states besides Indiana constitutionally provide for the election of the Lieutenant Governor. One state, Utah, has combined the office with that of Secretary of State by statutory provision. In Tennessee, the Senate elects a speaker from its membership who also serves, by statute, as Lieutenant Governor. The remaining six states do not have the office.

Thirty-six states join Indiana in having a Secretary of State provided for by the State Constitution. The remaining thirteen states do not have the office.

Thirty-nine states, including Indiana, elect the State Treasurer or the office which performs those functions, all but one according to the State Constitution. The Legislature elects the Treasurer in four states, the Governor appoints persons to the position in six states and the remaining state, Hawaii, does not have a comparable office.

Indiana's method for selecting the Attorney General is consistent with forty-three other states, although only two other states besides Indiana have the office as elective due to legislative authority rather than constitutional authority. In four other states the governor appoints the Attorney General; in Maine the Legislature designates; and in Tennessee the Supreme Court makes the selection.

Indiana is one of the twenty-five states that has an elected Auditor. A variety of organizational structures is used by the remaining states. The most common involves the Governor having some role in the selection. All of the states with elected Auditors have constitutional provisions for their elections.

Only a minority of states today select the chief administrative officer of their educational system by the ballot. Of these eighteen states, Indiana is the only state which elects the Superintendent of Public Instruction due to a statutory requirement. The others follow provisions in state constitutions.

Before returning to a more in-depth examination of Indiana's system, let us look at the personalities who have served at the apex of the executive system. Their impacts on the traditions and practices of state government are imbedded in today's operation of state government.

Characteristics of Indiana's Governors

Although no single mold has produced the forty-three Governors who have served Indiana, some common patterns of those who have served in the state's top executive role are apparent. Age, profession, partisanship, experience, post-gubernatorial service and election characteristics can provide an insight into those who have held the state's top political office.

At the time of assuming the responsibilities of Governor, the average age of the chief executive has been forty-eight years. The youngest Governor, James Ray, took office in 1825, just one week before his thirty-first birthday. James Williams, who took office just eight days before his sixty-ninth birthday, was the oldest of the forty-three Hoosier Governors at the time of his initial term as Governor. Williams died with less than two months remaining in his term in 1880. Overall, eight of Indiana's Governors were in their thirties at the time they became Governor. The last two of these, Oliver Morton and Conrad Baker, succeeded to the office of Governor from the office of Lieutenant Governor in 1861 and 1867, respectively. The six who were elected Governor while in their thirties were among the first eleven Governors, with the last of these, Ashbel Willard, assuming office in 1857. Contrary to common expectations about youth, Ashbel Willard died in office with a little more than three months remaining in his term. Selection of young Governors is not an historical pattern or current trend. Fourteen men assumed the office while in their forties and seventeen took their oath of office while in their fifties. Only four persons have undertaken the responsibilities of Governor after the age of sixty years. Besides James Williams, Alvin Hovey (sixty-seven years old in 1889), Roger Branigan (sixty-two years old in 1965), and Robert Orr (sixty-three years old in 1981) began their terms while sixty years old or older. Henry Schricker, who had been in his fifties when he held office for the first time, was sixty-five when he began his second term in 1949. There has been a preference for a mature government leader in Indiana in the 20th century.

The legal profession is well established as the most predominant occupation for persons who enter politics and hold elective office. Thus, it is not unusual that thirty-one of Indiana's Governors have been lawyers. Persons engaged in some form of business activity, education, and agriculture are the other occupations represented in the Governor's office with some regularity. By including bankers and publishers with general business, fourteen Governors had a background in private sector enterprises; six had been engaged in education; and seven came from agriculture. Otis Bowen and Paris Dunning are the two medical doctors who became Governor. Two Hoosier Governors, Isaac Gray and Alvin Hovey, had distinguished military careers in addition to their legal professions. Ira Chase's ministry served as a basis for his rise to prominence and election as Governor. He is the only person of the cloth to serve as the State's Governor. Although no pattern on occupations of Indiana's Governors appears, excepting the dominance of the legal profession, it is noteworthy that in recent years business and other non-legal careers have been more predominant.

When electing Governors, the Hoosier electorate has been uncannily bipartisan. Figure 4.1 shows the electoral patterns in Indiana's gubernatorial elections. Although the choices of the electorate have historically swung like a pendulum in party occupancy of the Governor's office, the overall time of party occupancy is virtually equal. The first five Governors came from the Democrat-Republican Party, followed by two Whig Governors. The next five Governors were Democrats. From the election of one-time Hoosier resident, Abe Lincoln, as President of the United States, to World War I, the two political parties virtually shared the Governor's mansion. Then from the election of James Goodrich (1917–1921) through Henry Leslie's term of office (1929–1933), Republicans were five times elected to head state government. Again, since Paul McNutt's election in 1932, the Democrats and Republicans have virtually shared the state's high-

Figure 4.1. Indiana gubernatorial elections

Election Year						
1816	Jennings (DR)	5,211	57.0%	Posey (DR)	3,934	43.0
1819	Jennings (DR)	9,168	81.4	Harrison (DR)	2,007	17.9
1822	Hendricks (DR)	18,340	100	———		
1825	Ray (DR)	13,852	53.2	Blackford (NR)	12,165	46.7
1828	Ray (DR)	15,131	39.2	Moore (NR)	10,898	28.5
				Canby (DR)	12,251	32.0
1831	Noble (NR)	23,518	45.6	Read (DR)	21,002	40.0
				Stapp (NR)	6,984	13.6
1834	Noble (W)	36,773	57.4	Read (D)	26,257	42.6
1837	Wallace (W)	46,067	55.5	Dumont (D)	36,915	44.5
1840	Bigger (W)	62,932	52.7	Howard (D)	54,276	46.3
1843	Whitcomb (D)	60,784	50.2	Bigger (W)	58,721	48.4
1846	Whitcomb (D)	64,104	50.7	Marshall (W)	60,138	47.5
1849	Wright (D)	76,996	52.3	Matson (W)	67,218	45.6
1852	Wright (D)	92,576	54.6	McCarty (W)	73,641	43.4
1856	Willard (D)	117,981	51.7	Morton (R)	112,139	48.7
1860	Lane (R)	136,725	51.9	Hendricks (D)	126,768	48.1
1864	Morton (R)	152,084	53.7	McDonald (D)	131,201	46.3
1868	Baker (R)	171,575	50.1	Hendricks (D)	170,614	49.9
1872	Hendricks (D)	189,424	50.1	Browne (R)	188,276	49.8
1876	Williams (D)	213,219	49.1	Harrison (R)	208,080	48.0
1880	Porter (R)	231,405	49.1	Landers (R)	224,452	47.7
1884	Gray (D)	245,140	49.5	Calkons (R)	237,748	48.0
1888	Hovey (R)	263,194	49.0	Matson (D)	260,994	48.6
1892	Matthews (D)	260,601	47.4	Chase (R)	253,625	46.2
1896	Mount (R)	320,932	50.9	Shiveley (D)	294,855	46.8
1900	Durbin (R)	331,531	50.5	Kern (D)	306,368	46.7
1904	Hanley (R)	359,362	53.5	Kern (D)	274,998	41.0
1908	Marshall (D)	348,849	48.9	Natson (R)	334,040	46.9
1912	Ralston (D)	275,352	42.9	Durbin (R)	142,850	22.3
				Beveridge	166,124	25.9
1916	Goodrich (R)	337,831	47.8	(PR)	325,060	46.0
1920	McCray (R)	683,253	54.6	Adam (D)	515,253	41.2
				McCulloch (D)		
1924	Jackson (R)	654,784	52.9	McCulloch (D)	572,303	46.3
1928	Leslie (R)	728,203	51.3	Dailey (D)	683,545	48.1
1932	McNutt (D)	862,127	55.0	Springer (R)	669,797	42.8
1936	Townsend (D)	908,494	55.4	Springer (R)	727,526	44.3
1940	Schricker (D)	889,620	49.9	Hillis (R)	885,657	49.7
1944	Gates (R)	849,346	51.0	Jackson (D)	802,765	48.2
1948	Schricker (D)	884,995	53.6	Creighton (R)	745,892	45.1
1952	Craig (R)	1,075,685	55.7	Watkins (D)	841,784	43.6
1956	Handley (R)	1,086,868	55.6	Tucker (D)	859,393	44.0
1960	Welsh (D)	1,072,717	50.4	Parker (R)	1,049,540	49.3
1964	Branigan (D)	1,164,620	56.2	Ristine (R)	901,342	43.5
1968	Whitcomb (R)	1,080,271	52.7	Rock (D)	965,816	47.1
1972	Bowen (R)	1,203,903	56.8	Welsh (D)	900,489	42.5
1976	Bowen (R)	1,236,555	57.1	Conrad (D)	927,243	42.9
1980	Orr (R)	1,257,383	58.0	Hillenbrand (D)	913,116	42.0

Notes: DR—Democrat Republican; NR—National Republican; PR—Progressive; D—Democrat; R—Republican; W—Whig

Source: Roy Glashan, *American Governors and Gubernatorial Elections, 1775–1975* (Stillwater, Minn. The Croixside Press, 1975)

est office, with six Republicans and five Democrats. Totally, the Democrats have been represented by sixteen different Governors, while twenty Republicans have held the office of Governor. In tracing the evolution of American political parties, it is commonly accepted that the Democrat-Republican party preceded the Democrat party and that the Whig party was one of the groups that merged into the Republican party. By including these evolutionary patterns of political party alignment, the forty-three individual Indiana Governors have nearly equally represented the two political parties, with twenty-one Democrat occupants of the office and twenty-two Republican chief executives.

Governors generally are not elected without having some previous experience in public office. The two most common forms of political experience include service in the legislative branch of state government and in state elective office. Twenty-four of Indiana's Governors have served in the General Assembly: fourteen served in the House of Representatives, seven in the State Senate, and three served in both chambers of the General Assembly. In addition, one Governor served in the Territorial Assembly. It is common for those coming from a legislative experience to have served in a leadership role in the General Assembly. Otis Bowen, who was the third House Speaker to be elected Governor, is typical of this pattern. Thirteen Governors had prior experience as the state's Lieutenant Governor. Of these, six were independently elected to the governorship while the other seven assumed gubernatorial responsibilities through succession to the office. Two of those who served out a governor's term of office, Morton and Baker, were subsequently elected in their own right to the office. Three other governors served as Secretary of State earlier in their political careers. No other state elective office has ever served as a steppingstone to the governor's office.

In addition to the Indiana General Assembly and state elective offices, Hoosier governors have had some previous background in federal positions. Indiana's first governor, Jonathan Jennings, had served as a delegate to Congress prior to statehood. Eight governors had served in the U.S. House of Representatives, with one, Thomas Hendricks, having served in the U.S. Senate. Seven held one or more federal appointed positions before assuming governorship. In addition, six governors had been judges, eight had held local government office, two had served as officers in the state's constitutional convention—President (Jennings) and Secretary (Hendricks)—and one, Alvin Hovey, had been a delegate to the State Constitutional Convention of 1850.

Only nine men have risen to the state's highest office without prior elective office experience. Seven of these had extensive experience in their political party organization.

Following their terms of office as governor, sixteen continued their service by holding one or more public offices. Two former governors were elected to the U.S. House of Representatives and seven to the U.S. Senate. It is worthy to note that Samuel Ralston is the only former Governor to win a seat in the U.S. Senate since the adoption of the 17th Amendment to the U.S. Constitution; the direct election of the U.S. Senators (1922). Two former Governors have become Vice President of the United States, Thomas Marshall and Thomas Hendricks. Five former governors served the U.S. government in appointive positions or on various commissions. Most notable are appointments as ministers to foreign nations.

Historically, the electoral road to the Governor's mansion has been against the pattern found in other states. Indiana was the very last state to abandon the state political party conventions as the sole method for nomination. Although the direct primary was used briefly to nominate Governors earlier in the twentieth century, it was soon abandoned. For Governor and Lieutenant Governor, the direct primary was reinstated with the 1976 gubernatorial nomination. The other state executive offices continue to be nominated by the convention system.

Once past the initial hurdle of the political party's nomination, the state's executive officials are elected at the general election. One recent modification in this process was the constitutional amendment which requires that the Governor and Lieutenant Governor candidates run as a team. Used for the first time in the 1976 election, this eliminates the prospects for the top two offices being filled by persons from different political parties. Although this has occurred in Indiana on several occasions—most recently in 1961–65 when Richard Ristine, a Republican Lieutenant Governor served with Democrat Governor Matt Welsh—it has also been a recent problem in several other states, most notably in California where the Democrat Governor Brown and Republican Lieutenant Governor Curb constantly battled over the powers and prerogatives of the Lieutenant Governor as acting Governor when the chief executive is out of state. Twenty states join Indiana with the joint election method while twenty-two have a system which permits persons from different political parties to hold office.[5]

A plurality vote of the Indiana electorate will elect the governor. Eleven times Hoosiers have selected a Governor who did not have a simple majority of the votes cast for that office. Although the closest contests were decided by 2 votes out of each 1,000 votes (1868 and 1940),[6] the constitution does provide a mechanism for a situation where a tie would occur in the general election. The Indiana General Assembly is required to select the Governor and Lieutenant Governor from among those who were tied. As the first order of legislative business following their organization, the General Assembly's selection would come from a majority vote of the combined membership (150) sitting in a joint session.

Conditions and Provisions of Indiana's Executive Officials

Qualifications

Aspirants to the Governor's chair must meet the legal qualifications imposed by the State Constitution. Like thirty-seven of the states, Indiana requires the Governor to be at least thirty years of age.[7] Only Oklahoma has an older age requirement (thirty-one years of age), while seven states have lower age requirements. Indiana is among the thirty-six states which require the Governor to be a U.S citizen. For Hoosiers, a Governor must have been a citizen for at least five years. A third requirement imposed by the Constitution is that the Governor must have been a state resident for at least five years preceding the election. Only seven states do not impose such a requirement on the Governor. Indiana's five-year requirement is shared by seventeen states. Of the thirteen states with longer resident requirements, Missouri has the longest with ten years. Rhode Island's one-month requirement is the shortest among the twelve states with less state citizenship or residency required. The same constitutional requirements apply to the Lieutenant Governor.

Other elected officials in Indiana have no constitutional requirements for holding office. Besides being an eligible voter, an implied age requirement of eighteen years, only the Attorney General has additional statutory requirements which are U.S. citizenship, state residency, and a license to practice law.

Succession

By an overwhelming vote of 700,801 to 143,650 the citizens of Indiana adopted a constitutional amendment on November 2, 1978, which revised the vague constitutional language about gubernatorial succession and the inability of the Governor to perform the duties of the office.[8] Similar to the constitutional changes made by the 25th Amendment to the U.S. Constitution in 1967, it satisfied the interest in clarifying the transition of executive powers. Several situations of transition are possible, with each presenting a somewhat different solution.

Figure 4.2. Experience of Indiana governors

Governor	Previous Public Office									Subsequent Public Office
	Lieutenant Governor	State Legislature	State Executive (elective)	State Executive (appointive)	Judiciary	Local Government	Constitutional Convention	Federal (elective)	Federal (appointive)	
Harrison										President of U.S.
Gibson							X		X	
Posey		S*								Indian Agent/U.S. Senate
Jennings							Pres X	X		U.S. Congress
Boon	X	H				X				U.S. Congress
Hendricks, W		TA					Sec X	H		U.S. Senate
Ray		Pro Team S								
Noble		H				X			X	
Wallace	X	S								U.S. Senate/Judge/State Constitutional Convention
Bigger		H			X					
Whitcomb, J		H				X			X	U.S. Senate
Dunning	X	H/S								
Wright		H/S				X		H		U.S. Minister to Prussia/U.S. Senate
Willard	X	H								
Hammond	X				X					
Lane		H						H		U.S. Senate/Indian Commission
Morton	X				X					U.S. Senate
Baker	X	H								
Hendricks, T.		H						H/S	X	Vice President of U.S.
Williams				X		X		H		
Gray		S								U.S. Minister to Mexico
Porter					X			H		U.S. Minister to Italy
Hovey					X		X	H	X	
Chase	X									

Figure 4.2. Continued

Governor	Previous Public Office									Subsequent Public Office
	Lieutenant Governor	State Legislature	State Executive (elective)	State Executive (appointive)	Judiciary	Local Government	Constitutional Convention	Federal (elective)	Federal (appointive)	
Matthews		H	Sec X							
Mount		S								
Durbin										
Hanley		H						H		
Marshall										Vice President of U.S.
Ralston										U.S. Senate
Goodrich										Served on several national gov't committees and commissions
McCray										
Branch	X	Speaker H								
Jackson			Sec X		X	X				
Leslie		Speaker H				X			X	
McNutt										U.S. War Manpower Chief/ Ambassador to Philippines
Townsend	X	H							X	
Schricker	X	S								
Gates										Nation Republican Executive Committeeman
Craig										
Handley	X	S								
Welsh		H/S							X	U.S.-Canada International Joint Commission
Branigan										
Whitcomb, E			Sec X							
Bowen		Speaker H								
Orr	X	S				X				

Should a Governor-elect be unable to assume office through death or resignation, the Lieutenant Governor shall become Governor and hold office for the unexpired term of the person he succeeds. In case the Governor, once having taken office, is unable to discharge the responsibilities of his office due to death, resignation, removal from office, or disability, then the Lieutenant Governor shall assume the powers and duties of the office as acting Governor.

In a situation where the Governor can and does declare that he is unable to discharge the duties and powers of his office, he shall transmit this message through a written declaration to the President Pro Tempore of the Senate and the Speaker of the House of Representatives. At that time, the Lieutenant Governor assumes the powers and duties of the office as acting Governor. The Governor will resume his powers and duties upon submitting a written declaration again to the President Pro Tempore of the Senate and the Speaker of the House of Representatives that no inability exists.

In a situation where the Governor is unable to communicate or is unaware of his disability, the Constitution provides for the Speaker and President Pro Tempore to take action to remove the powers and duties from the Governor to the Lieutenant Governor on an acting basis. This is accomplished by their filing a written statement with the state Supreme Court suggesting that the Governor is unable to discharge his responsibilities. The Supreme Court shall meet within forty-eight hours to decide the question, with their decision being final. Whenever the Governor files a declaration of his fitness to discharge his duties with the Supreme Court, again the court must decide the question in forty-eight hours, with the decision being final. Whenever a decision that no disability exists is made, the Governor assumes the full powers and duties of his office.

Should there be a vacancy at the same time in the offices of Governor and Lieutenant Governor, the constitution provides for the General Assembly to resolve the problem. The legislature is to meet in joint session within forty-eight hours and elect a Governor from and of the same political party as the immediate past Governor. In selecting the Governor, each house must cast a majority vote for the successful candidate. From the point of time that both offices of Governor and Lieutenant Governor were vacated and until the General Assembly selects a successor, the President of the Senate (President Pro Tempore since the office of Lieutenant Governor, the President of the Senate, is vacant) serves as acting Governor. Should there be no President of the Senate, the Secretary of State shall convene the Senate for the purpose of electing one.

Should a vacancy in the office of Lieutenant Governor occur, the Governor is responsible for nominating a Lieutenant Governor, who shall be confirmed by the General Assembly. This requires a majority vote in each chamber of the Legislature. The new Lieutenant Governor holds office for the completion of his predecessor's term. In the event that the General Assembly is out-of-session, the Governor shall call it into special session to receive and act upon the nomination. Until the vacancy is filled, the State Auditor shall fulfill the Lieutenant Governor's duties on any commissions or boards.

Transition

In transferring the executive power of Indiana from one administration to the next, the state has provided some assistance for an orderly transition, similar to action taken in thirty-two other states. For nearly two months the staffs of the incumbent and Governor-elect can arrange for this shift. The transition begins after the General Election (first Tuesday after the first Monday in November) and continues until the term commences on the second Monday of January. Indiana statutes provide for a $40,000 transition fund to be established and used by the new administration. This enables the Governor-elect to hire a staff of persons to organize the new administration. Oftentimes, these are the key persons from the Governor-elect's campaign staff. The transition staff participates in preparing the budget for the coming fiscal year. This is especially important when considering a biennium budget. Because the budget to be considered by the legislature during the early months in the administration will run the government to a period of time which is two and one-half years into the term of office, the new Governor must move swiftly to influence the budget direction of his administration. Without quick action, he could conclude his term with only one and one-half years of real budget influence.

The transition team is also allowed to utilize state personnel, become acquainted with office procedures and routines, and provide for the transfer of government information and files. Transition provisions in the statutes encourage cooperation in the changing of state leadership.

Compensation

Only North Dakota paid its Governor less than Indiana in 1980.[9] Indiana's Governor Bowen received a $30,000 a year salary plus $6,000 for expenses, just $2,500 more than his North Dakotan counterpart. When considering, however, the $17,000 supplement received by the Governor of North Dakota, Indiana may well have been the lowest in 1980. A 1977 legislative statutory change altered the pay beginning in 1981 to $48,000. The Governor is allowed $12,000 for office and other discretionary expenses in addition to his salary. In comparison to other states, Indiana is below the medium.[10] Thirty-one states, with New York at $85,000 and Texas at $71,400, offer their Governors more financial incentives than does Indiana. In addition to the one state that shares the Indiana level of compensation, the remaining seventeen states pay their Governor less than Indiana.

Indiana's Lieutenant Governor, prior to 1981, was paid a modest salary, $23,500 plus $44 for each day of the General Assembly. The salary changes adopted by the 1977 statute put the salary at $34,000 and eliminated the supplemental compensation for legislative duties. Maryland's $60,000 and Texas's $7,200 are the extremes among the states, with Indiana's new salary placing Indiana among the moderate paying states.[11] The same can be said about the other state elected officials in Indiana. The Secretary of State's salary ranges from $20,000 (Connecticut) to $60,000 (Michigan), the Attorney General from $25,000 (Missouri) to $60,000 (Michigan and New York), the Treasurer from $20,000 (Connecticut and Missouri) to $50,000 (Ohio), the Superintendent of Public Instruction from $27,500 (Arizona) to $61,685 (New York) and the Auditor from $20,000 (Connecticut) to $48,000 (Illinois).[12] All Indiana state elected officials receive $34,000.

Figure 4.3. Salaries for governors, 1980

Salary Level	Number of States
$80,000–up	1
$70,000–$79,999	1
$60,000–$69,999	10
$50,000–$59,999	18
$40,000–$9,999	13
$30,000–$39,000	7 [Indiana: $30,000 + $6,000]

Source: Compiled from information in the Council of State Governments, *Book of States,* 1980–81.

Figure 4.4. Salaries for state elected officials (Number of states by salary range)

	Lt. Gov.	Secretary of State	Attorney General	Treasurer	Auditor	Sup. of Pub. Instruction
$60,000–$69,999	0	1	2	0	0	0
$50,000–$59,999	1	1	5	1	0	1
$40,000–$49,999	11	8	14	9	4	7
$30,000–$39,999	9	15	20	16	2	7
$20,000–$29,999	6	12	2	12	4	3
$10,000–$19,999	12	0	0	0	0	0
Below $10,000	2	0	0	0	0	0
Indiana	$34,000	$34,000	$34,000	$34,000	$34,000	$34,000

Source: Compiled from information in the Council of State Governments, *Book of States,* 1980–81.

Formal Powers of the Governor

Most observers recognize that a leader's true powers often emerge from the individual's skills in acquiring and using authority which is not formally sanctioned. Whereas this informal power is vital to a Governor's success, it is often built upon a foundation provided by the formal authority or source of power in the Governor's hands. Joseph Schlesinger identified four primary sources of formal powers in his writings on the Governors.[13] Although he indexed these for inter-state comparison purposes, we will examine the power as a basis for reviewing the authority of Indiana's chief executive. Powers examined are tenure, legislative (veto), personnel (appointment) and budgeting.

Tenure Power

A willingness to accept and follow policy directions by those within, as well as those outside, government is primarily based upon a perception that the leader will be around long enough to see the policy executed. A leader who cannot succeed himself is weakened by the potential that the policy directions may be ignored, stalled, or adjusted long enough for the impending leadership change to take place. The longer the tenure in office or the potential for tenure in office, the greater the likelihood that policy directions will be implemented. An additional consideration is the longer the service of a leader, the greater the ability to systematically work toward policy change and implementation. Incremental shifts in policy and administration can provide the basis for future shifts. Over a period of time, significant changes can take place through policy and administrative "fine tuning." To acomplish the same goal during a short tenure could possibly cause a disruption in service and a need to quickly remove administrative barriers while leaving the end product vulnerable to new changes before the policy changes have had an opportunity to effectively demonstrated and evaluated.

Thus, the length of the Governor's term of office and the ability of the Governor to succeed himself becomes an important measure of power. Prior to 1972 Indiana had one of the weaker Governors among the states in tenure power. In the General Election of that year, by a vote—one which demonstrates a strong minority viewpoint of continuing to restrict the Governor's terms of office—of 633,577 in support and 497,458 in opposition, the tenure provision of the Governor was amended. Since the Constitution of 1851, Indiana Governors have been elected to four-year terms of office. With the change in 1972, a Governor can hold office for not more than eight years of any twelve-year period. The previous language restricted the Governor to no more than four years in any period of eight years. Only Henry Schricker was ever elected a second time under this provision, 1940 and 1948. Matt Welsh was the only other to attempt re-election when he unsuccessfully tried to reclaim the office in 1972, twelve years after his election as Governor.

Before the adoption of Indiana's second constitution in 1851, the tenure provision permitted succession for the Governor's three-year term of office. Governors Jennings, Ray, Noble, and Whitcomb all were elected to second terms. Only Governor Samuel Bigger was unsuccessful in a re-election contest when he lost to James Whitcomb in 1843. Governor Joseph Wright's second election in 1852 came after the change in the State's Constitution. As a result, he was elected to one three-year term and one four-year term.

Governor Otis Bowen is the first Governor to have the constitutional ability to be immediately elected to a second four-year term of office. Although this provision does not permit a third successive election, it does provide that Bowen could hold additional terms of office. He could again be Governor for every other term of the office and exceed the constitutional language of not "more than eight years in any period of twelve years."[14]

Today Indiana's tenure provisions are comparable to those in other states. Like forty-five other states—only Vermont, Arkansas, New Hampshire, and Rhode Island are excluded—Indiana has a four-year term of office.[15] The longer term is considered to be a source of strength for the Governor. Limitations on succession still serve to differentiate among the states' sources of power. The most power is thought to be found in states with no limitation on succession and the least power in states where no succession is permitted. On a comparative scale of states, Indiana has improved but continues to have a less powerful Governor than most states.

Legislative Power

Traditionally, the executive and legislative branches have competed for government authority as well as interacting within the checks and balances which are built into a separation of powers doctrine. A Governor is required to examine his arsenal of authority to find weapons which are useful in insuring that the legislative branch follows his leadership in state policy matters. For this discussion, official and formal authorities can provide some insight. It is well to keep in mind, however, that much of a Governor's leadership with the legislature is not reflected in formal authority. We will return to the informal influence later.

Figure 4.5. Tenure power of Indiana in comparison to other states

Terms of Office	States with succession unlimited	States with consecutive 2 terms limit	States with 2-consecutive term and must wait 1 term	States with absolute 2 term limit	States with no succession
4 year terms	18	17	2 [INDIANA]	3	5
2 year terms	4	—	—	—	—
	22	17	2	3	5

Note: Indiana's 8 years in 12 years provision gives it a 2 consecutive terms limit, but the Governor would not necessarily be eligible for 2 additional consecutive terms.

Source: Compiled from information in the Council of State Governments, *Book of States,* 1980–81.

Indiana's Governor has two principle measures for interacting with the General Assembly. In January of each year, usually early in the legislative session, the Governor appears before a joint session of the General Assembly for the purpose of giving the "State of the State" message. This complies with the state constitutional language which says the Governor "shall, from time to time, give the General Assembly information touching the condition of the state, and recommend such measures as he shall judge to be expedient."[16] The Governor's legislative package for the session is commonly outlined in the presentation. This provides the Governor with an opportunity to lead the policy decision-makers of the legislature. Whether or not they follow greatly depends on his informal powers.

The second but somewhat associated power is the governor's veto authority. More than anything else, this is a power the governor can use to bargain with the legislature. The greater the difficulty in overriding the governor's veto, the greater the bargaining position of the governor. The governor can bargain for revisions in a particular bill or can bargain for passage or non-passage of other legislative measures. Whatever strategy the governor may want to use, it is the formal authority and its potential use which sets the foundation.

Schlesinger used the veto power as a measure of the governor's legislative power. Two factors in the veto power are important: what can be vetoed and the difficulty of sustaining the veto. A governor who has the item veto has more formal legislative power than does a governor who does not. The item veto permits the governor to veto only portions of a bill and allows the remaining parts to become law. The governor can be very selective when using this authority. It provides considerable leverage over the legislature in the forming of specific legislation. An alternative version found in some states is where a governor can write a proposed amendment to a bill and return it to the General Assembly. This is referred to as the executive amendment and gives the governor the advantage of forcing the legislature to vote on his language for the bill. The weakest position for the governor is when he must veto all of a bill. The Governor may have to sacrifice some provisions with which he is in agreement in order to eliminate a section that he does not find acceptable. Indiana's Governor is one of only six who does not have an item veto provision.[17] In Indiana, the Governor must act upon the complete bill.

The second measure of the veto power is the ease by which the legislature can override the Governor's action. The more difficult an override action, the greater the Governor's formal power. The veto override requirement which gives the greatest power to the Governor is one which requires 2/3 vote of the elected membership to each chamber of the legislature. In addition to the twenty-six states with this requirement, eleven states require 2/3 vote of those members of each chamber who are present at the override vote.[18] Five states use a 3/5 vote of the elected members while one state provides for a 3/5 vote of those members present at the vote.[19] These forty-three states place an extraordinary burden on the legislature for enacting legislation which the Governor does not desire. In each, the Governor's position is strengthened by the additional difficulty in securing sufficient support to pass a controversial statute. Indiana is joined by five states in requiring that a simple majority of the elected chamber membership is sufficient to override the Governor's veto.[20] In these states the Governor's formal power is not enhanced since the legislature needs only the same number of votes received during the original passage of the law. Only the informal influence of the Governor to dissuade legislators from their previous position can make the veto meaningful.

Among the states, Indiana's Governor has the second weakest position of authority of legislative veto power. South Carolina's Governor, who has no veto power, is the only Governor in a weaker position. Indiana is the only state of the six without an item veto authority that requires only a simple majority of elected legislators to override a veto. There are ten states that are weak in either the flexibility of what is vetoed or in the vote requirements for an override. But none is like Indiana and weak in both.

Regardless of the formal strength of the veto power, its real strength is determined by the user of the power and the means by which it is used. A review of the legislative sessions in the 1970's and early 1980's reveals the practice of the veto power in Indiana (see Figure 4.6). During these eleven legislative years, only 117 legislative measures were vetoed by the Governor. This represents a minimal amount compared to the 3,240 bills passed by both houses of the General Assembly (3.6%). Even with a relatively weak legislative power, the Governor was able to have his will sustained on most of those measures. Only eleven times of the possible 117 was the Governor's veto overridden. Thus, on about one-third of one percent of all bills enacted into law was the Governor's veto power used and overturned by the legislature. The Governor's effective use of the veto was evident on 106 bills (3.3% of the total bills passed). Of special interest is the tenure of Otis Bowen, where only 2 of 82 vetoes were overridden by the General Assembly. They both came when one branch of the legislature was controlled by the opposing party. During the last two years of Governor Edgar Whitcomb's administration, 9 of 28 vetoes were overridden by the legislature. It suggests that the real use of the veto is influenced by events, partisan control of the General Assembly, individuals, and the selectiveness of a Governor's choice in using the veto power. All are beyond the formal authority of the Governor.

Figure 4.6. Indiana governor's veto power

	Bills Introduced	Bills Passed	Governor Signed	Became Law Without Governor's Signature	Bills Vetoed	Vetoed Bills Overridden
1971	1688	499	478	5	16	5
1972	794	249	231	2	12	4
1973	1263	355	336	11	8	0
1974	697	167	157	2	8	0
1975	1706	376	388	12	26	0
1976	926	165	157	2	6	0
1977	1785	375	359	5	11	2
1978	939	164	157	3	4	0
1979	1706	337	318	1	18	0
1980	959	224	219	4	1	0
1981	1628	339	330	2	7	0
	14091	3240	3130	49	117	11

Source: Indiana Legislative Council

Appointive Powers

The third formal power of the Governor relates to his ability to direct or control the administrative agencies of his administration. In Schlesinger's review of formal power of the Governor, he identified the appointment power of the Governor as an indicator of the Governor's strength in managing the state administrative system. As noted in the case of *Tucker v. State,* the legal structure of Indiana government recognizes the power of the chief executive to control appointments of his principle policy-making subordinates.[21] The practice of this doctrine places Indiana's Governor as one of the more powerful in personnel management. In Schlesinger's study, Indiana ranked behind only New Jersey in terms of the Governor's strength in appointment power.

The strength of the Governor can be measured by his control over the appointment of subordinates in major state agencies. In Schlesinger's study, sixteen separate state functions were examined to determine the Governor's power to appoint. The Governor was considered to have the greatest control when the agency head was directly appointed by the Governor. A Governor who could appoint an agency head upon the confirmation by one or both houses of the General Assembly would find his position weakened in the appointment of power. This is true since the legislature would be able to coerce the Governor by withholding their confirmation of his appointments to major offices. It was also accepted that a Governor would be less able to control the management direction of state government if he shared his appointment power with one or more agencies, boards, or commissions of state government. For example, a Governor who nominates a person for appointment to head a state agency but must have the approval of the overseeing board or commission would find himself sharing the authority to appoint the department administrator. Less desirable situations related to appointment power are where boards or commissions nominate chief administrative officers who are then confirmed or appointed by the Governor. This permits the board or commission to select the agency head and give the Governor only those choices for appointment that the commission or board wants him to have. Any sharing of the appointment authority with other agencies of state government places the Governor in a position of not having control or responsibility for those persons who hold executive appointments within the administration. Even less desirable situations of gubernatorial appointment authority would be the election of state officials who have responsibility for an administrative function of state government. This is considered to be the weakest position of the Governor in the appointment power since he obviously has no capacity to direct those persons who are beholden to the voter of a state rather than to the Governor's authority.

A secondary influence on the Governor's power to control the management of his administration is the tenure of subordinate officials. Subordinates who serve at the pleasure of the Governor obviously remain more directly under control of the Governor during his administration. However, situations where subordinates are appointed for specific terms of office place the Governor in a less influential position when it comes to directing activities of that agency. The ability of the Governor to remove subordinates without cause as opposed to the necessity for showing cause also strengthens the Governor's control over the bureaucracy. The significance of this is that removing without cause permits the Governor to make changes for purely policy reasons.

Borrowing from Schlesinger's list of functions of state government, we can review Indiana's gubernatorial authority over appointments. With the exception of the six positions which are elected by the voters and the one function which is incorporated with other functions of the state government, the Governor of Indiana can directly appoint agency heads for the other nine functions. A review of these positions and the method of selection along with other significant functions of state government can be found in Figure 4.7.

Figure 4.7. The governor's appointment power in Indiana

Major State Functions (Schlesinger Study)	Agency	Chief Administrative Official Selected by
Administration	Dept. of Administration	Governor Appoints
Agriculture	Commissioner of Agriculture	Elected (Lt. Governor)
Attorney General	Attorney General	Elected
Auditor	State Auditor	Elected
Budget Officer	Budget Agency	Governor Appoints
Conservation	Dept. of Natural Resources	Governor Appoints
Controller	(performed by auditor)	-------------------
Education	Supt. of Public Instruction	Elected
Health	Board of Health	Board of Health/Gov. Approval
Highway	Dept. of Transportation	Governor Appoints
Insurance	Insurance Department	Governor Appoints
Labor	Division of Labor	Governor Appoints
Secretary of State	Secretary of State	Elected
Tax Commissions	State Board of Tax Commissioners	Governor Appoints (3)
Treasurer	State Treasurer	Elected
Welfare	Dept. of Public Welfare	Governor Appoints
Other Major State Functions		
Commerce	Department of Commerce	Elected (Lt. Governor)
Planning	State Planning Services Agency	Governor Appoints
Utility Regulation	Public Service Commission	Governor Appoints (3)

The influence of the Governor over the state personnel system is of some significance when viewing the number of persons who are employed by state government. Indiana employed 62,059 full-time equivalent employees in 1978[22] and ranked 19th in the number of state employees among the states.[23] Whereas in actual numbers this may seem large, there are only five states which have fewer employees for each ten thousand of population than does Indiana.[24] For every ten thousand residents of Indiana, there are 115 state employees as compared to the national average of 136 employees for each ten thousand citizens of a state.

As might well be expected, the bulk of these state employees are found in education. Nearly 50 percent of Indiana's state employees are found in institutions of higher education (29,242 of 62,059). An additional 3,314 employees work in the field of education within state government. Outside the field of education, a significant number of employees can be found in the health and highway functions of state government. A review of state functions and Indiana's level of state employment is in Figure 4.8.[25]

For the past decade, Indiana state government has grown in personnel. This rise in number of full-time employees indicated the increasing significance of the roles and functions of state government. Although information supplied by the Department of Administration, Personnel Division, indicates a rise in the number of full-time employees, there is not a substantial rise, particularly in the last three years, in the number of full-time positions in state government. A review of Figure 4.9 shows the trends in state employment for functions other than education.

Figure 4.8. Indiana state government employees (full-time equivalent) by selected functions

	Indiana	U.S.
Institutions of Higher Education	29,242	907,346
Other Education	3,314	108,391
Highways	5,412	259,884
Public Welfare	1,171	169,174
Hospitals	9,707	537,706
Corrections	2,186	138,947
Police Protection	1,536	71,474
Natural Resources	2,379	161,432
Financial Administration	1,823	121,091
General Control	621	82,580
All Functions	62,059	2,965,961

Source: Council of State Governments, *Book of States,* 1980–81, Table 5, p. 273. Taken from U.S. Bureau of the Census, *Public Employment in 1978.*

Figure 4.9. Indiana full-time state positions and employees (excluding education)

	No. of Full-time Positions	No. of Full-time Employees
July, 1980 (Estimated)	32,298	29,104
July, 1979	32,669	27,994
July, 1978	32,421	28,309
July, 1977	31,202	27,536
July, 1976	30,666	27,339
July, 1975	28,903	26,359
July, 1974	27,265	24,447
July, 1973		24,022
July, 1972		23,914
July, 1971		23,646

Source: State of Indiana, Department of Administration, Personnel Division.

Appointments to positions in Indiana state government can come under the classified or unclassified service. The distinction is made by statutory definition of what positions fall under the State Personnel Act or merit positions. These positions under the classified service are subject to the provisions of the State Personnel Act.[26] The State Personnel Act is:

> to insure the appointment of qualified persons to the state service . . . solely on the basis of proved merit, to offer any person a fair and equal opportunity to enter such state service, and to afford the employees in such state service an opportunity for public service in individual advancement according to fair standards of accomplishment based upon merit principles, and to which ends there is . . . established a personnel system based on merit and scientific methods relating to the appointment, compensation, promotion, transfer, layoff, removal and discipline of employees and to other instances of state employment.[27]

The State Personnel Act applies to all members and officers in those designated agencies with the exception of the chief administrative officers; persons in positions of appointing authorities, deputies, or assistants reporting to appointing authorities; and members of boards and commissions.

Those state agencies which fall outside the state classified service and into the unclassified service do not, then, come under the terms of the State Personnel Act. Employees in unclassified service serve at the pleasure of the appointing authority. Although the personnel classification and salary policy provisions apply technically only to the classified personnel service, in practice the State Budget Agency has merged the classified and unclassified systems. From a practical standpoint the primary differences between the two is that classified positions require competitive exams or ratings of individual candidates by some means before appointment, where the unclassified positions do not. In the unclassified system the appointing authority has greater flexibility in making appointments, although this does not mean that the appointments are any less qualified. The other primary difference is classified personnel's right to the personnel appeals and grievance system, whereas unclassified personnel are not entitled to use these procedures.

Budget Power

The final element of gubernatorial authority and power suggested by Schlesinger's study was the budget power. Schlesinger used the Governor's role in preparation of the state budget as a measure of the Governor's influence and control over the budgetary process. Whereas the Governor of Indiana was seen to be significantly influential in the appointment process, he fails to attain the same level of authority in the budget-making process. A Governor with significant authority would have an executive budget. This is a budget prepared by the Governor or by his direct staff where the Governor has substantial involvement in the formation of the budget before it is transmitted to the legislative branch of government. The Governors with power to make budgetary recommendations and decisions find themselves somewhat more influential in directing the appropriations of state expenditures. Governors who play a limited role in the budget preparation process or share that authority with other state officials or agencies find themselves limited in their ability to influence the direction of the budget proposal. Indiana is such a state. In forty-six states, the Governor either has exclusive power to formulate the budget or shares this with one agency head or appointed official.[28] Indiana is among the four states which are classified as weakest in gubernatorial authority over the budget function.

In Indiana, the primary responsibility for preparing the state budget rests in the State Budget Committee. The State Budget Committee is composed of the State Budget Director, who is appointed by the Governor and serves at his pleasure, and two members from each legislative chamber. The Senate members are appointed by the Senate President Pro Tempore, with one member from each political party. The State Budget Committee is composed of the State Budget Director, who is appointed by the Governor and serves at his pleasure, and two members from each legislative chamber. The Senate members are appointed by the Senate President Pro Tempore, with one member from each political party. The minority party leader nominates the person from his party who is then selected by the President Pro Tempore. In the House of Representatives it is the Speaker who makes the appointment with the same conditions placed upon his appointment of the minority member. In addition to the four members from the legislature who serve on the committee, there are four alternate members, one from each of the political caucuses, to serve in the absence of the regular appointed member from the General Assembly. In formulating the state budget, it is this committee that makes decisions. In terms of formal power, this procedure places the legislative branch of government in a superior position in influencing budget preparation—since they have 80 percent of the committee's membership. Where it is possible for the legislature to dominate, it is not probable in a strong partisan state like Indiana. The Governor has two members from the legislature of his own political party in addition to his state budget director as members of the committee. Whereas he may not be able to formally dictate the preparation of the state budget, he is in a politically superior position to influence the development of the state budget through his leadership role in the political party.

The role of the State Budget Committee is to obtain from the various state agencies, boards, and commissions the proposed biennium budgets which are reviewed during the summer and autumn of the year prior to submission to the General Assembly in January. The State Budget Committee holds hearings where the administrative agencies defend and promote their budget proposals. The committee most often reduces the amount of money requested by the state agencies before submitting the budget to the General Assembly. Upon completion of its task, the committee transmits its work to the Governor who officially has the responsibility for sending the state budget to the General Assembly for review. Since the legislative branch is heavily involved in the preparation of the budget proposal through the State Budget Committee, the legislature enters this stage of the budget process with a good understanding of the budget, unlike those states where the legislature has not seen a budget until the Governor transmits his executive budget to them.

In Indiana, the budget is first submitted to the House of Representatives where it is assigned to the House Ways and Means Committee for hearing and recommendations. The common practice is for the House Ways and Means Chairman to be a member of the State Budget Committee. Therefore, he and his counterpart from the minority party have a thorough understanding of the budget when it comes to the committee. The committee normally holds hearings on the budget and commonly amends the budget before submitting the budget to the floor of the House of Representatives. Upon passage in the House of Representatives, the budget is referred to the State Senate where the State Senate Finance Committee proceeds to review the budget in much the same manner as did the House Ways and Means Committee. Once again, since the leadership of the Senate Finance Committee has normally been involved with the State Budget Committee, the committee begins the process with some significant understanding of the intricate parts of the budget. Upon completion of the budget and passage by the Senate, the budget is almost always referred to a conference committee where the House and Senate arrive at a common agreement about the level of state appropriations and which agencies should spend those funds. It is common practice for the Conference Committee to be composed of the same legislators who served on the individual committees and made decisions during the budget process.

In Indiana, the General Assembly has no limitations placed upon its review and altering of the budget once it is submitted to the General Assembly. In other states, the Governor's position is strengthened in the budgetary process when the legislature is limited in increasing the amount of appropriations suggested by the Governor.[29] For instance, in Maryland the legislature may decrease, but it cannot increase, the appropriations for the legislative and judiciary branches of government. In Nebraska, the state Senate may increase any of the Governor's recommendations, but may do so only by a 3/5 vote in favor of such action. However, Indiana's legislative budget authority, where the legislature has unlimited authority to alter the budget once it is submitted to the General Assembly, is typical of that found in most states.

In addition, the Governor's power over the legislative actions in the state budget can be influenced by whether or not the Governor has the item veto. As we noted earlier in our discussion, the lack of that power in Indiana limits the Governor's influence on the direction of general legislation and, more specifically, budgetary legislation. The lack of this additional power places the Governor in a weak bargaining position with the General Assembly when there is some dispute about the level of state appropriations and how that money should be spent.

One of the major debates between the political parties in the 1970's in Indiana was the question of whether to have a biennium or annual budget. The tradition in Indiana has been to have a biennium budget which can be reviewed for emergencies in the short legislative year. The biennium is a two-year budget as opposed to a one-year budget. The major argument for a biennium budget is that it sets the budgetary question aside for two years; therefore, the political struggles over allocating revenues and appropriating expenditures surface on a two-year cycle rather than going through annual battles. Since the legislative body meets only for thirty days in the short session, it is thought that there is not sufficient time to review the total state budget. The proponents of an annual budget argue that, due to changing needs, inflation and requirements imposed by the federal government, an annual review of the total state budget is desirable. In comparison, twenty states join Indiana with a basic biennium budget process.[30] The remaining twenty-nine states utilize the annual budget process. The approach in Indiana has been to restrict the opening of the budget in the second year to emergency items only. Common practice is for pet projects of legislators and administrative agencies to surface during the second year for consideration. It is then up to the General Assembly, working with the Budget Committee, to determine whether or not to meet the emergency, or whether it can be postponed to the next biennium. An extension of the budget preparation and adoption authority is the management of fiscal and financial resources from the time of appropriation to the time of expenditure. Operating on behalf of the Governor, the State Budget Agency controls the expenditure of budgeted dollars. State funds are allocated on a quarterly basis to state agencies for expenditure purposes. State agencies must request from the State Budget Agency their allocations for each quarter. The State Budget Agency may review that request and determine whether or not the revenues are available to meet the request, whether the request is in line with the adopted budget, and whether the agency needs the resources which it has requested. This is one means by which the State Budget Agency can control the expenditures of state government. Among the tasks of the budget agency during the period between budgets is to monitor the anticipated revenues to insure that sufficient revenues are available to meet the appropriations made by the General Assembly. In situations where the revenues do not appear to meet the appropriation levels, the Governor, acting through the State

Budget Agency, may cut back the expenditures of state agencies or freeze hirings in state agencies, as Governors Bowen and Orr did in 1980 and 1982 respectively when they froze state agencies. The Governor may also order a cutback in state expenditures, as Governor Bowen did in 1979 for the use of gasoline in travel by state agencies. In 1982, Governor Orr, likewise, ordered a freeze on equipment purchases and capital expenditures except for emergencies, ordered a reduction in out-of-state travel by 60 percent, instructed state agencies to put 10 percent of their budget in reserve, and established a task force to find other methods for reducing the appropriated budgets. The Governor's position in the general financial administration of the state is much stronger than it appears by looking solely at budget making authority.

Administrative Reorganization Power

An investigation into what powers Governors did not possess found that Governors most often thought they lacked the power to reorganize state agencies. Reorganization authority permits the Governor to shift personnel and functions of state government between agencies or among agencies for purposes either of consolidating activities or segregating activities as he deems desirable by the policies of his administration. In Indiana, the Governor has no independent authority to reassign functions of state government or to reorganize functions of state government within the administrative structure. All reorganization is the prerogative of the General Assembly. The Governor's role is simply one of recommending to the General Assembly reorganization efforts which he would like to see enacted. There is no requirement on the legislative body to act at all, much less positively, upon the Governor's recommendation. The authority of the Governor in reorganization of the state administrative agencies may well have become even less significant with the recent onset of sunset legislation. Sunset legislation mandates the legislative body to review state agencies on a regular basis, in the case of Indiana once every eight years, and to make changes as are necessary to maintain the function and responsibilities of the specific state agency. Since the legislature in operating under sunset provisions has the capacity to make reviews of state agencies, we can also expect them to make recommendations on the organizational and functional structures of state government. The Governor's role remains one of putting into the legislative branch his preferences for reorganization. If anything, Governors have probably lost authority in making recommendations to the General Assembly.

Formal powers are easily overemphasized due to the legal basis for their existence. That is not to exclude the many informal powers or influences from the list of significant weapons available to the Governor. The Governor can, and has, used these resources as integral parts in his overall managing of state government. Among these are several worth noting. The Governor has utilized the patronage concept in making appointments within the administration. This works in practice when the Governor receives a nomination for a vacant position in the administration or for a board or commission. The Governor clears the designated persons with the individual's home county party organization before making the appointment. It is common to also insure that the individual is approved by the Congressional District and State Committees, but for practical purposes it is the county organization that is usually the most significant. The use of this clearing procedure keeps the Governor in the good graces of his political party organization and strengthens his ability to use the party organization to advance his goals to the public and the legislature. In a similar activity, the Governor may choose to assist or not to assist his party's candidates for the General Assembly. If the Governor is popular, that aid can help in getting both campaign finances and votes.

In addition, the Governor and the administrators control an abundance of information that can be helpful to many others, particularly other elected officials. How and with whom the Governor wishes to share this information is of great importance. Likewise, the Governor can always get the news media to listen to his views. This ability to communicate directly with the people helps to keep challengers to his authority and policies at a minimum. It is the use of these, separately or in conjunction with one another, that inflates the formal authority granted to the Governor. A Governor who uses these well can greatly increase his power.

State Administrative Structure

Indiana's Governor presides over approximately four hundred different state agencies and boards. The list of these is too great to depict in any single illustration. The administrative volume is shared by six other elected state officials, five of them completely outside the authority or accountability line to the Governor. Since the Lieutenant Governor is elected with the Governor as a team, we may conclude that he is not truly independent of the Governor, although it is well to remember that the Lieutenant Governor is independently nominated. In addition, the administrative burden is shared by a large number of persons who serve in full-time, or more commonly in part-time, positions on the numerous boards, commissions, or councils of state government. These policy-making overseers of administrative agencies remove the Governor from direct involvement except as he works through the membership of these multi-member units. Finally, the administrative burden is shared by some administrative department heads who are directly appointed by the Governor and serve at his pleasure. Obviously, these situations provide for considerable policy and administrative guidance from the Governor. A general and simplified overview of Indiana's administrative structure is in Figure 4.10.

Even though the Governor appears to have only limited direct authority, in fact, he has extensive power. It extends throughout the executive branch and includes the power to review the independently elected officials and the number of commissions, boards and councils. The authority of the Governor has been defined to give him clear executive power. The most notable thing about the authority of Indiana's Governor is the unhindered appointment power of administrative officials and members of the boards, commissions, and councils. As noted earlier, none of his appointments need confirmation of one or both houses of the General Assembly. With the exception of the five independently elected officials and a relatively small number of persons who have staggered term appointments, the Governor has the opportunity to guide the leadership selection of each agency of state government.

The classic definition of gubernatorial power in Indiana came in 1941 in the case *Tucker v. State*. The State Supreme Court clearly made a distinction between the Governor and other elected administrative officials when it wrote:

> The drafters of the Constitution could not have thought of administrative state officers of equal rank with the Governor since the word Governor is defined as 'one who governs; a ruler or magistrate'; 'the person elected as chief executive official of a state in the United States'; and 'govern' is defined 'to direct and control the actions, or conduct of, either by established laws or arbitrary will; to direct and control, rule or regulate, by authority.'[31]

The court further declared that:

> The word 'administrator' as used in the Constitution is not synonymous with 'executive' but rather synonymous with 'ministerial' since both stem from the word 'minor' meaning 'inferior in importance', 'less', 'smaller'.[32]

Figure 4.10. Indiana state government: A general chart of selected functions

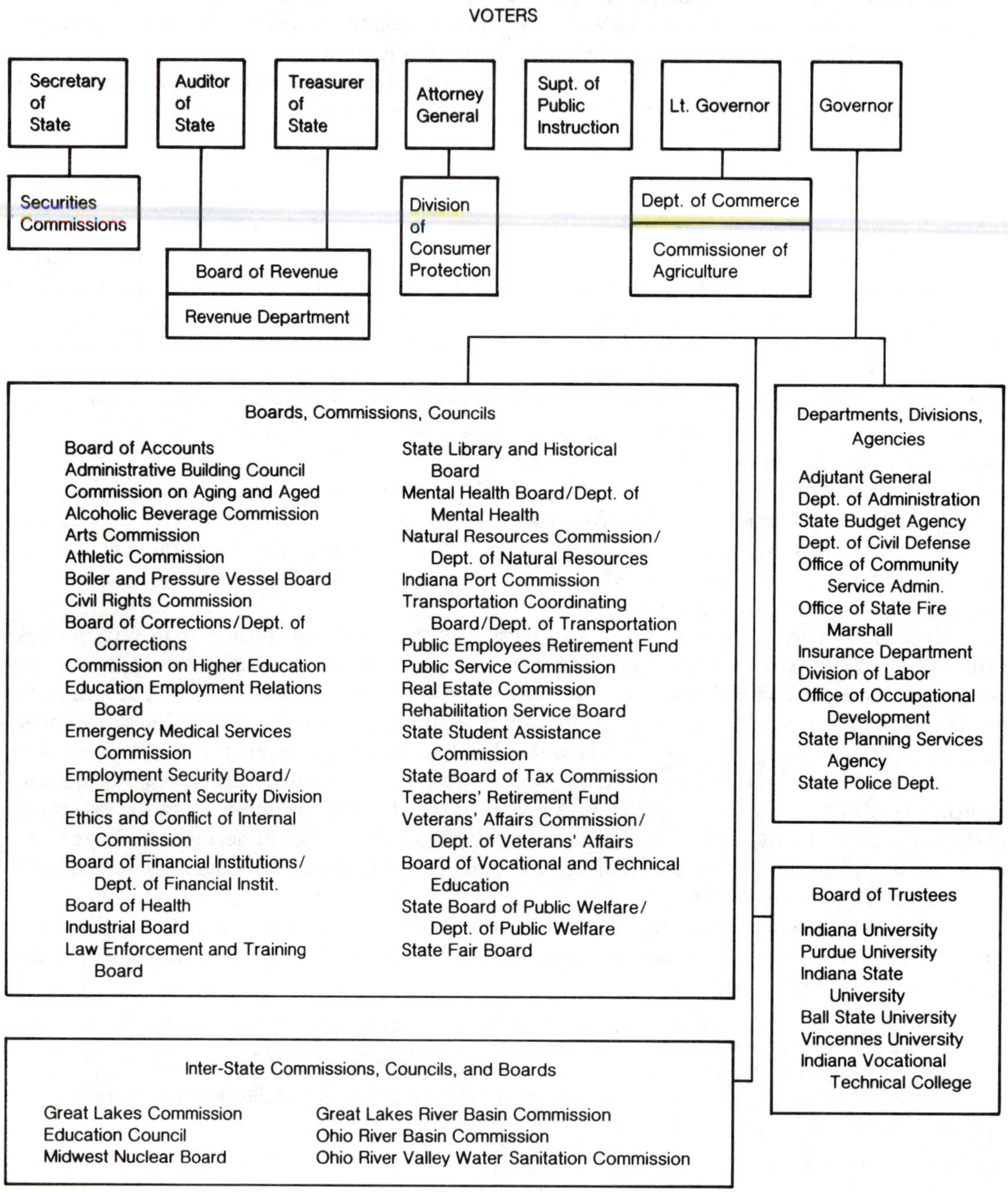

Therefore, the administrative offices which are elected are part of the executive department. They are to perform their ministerial and administrative functions independently of the Governor, but may not claim the broader executive duties which are vested solely in the Governor.

The executive power of the state belongs to the Governor. In *Tucker v. State* the court held:

> The executive power, vested in the Governor by the Constitution, is the power to execute the laws—to carry them into effect as distinguished from the power to make the laws and the power to judge them; and the power to appoint the subordinate officers and employees through whom the laws are executed is a necessary incident to the power to execute the laws.[33]

One of the means by which the Governor can use his executive authority is through executive orders. Issued by the Governor whenever official action is required to implement his authority, the orders are published in the *Indiana Register*. A review of the executive orders issued during the first eight months of 1980, shown in Figure 4.11, shows the common subject and nature of the Governor's use of executive orders.

Governor's Office

One of the principal components of the administrative structure of Indiana is the means by which the Governor organizes his office. Obviously, each Governor operates differently. Some have used a chief of staff structure while others have given a number of assistants equal authority. It is also feasible for a Governor to rely heavily upon the department heads as opposed to staff assistants in his office. The importance of the Governor's office staff is the proximity of the staff to him and the decision-making processes. How the personal staff is used will structure the real authority in the day-to-day operation of the administrative structure.

Figure 4.11. Executive orders January-August, 1980

Executive Order	Date	Subject
1-80	January 3	Establishment of Indiana Communications Study Commission
2-80	January 7	Establishment of Indiana Coordinating Council
3-80	January 15	Declaration of a state of energy emergency (Heating bill assistance)
4-80	Feburary 6	Creation of the Governor's advisory committee on libraries and information services
5-80	February 17	Creation of the Indiana Council on Physical Fitness and Sports Medicine
6-80	March 25	Activation of the Indiana National Guard
7-80	March 26	Deactivation of the Indiana National Guard
8-80	March 14	Promulgation for the acts of the second regular session of the One Hundred First General Assembly of the State of Indiana
9-80	March 31	Declaration of a road condition emergency
10-80	June 9	Amendment of Executive Order No. 4-74 creating an Illinois-Indiana Bi-State Commission
11-80	June 10	Continuation of the Governor's Water Resources Study Commission
12-80	June 19	Amendment to Indiana Criminal Procedure Law Study Commission
13-80	June 19	Amendment to Indiana Criminal Study Commission
14-80	June 30	Assignment of authority to Indiana State Police Department for seizure of all unlawful fireworks
15-80	August 5	Creation of the Governor's rural policy commission

Throughout the eight years of Otis Bowen's tenure, the Governor's staff played a significant role in the structure of the executive branch. Since there is no single means for organizing the Governor's office, a review of the Bowen years serves only as a sample of possible methods. Each of the six executive assistants, those personal staff persons who are located in the Governor's office, held co-equal status. Each was given a functional area of responsibility. This included the responsibility for the various boards, agencies, and departments within that area. Although there was no line of authority of the executive assistant over department heads, informally the executive assistant served as the liaison or contact between department heads and the Governor. Relationships varied between the executive assistant and department heads, with some department heads viewing the executive assistant as their boss, although the policy was that department heads would have access to the Governor. To view the executive assistant as superior could serve to insulate the department head from direct responsibility for things that went badly. Informationally, if not sometime in policy-making, the executive assistants served as a kitchen cabinet for the Governor. During the earlier period of the Bowen administration, the Governor's staff met twice weekly for 90-minute meetings. Besides the six executive assistants, these meetings also included the Budget Director, Revenue Commissioner, and Commissioner of Administration. The rise of one or two of the co-equal executive assistants to positions of prominence was partially the function of the issues which emerged as central to the administration. The assistants within these areas emerge as the more identifiable.

The staff of Governor Orr functions comparably to the staff of Governor Bowen. The structure of the office staff, however, has undergone some modification. Orr's has five principal staff members—his chief counsel and four executive assistants. Each executive assistant is responsible for specific areas of state administration. An administrative assistant is assigned to each executive assistant to assist in these responsibilites. In carrying out these day-to-day operations of state government, the Governor and his office staff rely upon the administrative departments and offices to implement state policy. A select few of the more prominent Indiana administrative units are briefly reviewed in the following paragraphs.

Department of Personnel

By a statute change in 1981, the personnel function gained independent department status after having been a division in the Department of Administration. Headed by a director appointed by the Governor, the department activities and policies are reviewed by the State Personnel Board. The department is responsible for developing personnel policies, methods, procedures, and standards for all state agencies. The state's personnel classification is administered by the department along with activities related to the allocation of positions to their proper classification and salary schedule. State employee performance evaluations, training, and career advancement functions are also assigned to the department. More commonly, it is the Department of Personnel that recruits; tests; and certifies the selection, transfers and promotions of employees in state government.

The first major result of Indiana's new sunset law is the Department of Transportation. Enacted by the 1980 General Assembly, the significant accomplishment of the sunset review was to reorganize the transportation functions. This structural reorganization brought most of the transportation-related functions under one department. Prior to this the Toll Road Commission, Aeronautics Commission, and Highway Commissions were all independent. In addition, the transportation planning function was relocated from the State Planning Services Agency to the Transportation Department. All state government activities for transportation planning, construction and maintenance now come under the jurisdiction of the Department of Transportation. Under the new statutes, the Transportation Coordinating Board will be responsible for the administration of this agency. It is composed of the chairman, the Director of the Department of Highways, the Director of the Department of Transportation and two citizen members. All of these are appointed by the Governor.

Department of Administration

The primary staff functions of state government are performed by the Department of Administration. Headed by a commissioner who is appointed by the Governor and serves at his pleasure, the department serves as the central agency for management services. Finance-related functions include state purchasing, supplies and insurance. Other activities include the state's telecommunication system, central services such as the motor pool, data processing, property management and the operation of the State House.

Board of Revenue/Department of Revenue

Composed of the Governor, State Treasurer and State Auditor, the Board of Revenue oversees the operation of the Department of Revenue. The Commissioner who serves as the Department's administrative head is appointed by the Governor and serves at his pleasure. The Department of Revenue collects and monitors the collection of the various state-imposed taxes—individual income, corporate income, local option income, local occupational income, sales, intangible, cigarette, motor fuel, alcoholic beverages, inheritance and petroleum severance.

State Planning Services Agency

The principal planning agency for the state is responsible for a comprehensive state plan and a long-range capital improvements program. In addition, planning and technical services, primarily land use, are made available to regional and local units of government. Governed by an executive council chaired by the Governor and composed of agency heads from transportation, commerce, health, administration, budget, and natural resources, along with the Governor and non-voting legislative members, the Speaker of the House of Representatives and President Pro Tempore of the Senate—the agency is headed by an executive director who is appointed by the Governor.

Board of Health

A wide range of health activities are administrated by the Board of Health including disease control, medical care administration, weights and measures regulation, health education, local health services, health planning, public health statistics and inspection and certification of sanitary standards related to food processing and handling. In addition, the Board of Health contains the environmental policy regulating agencies for the state: Environmental Management Board, Steam Pollution Control Board, and Air Pollution Control Board. The nine board members are appointed by the Governor and serve overlapping four-year terms. The chief operating officer of the Board of Health is the commissioner, who is appointed by the board with the approval of the Governor.

State Police

Protecting lives and insuring citizens' safety are the general purposes of the State Police. Much of the work of the State Police is in traffic safety enforcement on the state's highways. In cooperation with other state agencies, the State Police enforce laws on truck weight and size limits.

Local law enforcement agencies—county sheriffs and local police departments—work in conjunction with the State Police in the enforcement of criminal laws. The Governor appoints the State Police Superintendent who serves at his request. A bipartisan State Police Board of six members serving four-year overlapping terms oversees the Department.

Natural Resources Commission/Department of Natural Resources

Five public members and seven ex-officio government members compose the Natural Resource Commission which oversees the Department of Natural Resources. The Department's director is appointed by the Governor and serves at his pleasure. The Department issues restrictions for boating on waters of the state, registers off-road vehicles, issues permits for surface mining, manages the State Park system, establishes and maintains scenic and recreational river systems, is responsible for programs of flood control, conducts and updates geological surveys of the state, manages fish and wildlife resources of the state and has a variety of other related functions.

Employment Security Division

An employment service for the public is one of two major responsibilities for the Employment Security Division. The other is the administration of the state's unemployment compensation program required by the Federal Social Security program. A board of five members—two representing labor, one representing large employers, one from small employers and independent merchants, and one from the general public—serves as the policy-forming body. A director who administers the division is selected by the Governor.

State Board of Public Welfare/Department of Public Welfare

The State Board of Public Welfare sets general policy for operating the state and county welfare departments. These five bipartisan members are appointed by the Governor, as is the Department's director. Program responsibilities of the department include: aid to families with dependent children; child support; state supplemental assistance for the aged, blind and disabled; county home residents; Medicaid; family planning; child welfare; adoption resource exchanges and food stamps. Much of the operational activities of the Department is carried out by the County Welfare Departments.

Public Service Commission/Public Counselor

Regulating the services and rates of public utility and transportation companies in the state of Indiana is the primary activity of the Public Service Commission. Included on a limited basis are those utilities owned and operated by municipal governments. Utilities regulated include water, natural gas, electricity, telephone, and rural sewage disposal systems. In the transportation field, the Commission issues permits and regulates vehicles for hire which includes some rate setting, regulates intra-state railroad systems and oversees the safety laws affecting railroads, and supervises the collective bargaining agreements in the railroad industry. The three full-time commissioners are appointed by the Governor to four-year terms. No more than two can come from one political party and at least two must be attorneys.

The public or rate payers' position is presented to the Public Service Commission by the Public Counselor. The Governor appoints the Counselor, who serves at the pleasure of the Governor. State Board of Correction/Department of Correction.

The policy-making authority for the state correctional system resides with the State Board of Corrections. By law the board must include an educator, sociologist or social worker, attorney, psychologist or psychiatrist, a person knowledgeable of the juvenile area and two lay persons. The department is administered by a professional commissioner who is appointed by the Governor. Generally, the department is responsible for the custodial care of those sent to the institution and for their rehabilitation. For adult offenders, the state operates the Indiana State Prison (Michigan City), Westville Correctional Center (Westville), Indiana Reformatory (Pendleton), Indiana State Farm (Putnamville), and the Indiana Women's Prison (Indianapolis). Youth offenders are served by the Indiana Youth Center (Plainfield), Indiana Boys' School (Plainfield), Indiana Girls' School (Indianapolis, and Rockville Training Center (Rockville). Other facilities operated by the Department of Corrections include youth camps, juvenile diagnostic centers, day treatment centers, residential treatment centers, work release centers, and several parole offices throughout the state. The power for parole decisions belongs to the Indiana Parole Board which is appointed by the Governor. This five-member bipartisan board also reviews and makes recommendations to the Governor on clemency petitions.

Office of Lieutenant Governor

Indiana's Governor, as we noted earlier, shares administrative responsibility with several elected officials. Besides presiding over the State Senate as its President, the Lieutenant Governor serves as Director of the Department of Commerce and as Commissioner of Agriculture. As head of a major state agency, the Lieutenant Governor plays a vital role in promoting the state's economic interests. Among the functions which he oversees are promoting exports for manufacturing and agricultural products, acquiring investments from both domestic and international businesses in Indiana, promoting Indiana's tourism industry, informing the public about energy conservation and encouraging the development of energy alternatives. In his role as Commissioner of Agriculture, he is responsible for the State Fair Board, the Standardbred Board of Regulation, and the Commodity Dealers Licensing Agency. In promoting the economic interest of the state, the Lieutenant Governor serves on a variety of state boards and coordinating councils such as the Steam Pollution Control Board, the Executive Council of State Planning, and the Natural Resources Commission.

Office of Attorney General

Representing all state agencies in legal matters is the primary responsibility of the Attorney General. When a state agency uses an attorney other than someone from the Attorney General's office, the Attorney General must give his approval. Among his duties are to advise the Governor of the legality of state matters such as state contracts and laws passed by the Geneal Assembly. Although the Attorney General does not prosecute law offenders—this is done by prosecuting attorneys—he does represent the state in criminal appeals cases. A special authority of the Attorney General is his responsibility to respond to inquiries about the proper interpretation of the State Constitution and statutes and their application. These "official opinions" are provided to the Governor, state officers, and members of the legislature. They are considered to be the proper interpretation of the questioned law or constitution section until a court provides a different view. This presents the Attorney General with considerable policy potential. A list of opinions for a portion of 1980 indicates the nature of these (See Figure 4.12). Oftentimes, the Attorney General will respond to inquiries from local officials and public groups, but these are not considered as "official opinions." Among his other responsibilities is the direction of a division of consumer protection. This agency provides education about deceptive sales practices, investigates consumer complaints and takes appropriate civil action on behalf of consumers.

Figure 4.12. Official opinions of the Attorney General January-August, 1980

Number	Persons Requesting Opinion	Subject of Opinion
80-1	State Senator Wayne Townsend	Utilizing a lottery as a means of fund raising
80-2	H. P. Hudson, Commissioner of the Department of Insurance	Refunds to insurance companies for overpayment of gross premium privilege taxes
80-3	State Senator James R. Harris	One individual simultaneously holding the Office of Deputy Town Marshall and membership of the Town Board of the same town
80-4	State Senator Daniel A. Manion/State Rep. Robert J. Du Comb, Sr.	Transfer of public property
80-5	State Rep. Janet L. Hibner/Ralph C. Pichard, Technical Secretary Air-Pollution Control Board	Vehicle emission control standards—permanent inspection stations
80-6	H. P. Hudson, Commissioner of the Department of Insurance	Authority of Insurance Commissioner to adopt rules and regulations requiring membership of insurance companies in Indiana Basic Property Insurance Underwriting Association
80-7	State Senator Charles E. Bosman	Garnishment order including service fee
80-8	Joseph D. Cloud, Director Department of Natural Resources	IC 14-3-3.3-10, historic sites or structures
80-9	State Rep. Paul S. Hric/State Senator Frank Mrvan Jr.	Alterations of the bed of Lake George, North Township Lake County, Indiana; local ordinances
80-10	Harold J. Egenes, Executive Secretary, Public Employees Retirement Fund	Exclusively fee-basis official participating in the Public Employee's Retirement Fund
80-11	Jack P. Fitzgerald, Chief Executive Officer and Port Director, Port Commission	Status of the Indiana Port Commission under sunset legislation
80-12	Albert P. Tutsie, Chairman, Parole Board	Release on parole
80-13	Harold J. Egenes, Executive Secretary, Public Employees Retirement Fund	Sick pay plan excluded from federal social security
80-14	State Rep. William L. Soards	City of Indianapolis and Indianapolis-Marion County Building Authority legal relationship
80-15	Ronald G. Blankenbaker, M.D., Secretary, Indiana State Board of Health	House Enrolled Act No. 1617
80-16	Kenneth R. Beesley, State Examiner, State Board of Accounts	Public school corporation and the teacher's exclusive representative organization negotiate an agreement providing local retirement benefits
80-17	Richard L. Worley, Deputy State Examiner, State Board of Accounts	Township carrying comprehensive automobile insurance when the township neither owns nor hires an automobile
80-18	Harold J. Egenes, Executive Secretary, Public Employees Retirement Fund	Are Indiana state legislators considered to be full-time or part-time employees for social security purposes

Office of Auditor of State

The Auditor of State is the state's bookkeeper. All receipts and disbursements of state monies are processed by the Auditor. Before issuing any warrants to pay state obligations—checks are not used by the state—the Auditor pre-audits the disbursement to insure its legality and the availability of funds. A person wanting information on state employee earnings would find the information in the Auditor's office. Local governments, counties, cities, towns, and townships receive their disbursement of state collected funds—motor vehicle funds, cigarette taxes, and alcoholic beverage taxes—from the Auditor.

Office of Treasurer of State

Whereas the Auditor provides for the record keeping of the state's monies, it is the Treasurer's job to receive the funds, deposit them for keeping and to pay warranties when the state money is claimed. The key decisions of the Treasurer relate to the selecting of depositories for state monies. As custodian of state monies, the Treasurer designs and executes investment plans for the state funds while they are idle. This produces considerable revenue for the state. In 1979–80 alone, the state of Indiana earned $148,359,413.58 by investing idle state funds. How, where, and for how long these investments are made can mean substantial dollars to the state treasury.

Office of Secretary of State

All public documents of the State of Indiana—state laws, constitutional amendments, proclamations from the Governor—must be attested to by the Secretary of State as the custodian of official documents. It is in his office that the State Seal is housed. In addition, the Secretary of State's office receives official filing for state and federal offices, registers persons who lobby the General Assembly, administers the trademark registration law, and issues commissions granted by the Governor—the most common are those to the 100,000 notaries public. Issuing corporation charters and receiving their annual reports are also duties of the Secretary of State. A related role is the regulation of security trading and selling in the state and the administration of the Uniform Commercial Code.

Superintendent of Public Instruction

The state's public school system functions under the policy guidance of the State Board of Education, working through the Superintendent of Public Instruction. Within this function are the responsibilities of standards for teacher training, minimum standards for high school graduation, inspection and accrediting of schools, distribution of state funds to local districts, receiving and approving school sites and building plans, and the review and listing of acceptable textbooks for use in the state's schools. Whereas the Superintendent is an independently elected state official, the eighteen members of the Board of Education are appointed by the Governor for four-year terms. The three policy-making commissions, which are composed from the Board's members, are (1) Commission of General Education, (2) Commission of Textbook Adoption, and (3) Commission of Teacher Training and Licensing. In addition, the Superintendent works with an approved twelve-member advisory council for handicapped children.

Conclusion

The executive branch of Indiana State government under the authority of the Governor's office is evolving toward a more centralized model. Executive agencies in general and the Governor's office in particular are becoming more powerful and more important to the process of policy development and implementation. This new power and the centralized model that has evolved from it have come essentially because there is more work to be done. In recent years the state has taken on new functions and responsibilities, and the job of carrying out the new tasks has fallen in large measure to the Governor and to the executive branch in general.

The growth of responsibilities with the executive branch date from the "Great Society" programs of the mid-1960's. Since this period, the federal government has encouraged all states to undertake a multitude of new programs, and in most cases these programs have come under—directly or indirectly—the authority of the Governor. Indiana was slower than most states in acquiescing to federal demands, (especially in providing matching funds), and has consistently stood near the bottom of the list in terms of the per capita amounts of federal funds returned to the state; but it did not reject the federal programs, and the scope of state government grew during the 1960's and 1970's. The recently established Indiana State Department of Transportation, for instance, is an example of the newer directions in which the state has been moving. Thus, much of the power acquired by state executive agencies has been derived from federal government sources and funded with federally supported monies.

In order to accommodate these increases in responsibility, the state has been forced to make a number of changes in its structure and organization. The evolutionary process of strengthening the executive branch has been facilitated by the recent constitutional and statutory revisions that have mandated and/or permitted alterations in the organization and structure of state government. Further, not only have these changes permitted the state to accommodate the rounds of demands of the 1960's and 1970's, but they will help the state respond to the even newer demands that are likely to emerge in the 1980's and 1990's.

The strengthening and centralizing that has occurred within the executive branch parallels the changes that have taken place in the other branches of government. Indeed, the changes in the executive branch may be as much the result as the cause of the weakening of the state political party system, the strengthening and professionalizing of the state legislature and the reform of the state judiciary. In short, one reason why it was necessary for the executive branch to change might well have been its need to stay even in terms of its traditional relationships with the other branches of state government.

The changes that have taken place in the executive branch go beyond organization and structure. Program administration, particularly in the area of personnel management, has also been altered. New and innovative management systems have been introduced. With the decline in patronage has come a new interest in merit personnel principles and an increase in the level of activity of public employee unions. While Indiana is still regarded as a traditional state that lacks a highly developed civil service system or a strong network of public employee labor organizations, it is clear that the state is moving in these directions.

The election of President Ronald Reagan in 1980 is likely to mean that the state will have to undertake some further changes in the way the executive branch functions. A key element in President Reagan's program is a reordering of the relationship between the federal government and the states. He has called this approach "New Federalism," the basic thrust of which is to give states more power and authority in developing and administering programs that have traditionally been under federal control. The "New Federalism" approach envisions, in its initial stages at least, transforming many of the existing categorical grant-in-aid programs into broad block grants that the states would administer. Many of the existing federal requirements—including the requirements for state matching funds—would be removed. The trade-off, however, for this transfer of power from the federal government to the states is a significant reduction of federal support for the programs. Thus, while the states will have more discretion, they will also have less money. It remains to be seen how states like Indiana will respond to the "New Federalism."

Even if the full scope of the "New Federalism" proposals are never fully implemented, there can be little doubt that federal-state relationships in the 1980's and 1990's will go through some fundamental transformations. States, including Indiana, will have to assume greater levels of responsibility for providing basic social and other types of services and do so with smaller allocations of federal funds. As this transformation takes place, Indiana may find itself at a relative disadvantage to some other states. Indiana does not have the institutions and mechanisms in place to undertake the new responsibilities that are likely to be imposed. As the implementation of the "New Federalism" proceeds, Indiana will have to create these mechanisms and institutions. Fortunately for the residents of the state the initial steps have been taken and the state is in the position of having the flexibility to make future changes as they become necessary.

Notes

1. Constitution of Indiana, 1851. Art. 3, Sec. 1.
2. The Council of State Governments, *Book of States, 1980–81,* (1980), (Vol. 23), Lexington, Kentucky, pp 182–83.
3. *Ibid.*
4. *Ibid.*
5. *Ibid.*
6. Glashan, Roy. *American Governors and Gubernatorial Elections.* 1775–1975, (1975), Stillwater, Minnesota: The Croixside Press.
7. The Council of State Governments, *Book of States, 1980–81,* pp 186–87.
8. Constitution of Indiana, 1851. Art. 5, Sec. 10
9. The Council of State Governments, *Book of States, 1980–81.* p 171.
10. *Ibid.*
11. *Ibid.,* p 188.
12. *Ibid.*
13. Schlesinger, Joseph A. "The Politics of the Executive" in Herbert Jacob and Kenneth N. Vines (eds.) *Politics in the American States,* 2nd edition, (1971), Boston: Little, Brown.
14. Constitution of Indiana, 1851. Art. 5, Sec. 1.
15. The Council of State Governments, *Book of States,* 1980–81, p 70.
16. Constitution of Indiana, 1851. Art. 5, Sec. 13.
17. The Council of State Governments, *Book of States,* 1980–81, pp 110–111.
18. *Ibid.*
19. *Ibid.*
20. *Ibid.*
21. *Tucker v. State,* 218 Indiana Reports 614.
22. The Council of State Governments, *Book of States, 1980–81,* p 271.
23. *Ibid.*

24. *Ibid.*
25. *Ibid.*, p 273.
26. *Indiana Code* 4-15-2-1 to 4-15-2-46.
27. *Indiana Code* 4-15-2-1.
28. The Council of State Governments, *Book of States,* 1980–81, pp 202–5.
29. *Ibid.*
30. *Ibid.*
31. *Tucker v. State,* 218 Indiana Reports 614.
32. *Ibid.*
33. *Ibid.*

5

The Indiana Judiciary

Mary Louise Baker
Ralph Baker
Ball State University

St. Joseph County Court House
Courtesy of the South Bend Tribune

The Indiana Judiciary is a collection of court structures, judges, lawyers, other court actors and administrative practices. All of these facets are discussed in this chapter. Each facet is the product of the state's political system.[1] Political scientists have long ago broken the myth that politics are divorced from the law, judges and courts.[2] The state's judiciary, thus, should not be viewed as a separate entity but rather as an integral part of Indiana's political scene.

One study has compared the fifty state court systems on the basis of their legal orientations.[3] By legal orientations, the study included such factors as selection methods of judges in all state courts, state court organization, judicial administration, tenure of office for judges and the salary levels for judges. See Table 5.1. Comparatively speaking, Indiana ranks quite low. Despite this, we shall see that the state has made some rather dramatic improvements in its judiciary in the past fifteen years.

Table 5.1. Legal Professionalism in the American States

Rank of States		Composite Score
1.	California	21.7
2.	New Jersey	18.0
3.	Illinois	17.7
4–5.	Massachusetts, New York	16.7
6–7.	Alaska, Michigan	16.3
8–9.	Maryland, Hawaii	15.3
10.	Pennsylvania	15.0
11–13.	Colorado, Washington, Wisconsin	14.3
14.	Ohio	14.0
15.	North Carolina	13.7
16.	New Hampshire	13.4
17–19.	Arizona, Oregon, Rhode Island	13.3
20.	Nevada	13.0
21.	Connecticut	12.6
22–24.	Idaho, Minnesota, Oklahoma	12.0
25.	North Dakota	11.3
26.	Kentucky	11.0
27.	Iowa	10.9
28–29.	Maine, Wyoming	10.7
30.	Vermont	10.3
31–33.	Florida, Montana, Virginia	10.0
34–36.	Delaware, Louisiana, Missouri	9.6
37–38.	New Mexico, Utah	9.3
39–40.	Nebraska, South Dakota	9.0
41.	South Carolina	8.7
42–45.	Georgia, Kansas, Tennessee, Texas	8.0
46.	Indiana	7.6
47.	West Virginia	7.3
48.	Alabama	6.0
49.	Arkansas	5.3
50.	Mississippi	3.4

Source: Henry Robert Glick, Kenneth N. Vines *State Court Systems,* 1973 reprinted by permission Prentice-Hall Inc. Englewood Cliffs, NJ page 12.

The Indiana Court System

Numerous factors account for variations in the basic structure and complexity of state court systems. "In addition to the interests of political parties and competition between interest groups, judicial systems reflect the social environment in which they exist."[4] All fifty states, however, do have three general tiers of courts: state appellate courts whose primary function is to review decisions of lower courts, state trial courts which have broad jurisdiction, and various local trial courts of limited jurisdiction which hear minor cases. Despite these three common elements, state court systems vary greatly in complexity. The more preferred court systems are the modern and simplified court systems which include intermediate appellate courts, fewer types of trial courts of general jurisdiction and fewer types of trial courts of limited jurisdiction. On a comparative basis, Indiana's court system ranks in the category of a preferred modern and simplified system. See Table 5.2. The states in Group 2, including Indiana, are not considered as having court systems as meritorious as those in Group 1, however.

According to the Indiana Constitution as amended in 1970, the state's judicial authority is vested in the Supreme Court, the intermediate Court of Appeals, the Circuit Courts, and other courts as established by the General Assembly.[5] Pursuant to the constitutional authorization, the General Assembly has created Superior Courts with general trial jurisdiction and County Courts with limited jurisdiction. In addition, minor courts and specialized courts are found in many counties. Figure 5.1 outlines the Indiana Court System.

Table 5.2. Differences in State Court Organization

Simple and Modern ◄		► Complex and Traditional	
Group 1 N=6	**Group 2 N=20**	**Group 3 N=20**	**Group 4 N=4**
Arizona	*Alabama	Connecticut	*Arkansas
California	*Alaska	Idaho	Delaware
Illinois	*Colorado	Iowa	Mississippi
North Carolina	*Florida	Kansas	Virginia
Oklahoma	*Georgia	Kentucky	
Washington	Hawaii	Maine	
	*Indiana	Massachusetts	
	*Louisiana	Minnesota	
	*Maryland	Montana	
	*Michigan	Nebraska	
	*Missouri	New Hampshire	
	Nevada	North Dakota	
	*New Jersey	Rhode Island	
	*New Mexico	South Carolina	
	*New York	South Dakota	
	*Ohio	*Tennessee	
	*Oregon	Utah	
	*Pennsylvania	Vermont	
	*Texas	West Virginia	
	Wyoming	Wisconsin	

States marked with an asterik have intermediate appellate courts.

Source: Henry Robert Glick and Kenneth N. Vines, *State Court Systems,* 1973 reprinted by permission of Prentice-Hall Inc. Englewood Cliffs, NJ page 30.

Figure 5.1. The Indiana Court System (1981)

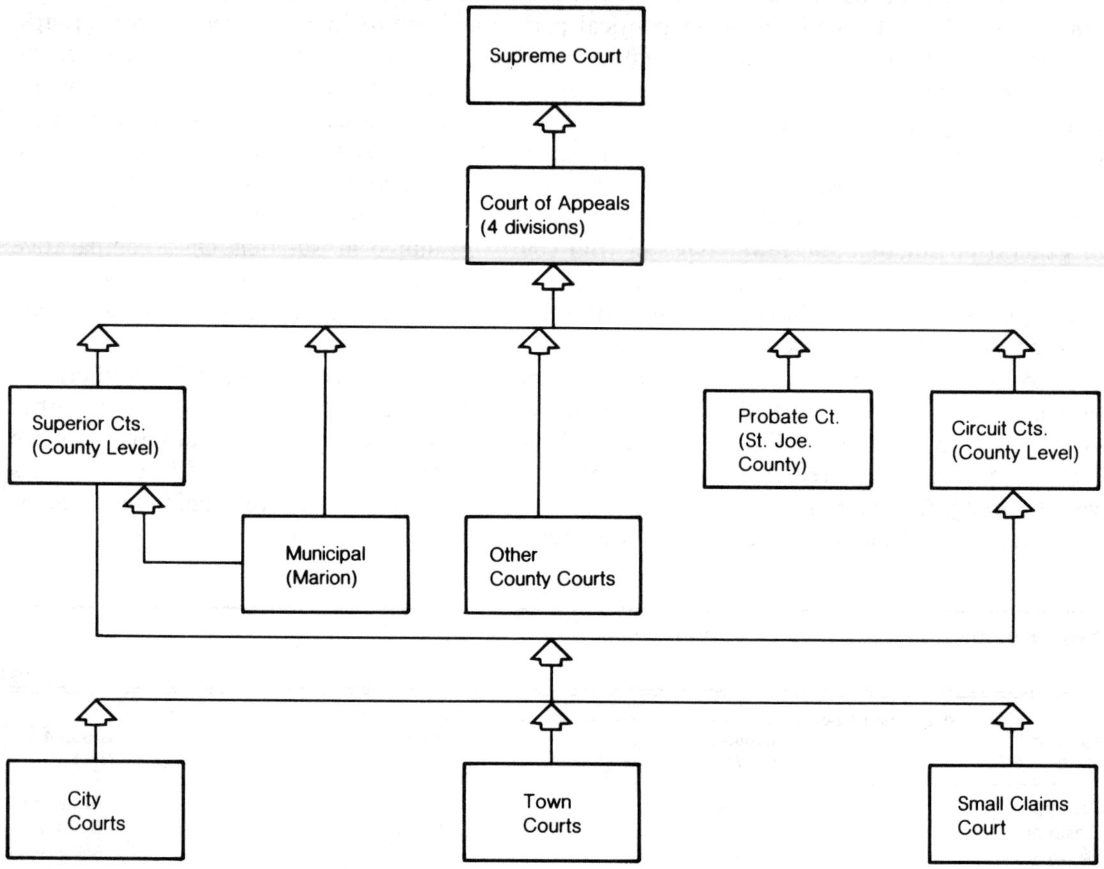

Indiana Supreme Court

The Indiana Supreme Court was first established in 1816 when Indiana became a state. During territorial days, a General Court of three judges served not only as the state's highest court but also participated with the Governor in enacting laws for the Indiana Territory. The importance of the Supreme Court was reflected in an early decision which enforced the new state's constitutional prohibition against slavery.[6] Originally the Court consisted of three judges. Due to the growing Court caseload, the number of judges was increased to four in 1853 and to the current number of five in 1872. According to the amended Constitution of 1970, however, the General Assembly was empowered to increase the size of the court from five members up to a maximum of nine members if they deem such an increase necessary. At present, the General Assembly has refrained from any such increase.[7]

The Supreme Court, consisting of a Chief Justice and four associate justices, is situated in a chamber located in the state capitol at Indianapolis. The court facility includes the judicial chamber, administrative offices, and the Indiana Supreme Court law library. The Supreme Court

Table 5.3. 1976 Supreme Court Caseload by Source of Case

	Dispositions Number of Cases	Percent of Total
Appeals brought under exclusive jurisdiction		
Opinions by Direct Appeal	137	57.0
Opinions by Original Action	11	4.5
Opinions by Disciplinary Cases	9	3.7
Sub-Totals	157	65.2
Actions brought through Petitions for Transfer		
Civil Petition Opinions	7	2.9
Criminal Petition Opinions	7	2.9
Criminal Petitions Denied Without Opinion	70	29.0
Sub-Totals	84	34.8
Grand Totals	241	100.0

Source: Indiana Judges Association, *Indiana Trial Court System,* Indianapolis: Indiana Judicial Center, (1978) page 157.

functions basically as an appellate court, being the ultimate interpreter of disputed cases brought to appeal when Constitutional issues or serious criminal penalties are involved.[8] Also the Court may review the decisions of the Court of Appeals. When the Supreme Court accepts an appeal, it proceeds to hear arguments and review the transcript of the record of the local trial. Having completed its review, the Court may sustain or overrule the decision of the lower court, giving the reasons for its decision in a written opinion. In some instances, it may order new trials under conditions correcting the original trial error.

The Indiana Supreme Court does exercise original jurisdiction in a limited number of cases as prescribed in the state Constitution.[9] Original jurisdiction extends to (1) admission to the practice of law; (2) discipline and disbarment of those admitted, (3) unauthorized practice of law; (4) discipline, removal, and retirement of judges; and (5) exercise of jurisdiction by other states.

Within the jurisdictional guidelines set by the Constitution, the Indiana Supreme Court has a rather heavy workload. To clarify the exact nature of that workload, Table 5.3 is presented indicating the caseload by source of case of the Court in a recent year. Studies of state supreme courts have shown that the types of issues heard by such courts depend not only upon jurisdictional provisions but also state socio-economic and political variables such as party competition, salaries of judges and legislators, proportion of the state population engaged in manufacturing, affluence and education levels.[10] Indiana was distinguished in this study by a finding that its Supreme Court dealt with more criminal issues in its caseload than any other state supreme court.[11]

The Court of Appeals of Indiana

This intermediate appellate court of Indiana was originally created in 1891 by an act of the General Assembly.[12] Then referred to as the Appellate Court of Indiana, it was created as a temporary judicial panel to last six years. Its purpose was to relieve the increasing caseload of the Supreme Court. In 1897 the court was continued on a temporary basis for an additional four years and finally in 1901 it was established as a permanent court. Through statutory changes in 1925 and 1959, the appellate court evolved into two panels of four judges each.

The current Court of Appeals was created by the 1970 amendment of the Judicial Article of the Constitution. Under Article 7, Section 5 of the document, the General Assembly was authorized to establish geographic districts for the Court consisting of three judges for each district. In 1971, the legislature created three such districts. The General Assembly also provided that cases would be placed on the dockets of the respective district panels according to the geographic districts from which the cases were appealed. The Court of Appeals, however, was authorized to transfer cases from one district to another to balance caseloads. In 1978, a fourth district panel of three judges was added, but the legislature provided that the fourth district would include the entire state geographically. This panel is authorized to handle cases from the entire state. The four district breakdown is thus as follows:

First District

Counties served: 53
Population served: 1,842,000

Second District

Counties served: 19
Population served: 1,724,400

Third District

Counties served: 20
Population served: 1,735,300

Fourth District

The Fourth District
includes the entire state[13]

Each district panel has a presiding judge elected by the members of that panel. The Court of Appeals as a whole has a Chief Judge elected for three years by the twelve members of the Court. Cases before the Indiana Court of Appeals are heard in the State Capitol Building at Indianapolis "or such other place as the Chief Judge of the Court of Appeals shall designate."[14]

The Court of Appeals has no original jurisdiction except that it may be authorized by rules of the Supreme Court to review directly decisions of administrative agencies. In all other instances, it exercises appellate jurisdiction consistent with Supreme Court rules. The appellate court function is quite important in Indiana because each individual is given the absolute right of one appeal. Table 5.4 gives an indication of the types of workload the Court has.

Circuit Courts

The first circuit courts in Indiana had their origin in the 1816 Constitution. Three circuits were initially created by the Constitution. Circuit courts from that time on have continued to be the only Indiana trial courts authorized by the state's Constitution. Presently, there are eighty-eight circuit courts with one circuit for each of the counties in the state except for four circuits which encompass two counties each.[15]

The circuit courts are trial courts of general jurisdiction in all cases except when exclusive or concurrent jurisdiction is conferred upon other courts. For instance, the circuit courts in Marion and Lake Counties have no criminal jurisdiction. With such few exceptions, however, the circuit courts' jurisdictions include cases in equity, criminal cases, divorces, and all other matters not specifically conferred by law on some other court or board. In all counties except those having a juvenile court (or where by special legislation the jurisdiction is given to a superior court) the circuit court has juvenile jurisdiction. Circuit courts also handle probate matters in most counties. In addition, the circuit courts in twenty-one counties are required by statute to maintain a small claims docket where civil claims of $1500 or less may be filed. A litigant on the small claims docket

Table 5.4. 1976 Court of Appeals

	Cases		
Fully Briefed Cases			
Pending 1/1/76		503	
Civil Cases Distributed		317	
Expedited Cases Distributed		43	
Criminal Cases Distributed		417	
			1280
Cases Disposed of			
By Opinion		639	
By Order		14	
			653
	Pending 12/31/76		
			627
	Opinions		
Majority		639	
Other		97	
Total Opinions Handed Down			736
Motions, Petitions For Time and Miscellaneous Orders Handed Down			
			2894
	Oral Arguments		
First District		43	
Second District		26	
Third District		15	
Total Oral Arguments Heard			84

Source: Indiana Judges Association, *Indiana Trial Court System*, page 164.

need not be represented by counsel because the trials are held in an informal atmosphere. In the remaining counties, the small claims dockets have been established either in the Superior or County Court in the county. Finally, circuit courts exercise appellate jurisdiction over appeals from City and Town Courts and, in Marion County, from the Small Claims Courts.

The circuit judge is a very important legal and political figure. Circuit judges name all employees of their courts and make appointments to several important county administrative boards in addition to carrying out their judicial duties. They have the power to request from the Governor the use of the state police to maintain order during a county emergency. They also exercise such powers as the regulation of the manner in which notice of sale of real estate in a probate matter shall be given and the making of decisions concerning adoption proceedings.

Superior Courts

Superior courts are trial courts which have been established by the General Assembly one at a time as local judicial needs change. The first superior court was established in 1871. Presently, eighty-three judges serve on the superior courts located in thirty-five counties.[16] Since the creation of these courts has been tied to local needs, their organization and jurisdiction vary from county to county. (This is one of the primary reasons that Indiana does not rank higher on the modern and simplified court structure scale presented in Table 5.2). Seventeen counties have more than one superior court or division. Ten of the thirty-five counties have one unified superior court with two or more judges. Nine counties have their small claims divisions within the superior court.

Although the superior courts generally exercise jurisdiction that is similar to that of the circuit courts, the jurisdiction does vary from county to county. In some counties, the superior court has not been given concurrent jurisdiction over certain matters that continue to be the exclusive jurisdiction of the circuit courts. For instance, superior courts in Clark and Marion Counties do not have criminal jurisdiction. In other counties, the superior courts have been given exclusive jurisdiction over certain matters which have been excluded from the circuit court's jurisdiction. For example, Boone, Hendricks and Vanderburgh Counties have superior courts with exclusive jurisdiction in probate matters. At this level in the Indiana court system, the jurisdictional lines become confusing.

County Courts

Following Indiana voter approval in 1972 of a constitutional amendment to remove the office of justice of the peace from the Constitution, the General Assembly in 1974 agreed to abolish all justice of the peace courts. To compensate for the loss of these much-criticized layman courts, a new system of county courts was created. Under the new law, three county courts were established in Lake County, two county courts were established in each of five counties, one county court was created in each of forty-two counties and joint county courts were established in each of nine pairs of counties. In addition, the "county court function" was placed in various courts in the remaining twenty-six counties.

The county court has original and concurrent jurisdiction in all contract and personal injury (tort) cases in which the damages do not exceed $3000, actions between landlord and tenant where the rent does not exceed $500 per month, all actions for the possession of property where the value of the property sought does not exceed $3000, criminal misdemeanor and infraction cases, lesser criminal felony cases, and violations of local ordinances. The county court also has a small claims docket like that of the circuit court. Each county court has a traffic violations bureau which expedites the processing of cases involving violations of motor vehicle statutes.[17] The law also provides for the use of six-member juries in both civil and criminal cases in the county courts and other courts with the county court function. Appeals from the county courts are taken to the Indiana Court of Appeals under the same rules and procedures prescribed for an appeal from a circuit court.

The county courts have been specifically precluded in cases involving the granting of injunctions, the partition of real estate, liens on real estate, paternity suits, juvenile matters, probate matters and dissolution of marriage. The county courts may, however, conduct preliminary hearings in felony cases.

Other Courts

City Courts

City courts had been targeted for extinction on December 31, 1979. By a 1978 legislative amendment, however, city courts could be continued in existence until December 31, 1983, if the city adopted an ordinance providing for such continuation before January 1, 1979. The exception to these regulations was that city courts in second-class cities, in counties with a population in excess of 500,000 (Lake County) were not to be abolished.

There are approximately ninety city courts operating in Indiana with varied jurisdiction depending upon the city's classification. Generally speaking, a city court's jurisdiction includes misdemeanor and criminal infraction cases, violations of city ordinances and civil claims up to $500. Appeals from most city courts are taken to the circuit or superior court and tried again as a new case, "trial de novo."

Town Courts

Identical with the situation of city courts, town courts were to go out of existence on December 31, 1979. The 1978 legislative amendment, however, gave towns the option of extending the life of their town courts for an additional four years. There are about nineteen town courts in Indiana. They have jurisdiction over town ordinance violations and state law violations for which the penalty cannot exceed six months imprisonment and/or a fine of $500. Appeals from town courts are taken to the circuit court or superior court and tried de novo.

Small Claims Court (Marion County)

The Marion County Small Claims Court was created on January 1, 1976, to replace the Justice of the Peace Courts. The court has eight divisions based on township lines and has a concurrent jurisdiction with the circuit, superior and municipal courts in all civil cases whose claim or value does not exceed $1500. Appeals are tried de novo in the circuit or superior courts.

Municipal Court (Marion County)

The Marion County Municipal Court has fifteen judges, fourteen trial judges and a presiding judge. It has jurisdiction in all misdemeanors, infractions and local ordinance violations. The court's civil jurisdiction includes contract and tort cases not exceeding $10,000. Appeals in civil cases are taken to the Court of Appeals and appeals of criminal cases are taken to the newly reorganized Marion County Superior Court. This criminal jurisdiction was formerly vested in the Marion County Criminal Courts.

Probate Court (St. Joseph County)

The St. Joseph County Probate Court has one judge and services original jurisdiction in all matters pertaining to the probate of wills, appointment of guardians, assignees, executors, administrators and trustees, settlement of incompetents' estates and adoptions. The Court also has exclusive juvenile jurisdiction.

Judges

The Judicial Role

The role of judge is one of the most important in our political system. The black robe and honorific form of address, "Your Honor," symbolically represent the American political maxim that "We are a government of laws and not men." Judges are more insulated from the political process than legislators, bureaucrats and executives, but they are still a part of it. As one author has written:

> Various research has shown, for example, that decisions often reveal a consistency in judges' policy preferences which suggest that attitudes, personal backgrounds, and other effects of the political environment are more important in determining the outcomes of litigation than the many legal sources usually cited in formal opinions. Furthermore, while many cases are routine and seem to affect only the litigants in the case, other decisions create new and far-reaching

policies which concern important interest groups, political parties as well as other governmental officials and their own policies. Finally, judges are linked to the political process via recruitment systems which involve various other political actors.[18]

Research has indicated, for example, that Republican state supreme court judges vote differently from their Democratic counterparts.[19] Republican judges are more likely to vote for business in government regulation cases; more likely to vote for the prosecution in criminal cases and more likely to vote for the landlord in landlord-tenant cases. It is also quite evident that judges, especially appellate judges, are linked to politics by their policy-making powers. Decisions concerning school busing and abortion are but just two examples of such powers.

It is not surprising that the great power and prestige associated with the judicial role causes many to take seriously the process by which judges are selected from the population.

Judicial Selection in Indiana

There are presently five different judicial selection systems in operation by the states. They are gubernatorial appointment in which the governor uses patronage, professional or other considerations; nonpartisan elections; partisan elections; the Missouri Plan; and the least frequently used method of legislative election in which the choice is made by the legislature on the basis of gubernatorial influence, patronage or other factors. At one time or another, Indiana has used all five selection methods.

Hoosier Appellate Court Judges

Initially, Indiana Supreme Court judges were appointed by the Governor to serve seven-year terms "if they should so long behave well."[20] Later in the 1851 state constitution, the selection method was changed to popular election for six-year terms. The current system for choosing Indiana Supreme Court judges was adopted in 1970 by constitutional amendment. It is a modification of the Missouri Plan. Incumbent judges are subject to statewide yes-or-no votes on the question of their retention in office. If they receive electoral approval, they begin ten-year terms and are subject to identical retention votes at ten-year intervals in the future. However, retirement is required at age seventy-five. If a vacancy occurs on the Court by way of retirement, voter rejection, death, illness or some other reason, the Constitution requires that a seven-member Judicial Nominating Commission recommend to the Governor three qualified individuals for each vacancy. The Governor then appoints one of the three individuals who will then serve for a minimum of two years before becoming subject to a retention vote at a general election. If the judge is approved, he begins a ten-year term. The Chief Justice of the Indiana Supreme Court is also selected by the Judicial Nominating Commission from the five members of the Court and serves for a period of five years subject to reappointment in the same manner.

To be eligible to serve on the Supreme Court, a person must have practiced law in Indiana for at least ten years or have served at least five years as a trial court judge. Considerations of the candidate's qualifications include such matters as legal education, reputation in the legal profession, legal writings, physical condition, financial interests and activities in public service.[21] In 1980 Supreme Court judges received a salary of $42,000 per year plus a $3000 subsistency allowance.

Judges serving on the Indiana Court of Appeals are selected in the same manner as judges of the Supreme Court. Members of the former appellate court were selected in partisan elections for four-year terms. The eligibility requirements, retirement age and salary for these judges are identical with those for members of the Supreme Court.

Hoosier Trial Court Judges

Initially, each circuit court in Indiana consisted of three judges, two associate judges and a president judge. The two associate judges were selected in partisan elections for a term of seven years whereas the president judge was elected by members of both branches of the legislature for a seven-year term. Today all circuit court judges are elected and serve a term of six years. Most of them are selected on a partisan basis, but in Vanderburgh County the judicial nominating commission for the Vandeburgh Superior Court selects two candidates for the circuit court judgeship. These two candidates then oppose each other in a nonpartisan election at the general election. Circuit court judges are subject to the disciplinary authority of the Indiana Supreme Court as are other trial court judges. Under its disciplinary authority, the Supreme Court may discipline a judge by removal, retirement or suspension without pay.

Superior court judges are elected on partisan ballots for six-year terms in thirty-one of the thirty-five counties having such judges. Judges in the other four counties are appointed by the Governor for an initial term of three years and then stand for election to a six-year term on a yes-or-no retention vote basis. Judicial nominating commissions select three nominees for each position. County court judges are selected in partisan elections for four-year terms. All other Indiana judges are also elected, except for the Marion County Municipal Court judges, who are appointed by the Governor for a four-year term. Each judge is selected from a list of three nominees selected by the Judicial Nominating Commission.

Assessment of Selection Methods

The selection systems adopted by states do not necessarily indicate how judges are chosen in actual practice.[22] Additional state informal practices often emerge to supplement the actual process of judicial selection. For instance, in many states having partisan and nonpartisan elections, many judges are initially appointed rather than elected. This is made possible by the governor's power of interim appointment and the general understanding that judges should resign or retire a short time before the end of their terms. In Indiana, a slight variation of this practice occurred with respect to county court judges. Fifty-six new county court judges were appointed by the circuit court judge of the county on January 1, 1976, to serve until the general election that year. Most of these interim judges were then retained by the electorate.

In other ways selection systems do not always operate as the reader might expect. Where nonpartisan elections are used to select judges, partisan influences are often present in the process. On the other hand, intense partisanship and vigorous political activity do not usually characterize the partisan selection of state judges. Indiana judicial elections are usually characterized by low key campaigns stressing professional qualifications, legal experience and "judicial temperament." Possibly as a result of such judicial campaigns, a study in the state of Texas has found that the electorate lacked the necessary information to make an elective judicial system function properly.[23] The Missouri Plan is usually praised as a "merit selection" plan and yet the political needs of the governor, the state judiciary and the state bar are certainly reflected.[24]

It is difficult to declare which selection system is best for the state of Indiana. One political scientist has systematically investigated and compared the characteristics of judges chosen under the five different selection systems. He found that judges selected under the different systems do vary but not always in the expected way. For example, judges chosen under the Missouri Plan are more localistic than other judges.[25] They also did not possess a better legal education than judges selected by other means. They did have greater previous experience as judges, whereas judges chosen by the state legislature or elected by partisan ballot were more likely to have other types of political experience.[26]

The contrast among the various forms of judicial selection methods is not as great as expected when comparisons are made of their impact. Whichever system is used, most state judges have certain characteristics in common. They have formal legal training, they are recruited and trained locally,[27] and they have prior political experience. In Indiana, one other characteristic stands out. The state judges are new to their jobs. A majority of Indiana state judges did not assume the bench before 1976. This is the result in part to the recent increase in the number of state judges.

Other Court Actors

Lawyers

There were 8,462 attorneys in 1980 who had paid their dues and were thus eligible to practice law in the state of Indiana. They represent clients in disputes that fall broadly into two categories—civil disputes and criminal disputes. Civil disputes involve conflicts between two private parties and are tied closely to the relationship between the parties.[28] The parties involved may be individuals or groups of individuals who share a particular interest. Lawyers representing such parties attempt to persuade judges to define, adjust, or establish the relationship between parties. The relationships in dispute may involve the terms of a contract, the determination of injuries in an automobile accident, the custody of children in a dissolved marriage or some other aspect of the private relationship between two parties. Criminal disputes, on the other hand, involve the definition or adjustment of the relationship between an individual and society as a whole. The conflict is based on the behavior of the individual which society has labelled "criminal." Since the public fears rising crime rates and is simultaneously fascinated and frustrated by the criminal justice process, we shall examine the lawyers who function in criminal disputes.

Prosecutors

The function of prosecuting criminals in Indiana is performed by locally elected prosecutors and the deputy prosecutors they, in turn, appoint. Prosecutors are representatives of the county government. They are selected by the voters in partisan elections for a term of four years. As of 1980, there were forty-seven Republican prosecutors in the state and forty Democrats. Prosecutors in Indiana may serve on a full-time or a part-time basis. Sixty-three are part-time while twenty-four serve as full-time prosecuting attorneys. A majority of the prosecutors in Class One and Class Two counties (the largest counties in the state), however, are full-time prosecutors. Elected prosecutors in Indiana appoint their assistant lawyers. As in most other states, the turnover rate among their assistants is high.[29] Most assistant prosecutors return to private practice after satisfying their need to serve, their need for experience or their need for a stable income while beginning their legal careers. Prosecutors exercise a great deal of discretion in determining which cases will be prosecuted and which charges will be introduced in a particular case. Many factors affect the use of this discretion such as (1) limited resources in terms of staff, money and time, (2) the importance prosecutors place on winning their cases, (3) law enforcement considerations such as dropping charges against one defendant in exchange for information, and (4) professional considerations such as a prosecutor's sense of professional ethics and feelings about collegial relations with other attorneys. When local cases are appealed, the State Attorney General's Office represents the state.

Defense Attorneys

No professional figure in the United States has a more ambivalent public image than criminal defense attorneys. In fiction and biographies, they are true American heroes, using their wits and hard work to save innocent clients from mistakes made by police, prosecutors, jurors and judges.[30] In reality, most criminal defense attorneys are rated low by their peers in terms of prestige. They are perceived to be tarnished by a lack of ethics, association with criminals and poor monetary returns. The one exception to this rule is a small group of well-known and successful criminal defense attorneys that usually defend rich and famous clients accused of unusual crimes.

The United States Supreme Court has ruled that poor individuals have the right to counsel in almost all criminal cases.[31] Indiana supplies attorneys to indigent defendants for criminal defense work in three different ways. Fifty-eight counties use the court appointment system and eleven counties contract with lawyers to conduct criminal defense work on a temporary basis. Both of these systems are considered inferior to the more permanent public defender system.[32] Thirty-two counties in the state of Indiana have public defender systems. The public defenders are appointed by the circuit court judge of the county and may serve on a full or part-time basis. Studies indicate, however, that the quality of representation even under a public defender system is inferior to that provided by private counsel.[33] Indiana also has an office of State Public Defender whose function is to provide legal representation for any inmate in the state who claims he is unlawfully imprisoned and is without sufficient funds to employ counsel.

Plea Bargaining

One of the great trends in the practice of law is that attorneys prefer to negotiate their lawsuits outside of court. Ninety percent of all civil cases and criminal cases are settled without trial. Indiana is no exception in this regard. Negotiations of this type in the criminal law are known as "plea bargaining."

Plea bargaining has become so prevalent because it has many advantages. It is the process whereby the defendant admits his or her guilt in exchange for a concession on the part of the prosecutor to reduce the original charge or recommend a lighter sentence. From a cost management perspective, it is very efficient. It also injects flexibility into the system allowing attorneys to view each case individually.

Plea bargaining also has its critics.[34] Some question its propriety. Is it proper for defendants to bargain away their rights in order to negotiate? Others criticize the practice because it is virtually invisible with no records being kept. Still others contend that plea-bargaining has replaced a system of criminal justice that has citizen input with a system dominated by bureaucratic specialization.

The Public

Plea bargaining has without question reduced the direct role of the public in the Indiana judiciary. Fewer trials means fewer opportunities for members of the public to serve as witnesses and jurors in trials. Of course, as spectators and critics the public continues to be just as important in providing support for the entire judicial system.

Trial juries in major courts in Indiana are composed of twelve members of the public drawn from a list of registered voters in the county. Jury decisions in the state must be unanimous. Juries are important judicial institutions because they allow parties to be judged by their peers. In criminal cases, they also serve as buffers between the accused and the state. The function of the trial jury is to ascertain the facts of the case and apply the appropriate law as instructed by the judge.

Members of the public might also serve on county grand juries. Grand juries in Indiana are composed of six members, selected in the same way as trial jurors except that the foreman is designated by the judge of the circuit court. The duties of the grand jury include such activities as bringing indictments against suspected criminals and investigating the conditions and management of jails and infirmaries.

Other Court Personnel

By a 1975 statute, the General Assembly provided for the appointment of a court administrator in any county having a population of more than one hundred thousand persons. Such court administrators are selected by a majority vote of the judges in the county and serve at their pleasure. In addition, their administrative duties are determined by the judges.

The clerk of the circuit court, commonly called the "county clerk," is elected by the voters of the county for a term of four years. They perform a variety of tasks such as the filing and recording of court orders, recording wills, receiving filings of candidacy from persons seeking elective office and the issuing of licenses.

Jury commissioners in Indiana are appointed by the judge of the circuit court. Two citizens, one representing each major political party, are selected in each county. The jury commissioners annually select the names of prospective jurors whose names are placed in a locked box and turned over to the clerk of the circuit court.

The Indiana court system also includes many other persons such as the sheriff, who serves warrants and subpoenas, court reporters, bailiffs and secretaries.

Administration of Indiana Courts

"The most important obligation of any court system is to resolve matters committed to its jurisdiction."[35] How well this obligation is met depends not only upon the types of courts in existence and the quality of the judges but also upon the administration of the courts. "Administration" in this regard refers to such activities as budgeting, planning, calendaring and the quality of caseload information.

Indiana Appellate Court Administration

The office of judicial administration was created by statute in 1975 to assist the Chief Justice of the Indiana Supreme Court in carrying out many administrative duties. The office of judicial administration consists of two divisions: supreme court administration and state court administration. The division of supreme court administration is headed by a supreme court administrator and the state court division is headed by an executive director. The members of both divisions are appointed and serve at the pleasure of the chief justice. The duties of the division of supreme court administration are "such legal and administrative duties for the justices as are determined by the justice."[36] The duties of the state court administration are more specific: "examine the administrative and business methods employed in offices serving state courts, collect and compile statistical data on the judicial work of the courts in the state, and prepare reports on the nature and volume of judicial work performed by the courts."

The administrative arm of the Supreme Court extends to many other agencies as well. The Board of Law Examiners helps the Supreme Court to determine the qualifications of law school graduates seeking admission to the practice of law in Indiana. The Disciplinary Commission's staff investigates complaints of lawyer misconduct and makes recommendations concerning appropriate disciplinary action ranging from disbarment or suspension to censure. The Commission on Judicial Qualifications oversees the conduct of judges having the authority to recommend retirement or removal for various causes including disability. The Judicial Conference of Indiana, created in 1967, is composed of "all justices of the Supreme Court, all judges of the Court of Appeals, all circuit, superior, criminal, probate, juvenile and county court judges, and all municipal court judges who are serving on a full-time basis."[37] The Judicial Conference was established to promote the continuing education of judges and a better understanding of the Indiana judiciary. The Indiana Judicial Center, created in 1971, sponsors educational conferences in legal and judicial administration and publishes many related documents.

The Court of Appeals shares with the Supreme Court the supreme court clerk, supreme court reporter and the supreme court sheriff. In addition, the Court of Appeals has an administrator and a court commissioner. The administrator prepares yearly caseload reports while the commissioner is involved in legal research.

Indiana Trial Court Administration

The administration of Indiana's trial courts varies from county to county and generally lacks the more professionalized nature of administration found in the state's appellate courts. Although a 1975 statute provided for the opportunity to appoint court administrators in counties having a population in excess of one hundred thousand persons, no study has been compiled as yet to analyze how these administrators have been used to improve the administration of trial courts in those counties adopting the position. We have a clearer picture, however, concerning the administration of trial courts in counties without administrators on the basis of a survey conducted in 1975.[38] This survey revealed that Indiana trial judges do not have large staffs. Sixty-eight percent of the judges responding had five people or fewer working for them. Most judges, more than eighty-two percent, prepared their own budgets to be submitted to the county council and board of county commissions. A large number of trial courts failed to compile caseload statistics and those that did rarely used them for any meaningful analysis of court management.[39] Sixty-one percent of the judges managed their own calendars but very few took part in court planning. Obviously, many Indiana trial judges do not stress court administration as a high priority item.

Conclusion

Analysts and commentators put forth suggestions for reform concerning most public institutions. The Indiana Judiciary has not been spared such recommendations. A few of these proposals will be discussed.

To improve the administration of Indiana's trial courts, a unified trial court for Indiana has been proposed.[40] Under such a system, the trial court system would consist of a single tier of courts, each having the same subject matter jurisdiction. This system would replace the current multiplicity of trial courts. The state court system would be divided geographically into districts, each district providing an administrative function. See Figure 5.2. The presiding judge could assign judges within the district and supervise financial affairs, continuing education for court personnel, and court planning. A few states such as California and Illinois have adopted unified court systems.

Another recommendation suggested is the abolition of partisan elections for the selection of Indiana trial judges. Under a proposed merit plan, a judicial nominating commisssion would convene to select the best two candidates who would then run against each other in a nonpartisan election.[41] In light of our earlier comments concerning the assessment of judicial selection plans, the authors have some doubts as to the impact of this merit plan.

Another popular recommendation is that local prosecutors and public defenders should be required to work full-time at their jobs. The argument is that the importance of their position demands no less. The fear expressed is that part-time prosecutors and public defenders will devote too much time to their more lucrative private practices under the present system. The problem with the recommendation would be the recruitment of lawyers to these positions unless salaries were dramatically increased.

A final recommendation to be discussed is the proposal to use six-member juries and allow less than unanimous verdicts in all Indiana trials. The United States Supreme Court has declared six-member juries to be consistent with the federal Constitution.[42] The advantages of six-member juries are the savings of money and time. It takes less time to impanel smaller juries. Less than unanimous verdicts have also been sanctioned by the United States Supreme Court.[43] Permitting less than unanimous verdicts increases the likelihood that a jury will be able to reach a verdict and reduces the impact of the obstinate juror. Changing the traditional nature of Indiana jury trials does not seem likely in the near future, however.

Notes

1. For an explanation of political systems theory, see Easton, David. *A Systems Analysis of Political Life,* New York: John Wiley, (1965).
2. The number of judicial behavior studies are too numerous to list. See, for example, Schubert, Glendon. *Judicial Policy-Making.* Atlanta: Scott, Foresman, (1965); Pritchett, C. Herman. *Congress Versus the Supreme Court,* 1957–1960. Minneapolis, Minn.: University of Minnesota Press, (1961); Ulmer, S. Sidney. "A Note on Attitudinal Consistency in the United States Supreme Court," *Indiana Journal of Political Science* XXII, (1961), pp 195–204; and Schmidhauser, John R. "Judicial Behavior and the Sectional Crisis of 1837–1860," *Journal of Politics* XXIII, (1961), 628.
3. Glick, Henry Robert and Vines, Kenneth N. *State Court Systems.* Englewood Cliffs, New Jersey: Prentice-Hall, (1973), pp 11–12.
4. *Ibid.,* p 33.
5. *Ind. Const.,* Art. 7, Sec. 1.
6. *State v. Lasselle,* 1 Blackf. 60 (1820).
7. *Ind. Const.,* Art. 7, Sec. 2.
8. *Ind. Const.,* Art. 7, Sec. 4.
9. *Ibid.*
10. Atkins, Burton M. and Glick, Henry R. "Environmental and Structural Variables as Determinants of Issues in State Courts of Last Resort," in Sheldon Goldman and Austin Sarat, eds., *American Court Systems.* San Francisco: W. H. Freeman, (1978), p 82.
11. *Ibid.,* p. 83.
12. *1891 Ind. Acts,* Ch. 37, Sec. 1, 39.
13. Indiana Judges Association, The Indiana Trial Court System, Volume 1, Indianapolis: Indiana Judicial Center, (1978), p 161.
14. *Ind. Code* Sec. 33-2.1-2-2(c) (1976).
15. *Ind. Code* Sec. 33-4-1-1 through Sec. 33-4-1-92 (1976). The counties which share a circuit court are Dearborn-Ohio, Jefferson-Switzerland, Crawford-Harrison, and Martin-Dubois.
16. This figure does not include the reorganization of the Marion County Superior Court.

17. *Ind. Code* Sec. 33-10.5-2-6 through Sec. 33-10.5-2-11 (Supp. 1977).
18. Glick, Henry Robert. *Supreme Courts in State Politics.* New York: Basic Books, (1979), p 3–4.
19. Nagel, Stuart S. "Political Party Affiliation and Judge's Decisions," *American Political Science Review,* 55, (1961), pp 844–850.
20. *Ind. Const. 1816,* Art. 5, Sec. 9.
21. Indiana Judges Association, *Indiana Trial Court System,* p 153.
22. Glick and Vines, *State Court Systems,* p 42.
23. McKnight, R. Neal, Schaefer, Roger C. and Johnson, Charles A. "State Judicial Elections," *Judicature,* 62, (1978), pp 94–99.
24. Watson, Richard A. and Downing, Randal G. *The Politics of the Bench and the Bar: Judicial Selection Under the Missouri Nonpartisan Court Plan.* New York: John Wiley and Sons, (1969).
25. Jacob, Herbert. "The Effect of Institutional Differences in the Recruitment Process: The Cases of State Judges," *Journal of Public Law,* 33, (1964), pp 104–119.
26. Watson and Downing, *op. cit.,* Chapter 6.
27. Volcansek-Clark, Mary. "Why Lawyers Become Judges," *Judicature,* 62, (1978), pp 167–175.
28. McLauchlan, William P. *American Legal Processes.* New York: John Wiley and Sons, (1977), p 9.
29. Alexander, C. E. *Survey of Local Prosecutors: Data Concerning 1,000 Local Prosecutors.* Raleigh, N.C.: National Association of Attorneys, General Committee on the Office of Attorney General, (1973).
30. Wood, Arthur Lewis. *Criminal Lawyer.* New Haven, Conn.: College and University Press, (9167), p 24.
31. *Argersinger v. Hamlin,* 707 U.S. 25 (1972).
32. Wice, Paul B. and Pilgrim, Mark. "Meeting the Gideon Mandate: A Survey of Public Defender Programs," *Judicature,* 58, (1975), p 407.
33. Rosett, Arthur and Cressey, Donald R. *Justice by Consent.* Philadelphia: Lippincott, (1976), p 177.
34. See Klein, John F. *Let's Make A Deal.* Lexington, Mass: Lexington Books, (1976).
35. American Judicature Society. *Indiana Trial Courts: Strategy for Cohesive Change.* Chicago: Judicial Study Commission, (1976).
36. *Ind. Code* Sec. 33-2.1-7-4, (1976).
37. *Ind. Code* Sec. 33-13-14-1, (Supp. 1977).
38. American Judicature Society, Indiana Trial Courts, p 6.
39. *Ibid.,* p 14.
40. Indiana Judges Association. *Indiana Trial Court System.* pp 59–69.
41. *Ibid.,* Volume 2, p 31.
42. *Williams v. Florida* 399 U.S. 78, (1970).
43. See *Apodaca v. Oregon,* 406 U.S. 404, (1972), and *Johnson v. Louisiana,* 406 U.S. 356, (1972).

6

Local Government in Indiana: A Study of Contrasts

William P. Hojnacki
Indiana University at South Bend

with *Lloyd Rowe*
Indiana University Northwest

Aerial view of downtown South Bend, Indiana
Courtesy of the South Bend Tribune

Local government is more important to the daily lives of Indiana residents than most people realize. Indeed, it is difficult for any Indiana citizen to avoid almost daily contact with some aspect of local government. It is local government that has the primary responsibility for raising and collecting property taxes, maintaining streets, roads, and public parks, running the schools, providing police and fire protection, regulating land use, and insuring the health and welfare of all Indiana residents.

Local government is pervasive. Most residents live within the jurisdiction of at least three and probably more local units. All residents live within the boundaries of a township, a county, and a school district. Most also live in a city or a town, and many live within the jurisdictions of one or more special purpose governments that provide services that range from soil and water conservation projects to public transportation. In all, Indiana has 92 counties, 1008 townships, 560 incorporated municipalities, and uncounted hundreds of special purpose governments, including school districts.[1]

The Indiana system of local government is complicated and difficult to understand. Indeed, at first glance it hardly seems systematic at all, and it is difficult to find any rational base for the structure, style, or divisions of responsibility that characterize it. For example, the same basic form of government is used to govern the smallest county in the state as is used to govern all the other counties of the state except the very largest. The County Recorder, who has no policy-making responsibilities, is elected while the County Engineer, who in large counties has major policy-making responsibilities, is appointed. Cities and towns may exist in all or part of one or more townships and bump into one another. Both counties and townships are given the same responsibility for undertaking property tax assessments. One form of public assistance, "poor relief," is a township function while another form, "public welfare," is a county function. Almost every municipality has its own police department, which means that in some of the larger counties there are more police chiefs than some small towns have police officers. It is quite possible for two neighbors living across the street from each other in identical homes to have several thousand dollars difference in the amount of property taxes each is expected to pay.

Actually, the Indiana system of local government is not nearly as confusing and irrational as it might first appear. Different units do serve different purposes, and different people in different parts of the state want different things. Many local government institutions, like the Board of County Commissioners, are products of history, carrying out functions that have been theirs since before the American Revolutionary War. Other institutions, like town managers and city government cabinets, have been created more recently in response to new and changing public demands. Local government in Indiana is a blending of old and new. If it appears to be somewhat confusing and irrational, it is because local governments do many different things, and they do them in different ways. Local government becomes less confusing when its purposes are understood.

Local government in Indiana, as elsewhere, has two important tasks to perform. The first task is to deliver public services at the local level. The second task is to manage the conflict that inevitably develops among individuals, groups, and communities when local government tries to deliver its services. In undertaking these tasks, the organizations of local government, in general, follow three basic principles. The first principle, known as "Dillon's Rule," is that local governments are the creations of the state in which they are located, and as such are totally responsible to their parent state government. This principle was articulated by Judge John F. Dillon of the Iowa Supreme Court in 1868.[2] Unlike the federal government or the individual governments of the fifty states, local units of government are in no way sovereign. The only powers they have are those the states either bestow upon them or allow them to exercise. Thus, in the United States each system of local government is distinct from the others, and each is responsible solely to the state that created it.[3] In Indiana, this principle has traditionally been rigidly applied. Cities, towns, counties and townships could do only those things specifically authorized by the State Constitution or by State Statute. In the late 1970's and early 1980's, however, the state began to loosen its tight reign of control over local government.[4]

A second important principle is that of local control over local affairs. This is a principle that was drawn from the British tradition of local self-government and strengthened by the American colonial experience of having to deal with a hostile central government located across the Atlantic Ocean. These historical factors combined to encourage the establishment of local governmental institutions that functioned, in large measure, independently of any central authority, at least as far as providing local services was concerned. Thus, throughout the United States today there are approximately 80,000 units of local government functioning independently of each other, and within the limits of the powers allowed to them under Dillon's Rule, independent of the central governing authority provided by their parent state. In almost all cases local units of government operate under the leadership of locally selected, either by appointment or election, public officials.[5] In Indiana alone there are over 2,000 units of local government, each performing a specific set of tasks over a particular geographic area and under the direction of locally selected leaders.

A third important principle of local government is the requisite for citizen participation in local affairs. This is a principle that began in colonial times as a combination of the British tradition of local self-government and the necessity, in the absence of a colonial professional civil servant class, of having to rely on citizens to provide many basic services on a voluntary basis.[6] Citizen participation became institutionalized as a result of the advent of "Jacksonian democracy," a basic tenet of which sought citizen rather than professional control over public affairs. This principle is maintained in local government throughout the United States today in two or three ways. First, it is manifested in the existence of the "long ballot" where many public officials are elected. It is common in some states to elect such minor officials as the drain commissioner, recorder of deeds, or the court reporter. At the local level in Indiana, citizens elect such officials as a county auditor, a city clerk, and a township trustee. A second way this principle is maintained is through the creation of autonomous or semi-autonomous boards and commissions that are given responsibility for making and carrying out various aspects of local public policy. Many of the boards and commissions are themselves special kinds of local units of government, while others are arms of more general purpose units of government. The authority of these boards and commissions ranges from advisory to administrative. Service on these boards is usually voluntary and without pay. In a typical Indiana community, citizens may serve on such diverse boards as the Drainage Board, Hospital Board, Human Rights Commission, Housing Authority, or the Board of Zoning Appeals. Even in a modest sized Indiana community, a hundred or more persons can participate in government through this means. The principle of citizen participation in local affairs also includes participation in the political process itself such as in voting, campaigning, working for a political party, and running for public office.[7]

In at least one aspect, local government is really no different from government in a democratic society at any level. While the primary responsibilities of local government are to deliver basic services and manage conflict, its responsibilities do not stop there. Local government serves, as George Blair has pointed out, as the "school room of democracy."[8] It represents that level of government to which citizens most easily gain access and in which citizen participation in public affairs is most likely to occur. It is this level of government where citizens learn how to participate in the political process. It is here where citizens gain their training and experience for participation in state and national affairs. Since local government forms the base of the state and national political system, it is the place where people most often begin careers in politics and public service.

Local government serves as the focal point for the social and economic organizations of any local community. Local governments come in different sizes and shapes and undertake varying responsibilities, because different groups of people need and want different things. Local government allows residents in different areas to come together and to behave like communities. Thus, different groups of citizens can draw boundaries between each other, provide themselves with wanted and needed services, and reach mutually agreed upon (or at least tolerated) decisions on the matters that affect their day to day existence.[9]

We expect our local units of government to deliver many different kinds of services and to do it as inexpensively, efficiently, and equitably as possible. We most often make judgments on the quality of local government based on the services it delivers. Too often the role of local government in managing political conflict is overlooked. In any democratic society, political conflict is inevitable, but this conflict is a dominant feature of government at the local level because of the high degree of citizen participation. Indeed, the management and resolution of local political conflicts may well be the most important role local government has to play. This role is reflected in the way that local government is organized. As local government in the United

States (including Indiana) has evolved over the years, the forms and procedures of government institutions reflect as much the role that government has assumed for itself in resolving conflict as they reflect the service missions for which they were originally created. The ideas of local control over local affairs and citizen participation in the political process imply the need for governmental institutions that can manage and resolve local political conflicts as well as deliver needed services.[10]

It is the diversity of local governmental roles and responsibilities that makes the study of local government a study in contrast. Systems of local government, in attempting to satisfactorily undertake all of their roles and fulfill all of their responsibilities, generate at first glance what appears to be confusing and contradictory institutions and approaches to running these institutions. The rational base of local government is often obscured. Local government today is a curious mixture of rational judgments on what citizens want and need and attempts at protecting various private interests that have evolved over a long period of history.

Historical Perspective of Local Government in Indiana

Local government in Indiana as we know it today evolved from the American colonial experience, and its evolution proceeded in response to a multitude of pressures. The existence of local government actually predates the organization of Indiana as a state in 1816. The first town in Indiana was Vincennes, established as a trading post and frontier fort prior to the American Revolution.[11] Beyond a rudimentary form of government created for this town and for a few other towns that were settled during the Revolutionary War era, the basic pattern of local government in Indiana was established by the Continental Congress of the United States during the period following the war.[12] The land ordinances of 1785 and 1787, known as the "Northwest Ordinances," were to Indiana local government the most significant pieces of legislation passed by the Continental Congress prior to the adoption of the current United States Constitution in 1789.

The ordinance of 1785 provided for the division of the entire Northwest Territory—the present day states of Indiana, Ohio, Michigan, Illinois, Wisconsin, and portions of Minnesota—into "Congressional" or "Survey" townships.[13] As the ordinance stated:

> "The surveyors . . . shall proceed to divide the said territory into townships six miles square by lines running due north and south and others crossing these at right angles as near as may be."[14]

The ordinance of 1787 further outlined a system of territorial and local government. One provision of the ordinance was for the organization of the congressional townships into counties as the population warranted; another provided for the appointment of commissioners to serve as the administrative officers of the counties.[15] This basic form of government, with some alterations, was incorporated in the first state constitution adopted in 1816 and carried forward by the second constitution adopted in 1851. The 1851 constitution does allow for the alteration of township and county boundaries, but such changes have rarely occurred. Counties and townships remain the basic units of government in Indiana primarily because they are geographically based covering the entire state and because they continue to deliver basic state-mandated services at the local level. Counties and townships, however, were conceived as a way of governing essentially rural and wilderness areas with sparse populations. They were never thought to be adequate for providing government services for places that had relatively large and concentrated populations such as modern urban areas. This task was given over to cities and towns.

Whereas the state's 1851 constitution is explicitly restrictive on certain matters concerning local government and mandates the election of several county officials, it is largely silent on the question of city government. Originally, cities were not even mentioned. Written for a simpler era when the major means of transportation was the horse and buggy, the only concession to the establishment of an urban community was the consideration that a county seat be situated a one-day round-trip buggy ride from the outreaches of the county. County governments, organized in 1851 to be administrative agents of state government, were not given authority to act independently or to provide many services. They were given primary responsibility for road building and peace keeping and little more. Townships were established in every county to provide for public schools and poor relief. Counties and townships still function primarily as administrative agents of the state.

The absence of any constitutional mention of cities and towns or municipal functions left a legal void for the organization and governance of cities as they emerged in number and size in the mid-19th century. This oversight was remedied somewhat when cities and towns were given constitutional status under Article XI, section 13, as "corporations other than banking" by court interpretation.[16] While this established cities' identities and gave them the authority to provide some municipal services, it also put some constraints on their activities such as a two percent limit on the bonded indebtedness for cities and a single tax requirement which forbids cities to vary the property tax rate within a taxing district regardless of the service level. The complex and protracted constitutional amendment procedure requiring that proposed amendments be passed in like form by two successive sessions of the General Assembly before they are submitted for referendum approval and the governor's signature has thwarted subsequent attempts to provide municipal authority through the constitutional process.

As a consequence of the absence of constitutional recognition, cities and towns trace most of their municipal authority to the Indiana General Assembly which first gave broad definitive status to municipal governments in the Cities and Towns Act of 1905.[17] Thus, in Indiana, virtually all of the structure powers and processes of city and town government are prescribed by state law rather than the State Constitution.

The concept of a city or county "charter" is unknown to the state law, and substantive "home rule," long a subject for debate by local officials, was not enacted until 1981. Legal recognition of the state's ascendency in the distribution of power was confirmed through Indiana's version of Dillon's rule which states in effect that local corporations are creatures of the state and can exercise only powers expressly granted to them by the state law.[18] Up until the 1981 statute, if any doubt existed it had to be resolved against the local unit in favor of the state.

As a consequence of nearly a hundred years of piecemeal legislation, there has been general application to local government of numerous overlapping and duplicative arrangements. Thus, there exists today a multitude of agencies, boards, and isolated officials that cannot cope with the exigencies of managing contemporary urban problems. The deeply felt effect of the General Assembly's policy of uncoordinated control over the affairs of local government was well stated by James Bryce over a half century ago:

> The aim deliberately was to make a city government where no officer himself should have enough power to do much harm. The natural result of this was to create a situation where no officer has power to do much good.[19]

The Design of Local Government

All units of local government in Indiana fall under the jurisdiction of the state. The range of responsibilities they undertake is set forth either by the Constitution or by statute. In Indiana the state has chosen to divide up responsibilities among different types of local governmental units.

There are two broad categories of local governmental units, "General Purpose" and "Special Purpose." General purpose units of local governments are counties, townships, cities and towns—the ones with which citizens are most familiar. The legislature has given units included under this category a wide range of responsibilities and relatively broad powers to carry them out. Special purpose units of government, on the other hand, are created by the legislature one at a time to undertake a specific single purpose service delivery function. Special purpose governments have no flexibility to alter the responsibilities they have been given. They are created when the legislature determines that a service needs to be delivered, usually to a specific geographic area, that would be inappropriate to deliver through some existing general purpose unit. The inappropriateness of using existing governmental units may stem from any one of a number of factors. One example would be the necessity of delivering a required service over a broad geographic area transcending the jurisdiction of a general purpose unit of government such as would be the case with soil or water conservation projects. These projects are likely to include more than one county or several cities, towns, and townships. The creation of a special purpose unit of government may also stem from the fact that the service to be delivered is simply different from what the existing government units normally do, or that funding for the service comes from special sources such as a particular federally funded program. Thus, special units of government have been created to administer the delivery of housing services (local housing authorities), transportation services (local public transportation corporations), and educational services (local school corporations). With special purpose units of government of this type, the service area is usually co-extensive with a general purpose unit of government, and it is oftentimes difficult to tell them apart.

General Purpose Units of Government

The major responsibility for delivering most local government services and for resolving local political conflicts rests with four types of general purpose units of local governments—counties, townships, cities, and towns. The four types can further be categorized as either quasi-municipalities or true municipalities. In Indiana, quasi-municipalities are counties and townships—those units of government that have as their primary responsibility serving an agent of state government at the local level. They are units of government whose primary responsibility is to deliver, at the local level, services that really are more the responsibility of state government than of local government. Cities and towns are considered true municipalities. They are recognized as "corporations" with variable geographic configurations that have as their primary responsibility the delivery of state-mandated or allowed local services.

Counties

If any unit of local government is basic to Indiana, it is the county. Counties in Indiana blanket the state and were established geographically without reference to population. The state constitution does allow for the alteration of county boundaries, but the geographic configuration of Indiana's 92 counties has not been changed since 1859. There is little sentiment for alteration today. These counties range in population from 765,233 in Marion County to 5,114 in Ohio County.[20] With the major exceptions of Marion County (Indianapolis) and the minor exceptions of St. Joseph County (South Bend) and Lake County (Gary), all counties have the same form of governmental structure.[21] Marion County government, of course, has been consolidated with Indianapolis city government to form the unique "unigov" system. St. Joseph County and Lake County incorporate variations of the traditional Indiana form of county government.

Counties and townships are different from true municipalities (cities and towns) because they have the dual responsibilities of serving as the agent of state government at the local level as well as providing some local services that are either mandated in the State Constitution or that the state legislature has from time to time allowed or required. In Indiana, this dual level of responsibility translates into counties serving as agents of the state for such functions, among others, as administering the trial court level of the state judicial system, conducting elections and recording such instruments as birth and death certificates, marriage licenses, and property deeds. At the same time, counties have the responsibility for maintaining county roads and highways, administering a "county home" for the aged and, if they choose, establishing building and zoning codes and administering public housing and development programs.[22]

The form of county government has changed little since Indiana was granted statehood in 1816. The Constitution of 1851 did little to alter the already established forms of county government. It incorporates eight elected "administrative" offices that form the basis of county government organization. The time-consuming and difficult process by which the state constitution is amended has worked against altering the fundamental organizational structure of county government, even when there was sentiment to do so.[23] While the legislature can create new offices, it cannot eliminate the constitutional offices without a constitutional amendment. Even the Indianapolis-Marion County "unigov" plan was implemented without altering the functions or roles of the constitutionally established county offices. These "administrative" offices are auditor, clerk of the circuit court, coroner, recorder, treasurer, sheriff, and surveyor.[24]

These were included in the constitution as elective offices primarily because of the largely rural state for which the constitution was written. Most counties were far removed from the state capitol in Indianapolis. Making these offices elected was the practical way the framers of the constitution felt they could insure the accountability of public officials who undertook sensitive and important tasks, even if those tasks did not encompass important policy making responsibilities. This approach was also consistent with the prevailing political theory inspired by both American political tradition and a basic tenet of "Jacksonian democracy" that local government ought to be locally controlled and encompass as broad a range of citizen participation as possible. It is primarily through the elected administrative offices plus the county level court officials that counties are able to undertake their responsibilities as agents of the state government at the local level.[25]

The most important county governmental body in all but Marion County is the Board of County Commissioners. Today all of Indiana counties, except Marion, are governed by three-member Boards of Commissioners, and in all of these counties, except Lake and St. Joseph, this board has both executive and legislative powers. In Lake and St. Joseph Counties they have executive powers only. County Commissioners are elected from single-member districts, but, except for St. Joseph and Lake County, all the voters of the county can vote for all three commissioners. They are elected for staggered four-year terms.

The focus of authority, at least as far as the service delivery function is concerned, in county government rests with the three-member Board of Commissioners. In addition to their statutorally defined legislative and executive responsibilities, they have the power to make appointments to a number of the most important county agencies, including the offices of the county attorney and the highway engineer. It is somewhat ironic that in all counties, except Marion where this board has been effectively eliminated, the position of commissioner is designated as "part-time," and pays only a minimal salary. Figure 6.1 is an organizational chart of a typical county government in Indiana.

Figure 6.1. Typical county government organization (simplified)

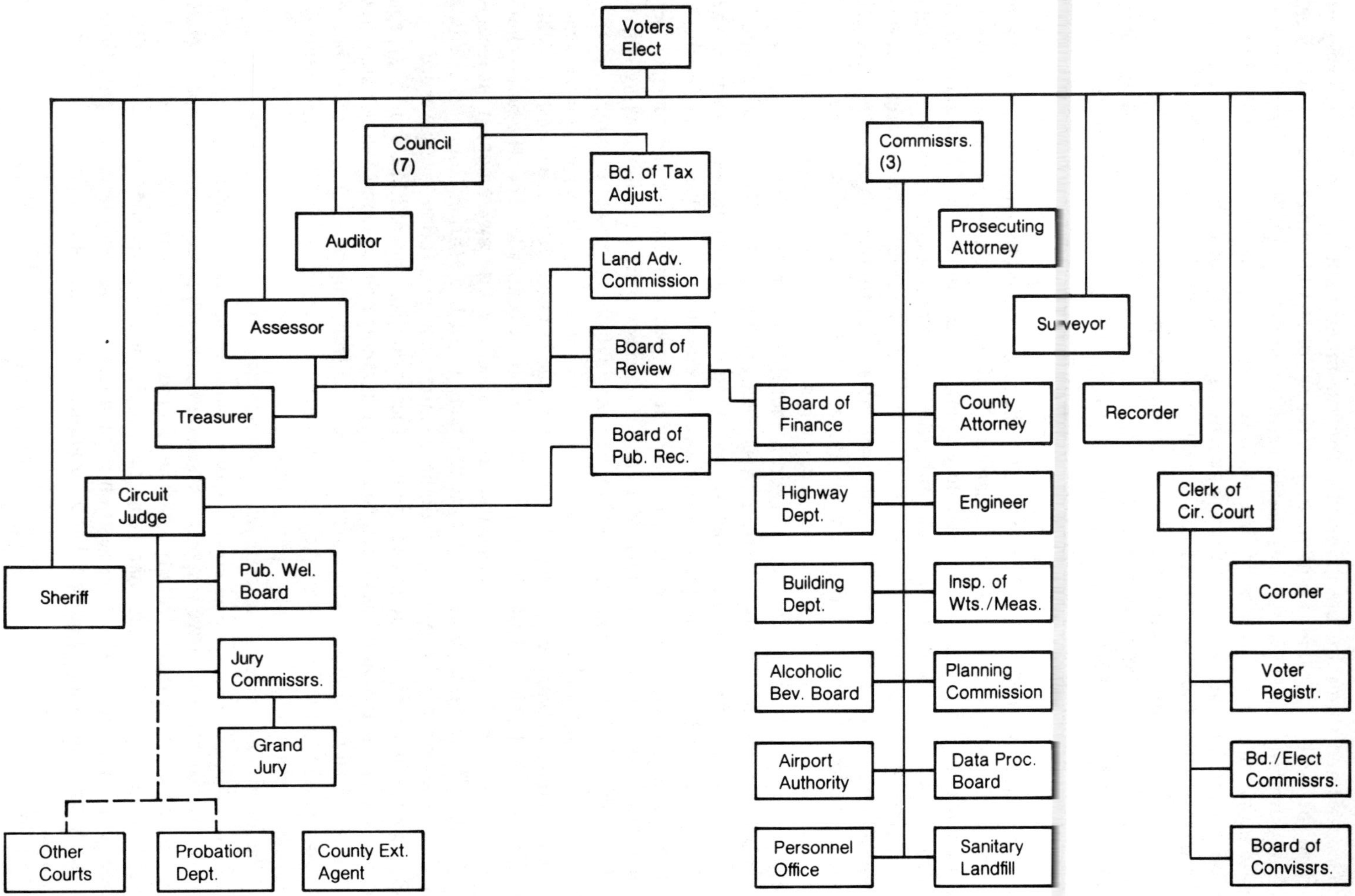

County councils are a relatively new institution, being established for the first time in 1897. County councils have in most cases very limited functions. Except for Marion, Lake, and St. Joseph County, they are not legislative bodies in the traditional sense. Their sole major responsibility is to appropriate county funds. In carrying out this responsibility, they also have the function of serving as a check on the budget-making responsibility of the Commissioners.

Figure 6.2 outlines the duties of the various elected county officials. As these descriptions point out, county officials have a variety of responsibilities and undertake a wide range of functions. The elected officials, however, are not the only persons responsible for administering county government. Administratively, many persons operating independently or through independent or quasi-independent agencies, boards, and commissions are responsible for undertaking the day-to-day tasks of county government.

Figure 6.2. Duties of Elected County Administrative Offices

County Assessor

The assessor has the responsibility for determining the value of property for taxing purposes in the county. In actual practice property tax assessments are made by township officials. Thus, the role of the county assessor is limited to supervising the township authorities and certifying their data.

County Auditor

The county auditor serves as secretary of the Board of County Commissioners and has the responsibility for keeping county accounts and issues warrants for the payments of the County Board of Review (of tax levies) and secretary of the County Council, and has responsibility for County-owned books, maps and other documents.

County Clerk—officially, the clerk of the Circuit Court

The duties of the county clerk revolve around the legal duties assigned to the county circuit court, and other county courts. The clerk is responsible for keeping court records, issuing marriage licenses, collecting and distributing child support payments in divorce cases and receiving filing of candidates for public office. The clerk also serves as an ex-officio member and secretary of the county election boards.

County Coroner

The chief responsibility of the coroner is to determine the manner of death in cases involving violence or the cause of death when an individual is found dead in unexplained circumstances. The coroner is also a peace officer and the only official who can arrest the Sheriff.

County Recorder

The primary responsibility of the recorder is to preserve public records. The recorder records such things as mortgages, liens, leases, articles of incorporation and military discharges.

County Sheriff

The sheriff is the chief "conservator of the peace," or law enforcement officer in the county. The sheriff is the head of the county police department that has primary law enforcement responsibilities in the "non-incorporated areas of the county." In addition to the law enforcement responsibilities, the sheriff serves as an officer of the court in serving papers issued by the court, collecting delinquent taxes, and housing prisoners.

County Surveyor

The surveyor is responsible for keeping a record of all "section corners" in the county in compliance with the requirements of the ordinance of 1789 and to supervise all civil engineering projects in the county.

County Teasurer

The county treasurer has the responsibility of collecting, retaining, and dispersing county funds. The county treasurer also serves as the ex-officio treasurer for cities of the second class.

Prosecuting Attorney

Prosecuting attorneys are assigned to each court district. The prosecuting attorney represents the State of Indiana and prosecutes violators of state statutes.

Source: *Here Is Your Indiana Government,* 20th Edition, Indianapolis, Indiana State Chamber of Commerce, 1981.

While the basic design of county government is the same, in 91 of Indiana's 92 counties some variation in the way the counties carry out their administrative responsibilities occurs. Variations exist because there are significant differences in the populations of Indiana counties and because the state legislature has from time to time enacted statutes that apply to only a few counties. For instance, commissioners of some counties; i.e., those where road maintenance and bridge repair are not handled by the county surveyor, have the option of creating the position of county highway supervisor; and larger counties have the further option of creating a "Department of County Engineering" with a full-time professional engineer as the director. All counties have a county commissioner of public records.

All counties also have the authority to appoint a part-time county attorney, and with larger counties the power exists to create and appoint directors of county purchasing and personnel departments. The commissioners further have the power to establish a data processing board, to appoint superintendent for the County Home (for the aged), and where countywide school districts exist, a superintendent of schools. In what potentially is one of the most progressive options available to county governments, the state legislature recently gave the commissioners the power to appoint a full-time county administrator, a position that when created assumes all of the powers otherwise granted to the commissioners. Most counties, however, have been slow in creating this position and filling it with professional administrators.

In addition to carrying out the administrative duties assigned to them by the state legislature, counties undertake specific functions flowing from their responsibility to serve as the agent of state government at the local level. Most of these responsibilities are consistent regardless of county size throughout the state. Unlike a county's administrative responsibilities that are given for the most part to the board of county commissioners, the duties associated with a county's role in serving as the agent of the state at the local level are undertaken by a variety of agencies and elected or appointed office holders.[26]

An important responsibility the state gives to counties is control over local taxing and spending activities. Much of the revenue utilized by all units of local government comes from property taxes. These taxes are paid by individual and corporate property holders based on a determination of the value of real and personal property and on a rate at which the taxes are to be paid; the rate being fixed at so many dollars and cents per $100 of the assessed value of the property (the assessed value is supposed to be one-third of the "true" market value of the property).

One method by which spending is controlled is through the county Board of Tax Adjustment. Its primary responsibility is to review and *revise* the budgets of the county and all the local governmental units within the county, cities, towns, townships, school corporations and others. This board has the power to reduce both the budgets and the tax rates of these units of government. It does not, however, have the power to increase them. In all counties, the Tax Adjustment Board is composed of seven members of whom not more than four can be of the same political party. One member must be the mayor of the largest city in the county or the mayor's representative—usually the city controller—and one member each is chosen by the County Council and the Board of School Trustees of the principal school corporation in the county. The other four members are chosen by a county judge.[27]

Counties have the responsibility for conducting all elections, and two election boards exist for this purpose: the County Election Board and the Board of Canvassers. The membership of both boards is identical; it is the clerk of the circuit court (the County Clerk) and two persons appointed by the clerk representing each of the two major parties as nominated by their respective county chairmen. As the County Election Board, these three are responsible for administering the voter registration office and running the periodic elections. Acting as the Board of Canvassers, they are responsible for tabulating the election results.

Three or four county agencies exist to assist in carrying out the state police power responsibility of protecting the health and welfare of Indiana residents. State law provides for local health departments to exist in all counties. (Some, however, are city rather than county agencies.) These boards are responsible for appointing a licensed physician to serve as the administrator. They work in the area of communicable disease control, retail food sanitation, and environmental health. Counties also have the option of establishing county hospital boards and hospital building authorities (either public or private) for the purpose of assisting in the construction and maintenence of public or private hospitals.[28]

Consistent with the state responsibility of protecting the health and welfare of Indiana residents, all counties are authorized to establish a county welfare department. In most counties the welfare department is the largest and most expensive unit of county government. Funding for the departments actually comes from three sources. In addition to locally raised (property tax) revenue, welfare departments receive direct state funding and funding from the federal government. Accordingly, welfare department programs must follow federally established regulations and procedures. County welfare departments are administered by a five-member board appointed by the Circuit Court Judge. The welfare departments are administered separately from township poor relief programs.[29]

One of the police powers that the state gives counties is that of public safety. In this field, however, county authority is limited, and much of what there is comes under the jurisdiction of the Sheriff and the County Police Department. The county commissions (or county councils in Lake and St. Joseph County) have the power to pass various public safety ordinances and give the enforcement of them over to the appropriate agency. Thus, it is possible to pass ordinances concerning environmental problems that the Board of Health will have to enforce or to pass strict building codes that a building department will have to enforce. Other areas that could fall under this category include dog control, noise control, control of junk and abandoned vehicles, and the licensing of a variety of private business establishments. The commissioners also have the authority to appropriate money to assist in construction and operation of community mental retardation and psychiatric treatment centers. Where appropriate, counties can establish a Mine Safety Board to insure the safety of miners.

The state mandates that a few offices exist in each county to exercise specific public safety functions. These offices include an Alcoholic Beverage Board to license drinking establishments and to enforce state laws dealing with the sale and consumption of alcoholic beverages and a county inspector of weights and measures to insure the accuracy of scales and other measuring devices operated in the county. Consistent with these roles is the role played by the county drainage board in maintaining ditches and culverts. Counties also have the authority to establish and appoint a County Veterinarian and a variety of inspector positions to enforce the various "public safety" ordinances that they pass.

One office that represents the state at the local level but has little to do with normal state level administrative functions is the County Extension Agent. In all counties, this agent is the local representative of the County Extension Service established through the U.S. Department of Agriculture. His primary responsibility is to assist the agricultural community. This office is unique in that it is established in cooperation with Purdue University (the state's land grant university), and the duties of the office are supervised by Purdue.

A number of options are available to counties that seek to expand their role in the service delivery area. These options were established by the state legislature, primarily for the benefit of the larger metropolitan counties that are receiving increasing demands for services. Some counties may, for instance, set up housing authorities to administer public housing programs, redevelopment commissions to undertake land use renewal programs, and development commissions to facilitate economic development.[30]

The suburbanization movement has resulted in an increased emphasis in many areas on land use control. Again, however, for most counties this responsibility is given over to different quasi-independent boards and commissions. This responsibility encompasses the enforcement of zoning and building codes as well as land use planning. Building code enforcement comes under a building department, while land use and zoning decisions fall under the jurisdiction of a quasi-independent planning commission and Board of Zoning Appeals. The planning commissions can be organized as either county, area (parts of a county), multicounty, or metropolitan commissions depending upon the perceived needs and size of the counties involved.

In addition, most counties also have the option to establish a limited number of other agencies that traditionally have been found with cities and towns rather than counties. These include park and recreation boards, economic development districts and transportation boards, among others.[31]

In general, county government in Indiana seems to be highly decentralized and cumbersome. Policy making and policy implementation authority is dispersed. The one unit that could perform these functions, the Board of Commissioners, is limited by the fact that many county activities are not under its control. Powers have been given to county government over the years on a piecemeal basis with apparently little thought given to the ways in which any one set of governmetal functions relates to all the other functions.

In recent years there have been some attempts to expand the powers of county government and to give counties latitude to determine for themselves what they ought to be doing and how the various functions ought to be done. In 1975, and again in 1981, the state legislature passed a "home rule" bill that allowed all counties to have some additional flexibility. Most counties, however, have been slow in taking advantage of those statutes. The multi-centered structure of county government makes it difficult to take advantage of such legislation.

Townships

Townships were originally created to bring local government even closer to the people than counties could do. They were created as sub-units of counties. In Indiana, although provisions do exist allowing county commissioners to alter township boundaries, it seldom occurs and most townships today are largely co-extensive with the original congressional townships outlined in the Land Ordinance of 1787. They are highly uniform in geographic size but vary greatly in population, ranging from the more than 205,000 persons in the Centre Township of Marion County to a mere 200 persons in the Boone Township of Crawford County.[32]

Originally, townships were given a limited version of the structure normally associated with general purposes units of government. They had an executive (Township Trustee), a legislature (Township Advisory Board), and a judiciary (Justice of the Peace) complete with a township law enforcement officer known as a Constable.

The operation of schools was an important historical township function. Townships had the power to raise and spend money from property taxes. Historically, they were given responsibility to "assess" property for tax purposes, provide for poor relief and provide limited services (volunteer fire departments). In largely rural Indiana, townships could function as the primary unit of local government.

As the state became more urbanized and transportation and communication improved, the importance of townships as general purpose units of government was greatly reduced. During the 1960's and 1970's, two important functions were removed from the jurisdiction of township authority. In the middle sixties, the state legislature mandated that local schools be reorganized to comply with federal guidelines for receiving federal funds. This reorganization resulted in the consolidation of most of the small township schools into larger independent school corporations that, in most cases, were organized on a multi-township or countywide basis and removed from the jurisdiction of township officials. Only in a few areas are schools still under the control of township officials. In the mid-seventies, the legislature initiated a judicial reorganization plan that since has had the effect of eliminating the justice of the peace courts and constables.

Townships today retain only some of their original government powers. It is these powers, however, that allow them to maintain volunteer fire departments and two important special powers, the power to conduct property tax assessments and the authority to provide poor relief for indigent persons. Townships also serve as the basic election units of the county (from which voting precincts are divided) and, in most counties, as the geographical unit in which school corporations are organized.[33]

The role of townships as the basic unit of government responsible for property tax assessments means that there are literally over 1,000 property taxing units in the state and that in spite of attempts to standardize procedures, residents are confronted with over 1,000 different tax rates and assessment procedures to determine property values. This approach has been criticized as contributing to inequity in tax assessments.

The responsibility of townships to provide poor relief has also been cited as a contributor to the inequitable distribution of government services and represents something less than an efficient and effective means of providing a basic service. The role of township poor relief dates to a period in American history when there was no assumption that government at any level had responsibility for providing assistance to indigent people. Thus, townships were authorized to provide only the barest minimum of temporary help to only the neediest people. The task of providing sustained income maintenance was instituted much later and given over to counties for administration through county welfare departments.

In practice, only a few townships are burdened with the responsibility for providing large amounts of poor relief. These townships, except in certain kinds of economic emergencies, are usually the ones in the hearts of the largest cities. Suburban and rural townships are usually free of such a burden. Thus, in any metropolitan county, only part of the property tax paying residents are responsible for paying for this service.[34]

With the exception of these two controversial functions, the role of townships is largely irrelevant to municipalities. There is little that townships do that is either complementary or contradictory to the functions of cities. Townships do, however, continue to play a significant, if not vital, role in suburban or rural areas. Townships can provide some services on a highly localized basis that either would not be provided at all or would become a county burden. Most of the rural and suburban townships provide their own fire protection, and some have sought to build such things as parks, community centers, and provide other highly localized amenities.

Cities

While many people continue to see Indiana as an agricultural state, in fact it is predominantly urban. As of 1970, the U.S. Census bureau listed Indiana as having 3,372,000 urban residents. Those persons live in cities and towns having a population greater than 2500; this figure represents 64.9 percent of the total statewide population of 5,193,669. Almost as many, 3,214,000 persons or 61.9 percent of the population, were considered to be metropolitan dwellers; that is, residents of places, both city and suburban, listed by the census bureau as being standard statistical metropolitan areas. These are the areas that encompass and surround the state's largest municipalities. With the 1980 Census, the proportion of the state's population that was considered urban went down slightly to 64.2%.[35]

While municipalities were created for the purpose of governing communities of all sizes, they are most relevant for urban areas where large numbers of residents are concentrated in relatively small geographic areas. Rather than being created by the state on a geographical basis as are counties and townships, the state simply allows municipalities to exist and prescribes the conditions and terms concerning how they can be created and then mandates their mode of operation. They have the legal status of a corporation (they can sue and be sued) and are established upon the initiation of the residents who want to be included in the incorporated municipality. Municipalities are described in geographic terms; they do occupy territory and, geographically as well as in population terms, they can range from very small to very large. All the persons who live within the described territory are considered residents of the municipality. Further, municipalities can expand their territory through a process called annexation. All of Indiana's largest cities, including Indianapolis, started as small towns and by the annexation process grew into the major metropolises they are today.

Municipalities occupy territory in one or more townships—in whole or in part—and they exist within the boundaries of a county. Municipal governments, however, are, with the exception of Indianapolis, administered independently of townships county authority. To be sure, municipalities, like counties and townships, must follow the dictates of state law; but state law gives them both greater service-related responsibilities and greater flexibility in carrying out their responsibilities. With the state Constitution being virtually silent concerning the form and functions of municipalities, the state legislature has, over the years, created different municipal forms, and today there is a great deal of variation in terms of the types of municipal governmental organizations that exist in Indiana. In Indiana, municipalities are called either cities or towns. (There are no legally constituted villages.) And cities, as a result, are divided into three different classes based in general on population. Towns and the three classifications of cities have plans of government organization slightly different from each other.[36]

Basis of City Classifications

First Class	More than 250,000 population
Second Class	35,000–250,000 population
Third Class	Less than 35,000 but more than 1,500

In general, municipalities with less than 1,500 population are towns.

The Indianapolis-Marion County form of government is the only first class city; eighteen Indiana cities are second class; the rest are third class.

The other 445 municipalities are towns. However, not all towns are small. In order for a town to become a city, it must apply to the state, and some towns, even though they would qualify as a city in terms of population, choose not to seek a change in status. Thus, there are some municipalities that were designated as towns when they were incorporated but have had a significant population growth over the last few years without a change in their legal status. The "town" of Merrillville in Lake County, for instance, had a 1980 population of 27,677, enough to be classified as a third class city.[37]

Indiana has four basic forms of municipal government—one for each of the three city classifications plus a form for town government. In actuality, the forms of government for cities in classifications two and three are quite similar. Among cities of these two classifications, the scope of operations and distribution of authority differs somewhat, but they encompass the same basic organizational components and have the same functional authority; only the forms of government employed by Indianapolis-Marion County at one end and the town governments at the other end are substantively different from the forms of city government in the other classifications. Figure 6.3 shows a composite organization chart for second and third class cities.

Professor Owen, in his chapter, analyzes the "unigov" system employed in Indianapolis-Marion County. Town government is considered separately later in this chapter. Thus, the focus here is on city government as it is used in second and third class cities.

Government organization in these two classifications of Indiana cities is quite traditional. Unlike county government in Indiana and some city governments in other states, city government in Indiana features a clear delineation between legislative and executive powers. In Indiana cities, executive authority is concentrated under one person, a popularly elected mayor, while the common council is given the authority normally accorded a legislative body. As at the county level, judicial authority is vested in the state judicial system and operates independently of municipal government. Only a few municipalities still maintain trial level courts oriented specifically to them. All Indiana cities are based on a partisan political system; all elected officials are nominated in the party primary (in May) and stand for election in a general election in odd numbered years preceding presidential elections (in November). All elected city offices are four-year, concurrent terms.

Common councils vary in size and composition depending on the classification of the city. Second class cities have nine-member councils, with six seats elected from single-member districts and three elected citywide or "at large." Third class cities over 10,000 population have seven-member councils with five seats elected from single-member districts and two elected "at large." Third class cities with populations under 10,000 have the option of having either a five or seven-member council.

By this method of apportionment, the common councils of Indiana cities are almost guaranteed to reflect a broad cross-section of any community, both in geographic and interest group terms. The role of the common council in any Indiana city is largely confined to budgetary and other legislative matters. Beyond providing a check on the executive branch, they have few administrative responsibilities. Thus, like legislative bodies at all levels of government, they are a forum through which individual and group concerns are expressed and issues are debated. They are the governing body of their cities.

The legislative responsibilities given to a city council means that it functions as the "policy-making body" of the city. The powers vested in common councils are virtually the same for all cities, and although they were given considerable discretion as a result of the 1981 home rule statute, most cities organizationally are still based on legislation passed by the Indiana General Assembly in 1905.[38] With the 1981 legislation, it became understood they could legislate in any area they chose, except those that either the General Assembly prohibited them to act in or in

Figure 6.3. Composite organization of a typical Indiana city (simplified)

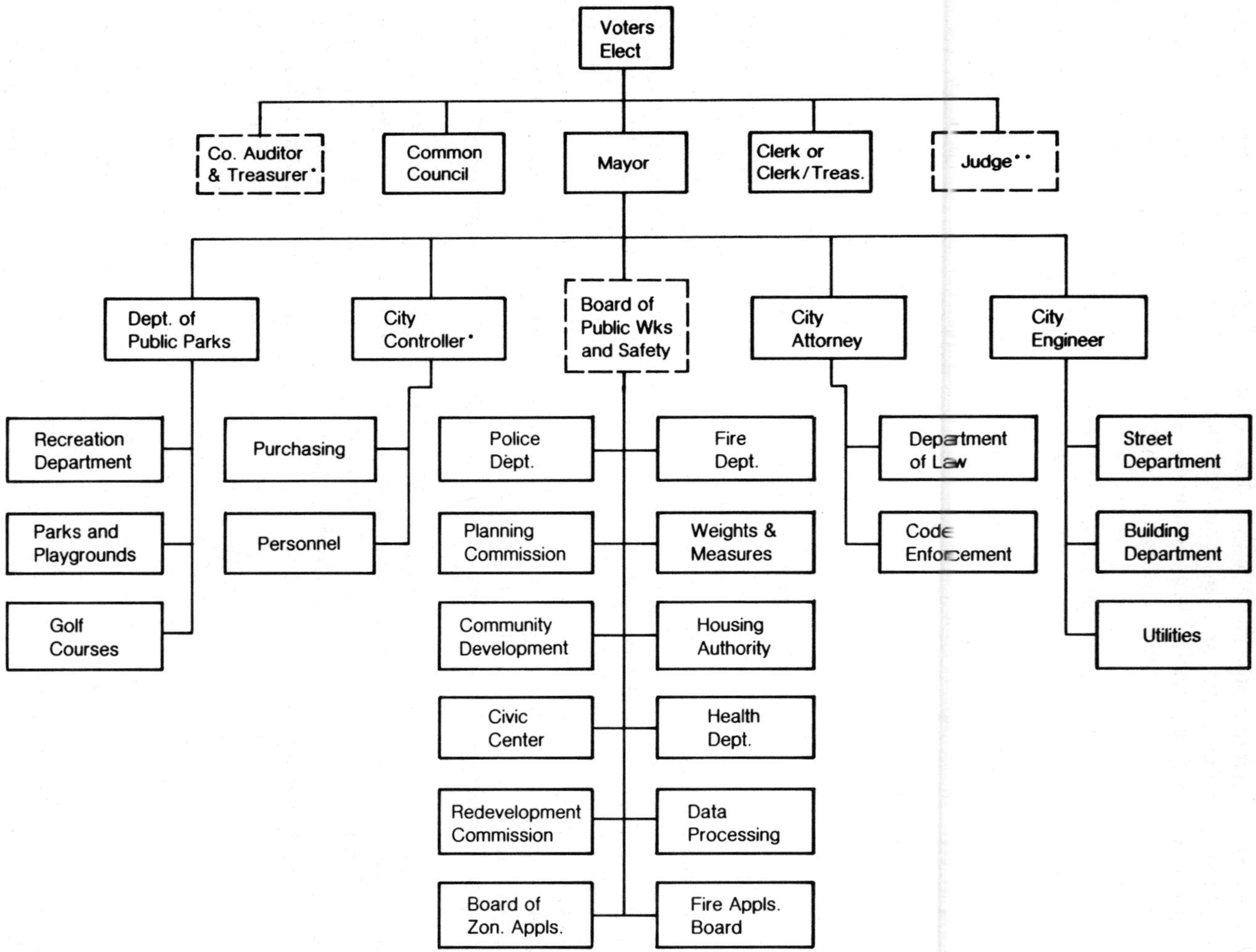

*City Controllers exist only in first, second and some third class cities. In second class cities the County Treasurer is the ex-officio City Treasurer.

**City Judges exist in only a few cities.

areas where the state pre-empted the cities.[39] Like counties, however, cities have been slow in taking full advantage of this legislation.

Administratively, cities are organized as service delivery units with the popularly and partisanly elected mayor designated to serve as the chief administrative officer.[40] Responsibility for administering the public works and public safety functions were given to an administrative board known as the "Board of Public Works and Safety." This is, in most cities, a three-member board required by state law to hold regular public meetings and public hearings on all important matters. The members of this board are appointed by and serve at the pleasure of the mayor. In some smaller cities the mayor will serve as the chairman. In most of the larger cities, however, it is composed of the city controller, city engineer, and city attorney. In second class cities, this board may be divided into separate boards of "Public Safety and Public Works." South Bend, for instance, has followed a plan of establishing a Board of Public Works composed of city officials and a separate Board of Public Safety composed of three "citizen" members. With the 1981 legislation, mayors can appoint anyone they choose to serve on either board.[41]

Regardless of whether the boards are combined or separate, they aggregately hold the same powers. These powers range from approving city expenditures to letting bids on all city contracts with outside firms and accepting the completed work. In the absence of police or fire department merit boards, they have the responsibility to set policy and administer discipline in the police and fire departments. The functions of this board which come under its "public works" jurisdiction include street, road, and sidewalk construction and maintenance, the construction and maintenance of city-owned property, and such diverse functions as traffic control and the licensing of various types of private enterprises. The public safety function, in addition to the administration of the police and fire departments, may include control of such things as loose dogs, junk vehicles, substandard building, civil defense, weights and measures, and again, some public safety related licensing.

This board, primarily because the people who serve on it are responsible directly to the mayor, is the most important administrative board in city government. In addition to its public safety and public works functions, it may assume control over such other city functions as personnel matters and general city purchasing, both under the official control of the controller in larger cities.

Outside of the common council and the mayor—and in a few cities a city judge—the only other elected city official is the city clerk. The clerk in second class cities has responsibility for keeping any records, including city court records if a city judge exists, and serving as the secretary to the common council. In most smaller cities, the office is known as the clerk-treasurer and has the additional responsibility for city monies. For second class cities, this fiscal responsibility is shared between the controller and the county auditor and county treasurer.

The parks and recreation function may be undertaken by one or two semi-autonomous boards. One is a "parks board" that operates as an arm of the city administration. The parks board budget is processed by the city's common council. In some cities there is a separate recreation board. This board may be a step further removed from direct city control in that in some cities its members come partly from the parks board and partly from the board of the appropriate school corporation. Parks and recreation boards are organized differently in different cities. In some cases they are independent of the mayor and have their own bonding authority.

The delivery of such basic services as water, sewage, and solid waste disposal are usually provided through municipal utility corporations. These utilities—and they may include electrical utilities as well as water, sewage, and solid waste disposal—may be organized as self-supporting (based on user fees) independent corporations, or simply as city departments. In most cities, whether or not they exist as independent bodies, the governing boards of the municipal utilities are the same people who serve as the Board of Public Works (or Works and Safety as may be the case).

Cities in Indiana do administer their own budgets. This power in larger cities is vested in the City Controller, who ranks as the city's second highest official. While the management of city funds in second class cities is shared with the County Auditor and the County Treasurer, it is the controller who has responsibility for administering the city budget. In smaller cities this responsibility falls to a clerk-treasurer.

City budgets can be complicated. Budgets include funds raised by property taxes, user fees and the issuing of various licenses as well as funds from different state and federal sources. Further, cities have the power to raise funds through bond issues, assessments for particular services, and through selling or leasing property. These powers too are administered by the city's chief fiscal officer.

All cities have a legal department under the control of the city attorney. This is usually a part-time position and includes several functions. The city attorney serves as the city's corporate council and has responsibility for insuring the enforcement of all city ordinances, advising the mayor and council on the legal aspects of city business and protecting against legal culpability of city personnel.[42]

The 1981 home rule legislation authorized cities to establish a deputy mayor position. Up to 1981 only Gary had such a position. They are to be prescribed by local ordinance.[43]

Over the years, many new functions have been assigned to cities in a piecemeal way in much the same way that new functions have been assigned to counties. For instance, cities were given the power to establish regulatory and licensing procedures and appropriate agencies to enforce them. In some cases, such as with health departments and building departments, cities share these powers with counties. As with counties, most of these powers at the city level are administered through independent or quasi-independent boards and commissions. Unlike in counties, however, in cities the appointive powers to these boards commissions have remained largely centralized in the hands of the mayor. Some of the agencies cities have been given the power to create include public transportation boards, health departments, building departments, human rights commissions, housing authorities, and development and redevelopment commissions. Cities have also been given the powers to create boards whose functions include administering such things as auditoriums, museums, civic centers, and historical collections. The powers of cities in this area have been expanded as a result of the 1981 home rule legislation.

With the 1981 home rule legislation, many of the responsibilities the state had mandated cities to undetake were put into the category of discretionary authority. In some areas, cities now enjoy the power to decide for themselves if they want to continue to operate according to state-defined procedures or to define procedures of their own. This legislation also gave, in most instances, more control to the mayor over the various boards and commissions that serve city residents.[44]

Indiana cities are two things. First, they are political units designed to provide a means for community level decision-making and problem-solving. Secondly, they are service delivery units and as such are provided with various mechanisms through which a variety of services can be delivered. The basic difficulty Indiana cities face is in making these two things consistent with each other. While cities have considerably greater potential for resolving this dilemma than do counties, they are still faced with the problems of decentralized administrative responsibilities and limited capability to effectively undertake new and innovative solutions to deal with these problems.[45]

Towns

Towns incorporate the least complicated form of municipal government in Indiana. Town government was designed for very small communities where service delivery needs are limited. At the same time, however, the statutory provisions for town government are quite flexible. Different towns can exercise different options in their plan of government, and thus some variation does exist in town government form throughout Indiana. One of the more progressive options available to towns is the provision for hiring a professional town manager. For most towns, both executive and legislative authority is vested in a single "Town Board of Trustees." The size of town boards may range from three to seven, and they may be elected "at large" or from single-member wards or in some combination of wards and "at large." The only other elected official is the town clerk. Candidates for town offices run as members of political parties but are nominated in party caucuses instead of a primary election. The 1981 home rule legislation also gave towns more discretion in determining their forms and functions.

Most towns, through the town council, hire a town marshal to serve as a law enforcement officer; and in some cases, the marshal can also serve as fire chief and street commissioner. In some towns, this position is the only full-time government position. Other towns, however, have established a police commission and thus are able to establish a professional police department. In many towns, the town clerk has been described as a full-time position, and a staff is hired to exercise the duties of the office. In towns with no town manager, the clerk may also assume some of the administrative responsibility of running the municipality.[46]

Town Management in Indiana

In 1971, the Indiana General Assembly passed enabling legislation which authorized Indiana towns to appoint town managers. With this legislation, Indiana joined all other states except Hawaii in authorizing at least some of its local governments to use the council-manager form. Under this form, local governing bodies, e.g., town boards, appoint administrators or managers to direct the daily activities of their municipalities and to assist them in the development of local policies. The Indiana legislation required town managers to do the following:

(a) attend the meetings of the board of trustees and recommend such action as he may deem expedient;

(b) hire all town employees who are authorized to be employed by the board of trustees in accordance with such pay schedules, standards and qualifications as may be fixed by the board of trustees, or applicable state law, and when, in his discretion, the welfare of the town requires it, suspend, discharge, remove or transfer any such employee. The town manager may delegate any such power to any employee responsible to him if he deems it advisable to do so. Nothing in this chapter shall affect any right given by law to the clerk-treasurers to select their own deputies, assistants and other employees;

(c) administer the execution and enforcement of all resolutions, orders and ordinances of the board of trustees, and see that all laws of the state required to be enforced through the board of trustees or other town officers subject to the control of the board of trustees are faithfully executed;

(d) prepare and submit to the board of trustees budget estimates as required from time to time;

(e) execute on behalf of the town all contracts which the board of trustees, or its officers, have the power to execute for goods, materials, services, construction, or improvements; provided that nothing herein shall be deemed to amend any laws pertaining to the necessary or proper appropriation of public funds prior to contracting, nor to amend any applicable laws requiring public notice for and receipt of competitive bids.[47]

Thus, the 1971 statute appears to grant Indiana town managers a broad range of responsibilities and an important role in those towns which choose to utilize this approach.

One of the key premises of the council-manager approach is that a professionally trained administrator should be hired to fill the manager position. Considerations such as partisanship and residency, for example, are not supposed to play a part in the selection. The 1971 Indiana statute required that town managers be employed solely on the basis of merit and, in addition, prohibited a residency requirement. In 1980, however, the Indiana legislature deleted the requirement that merit alone be considered in town manager appointments and eliminated the restriction against imposing a residency requirement. In effect, these new provisions give town boards the option of considering factors other than merit in the appointment of town managers.

The 1971 statute also provided that town managers could be employed for a definite period or simply at the pleasure of a town board. In addition, the statute provided that two or more towns might employ the same manager. The tenure of a town manager cannot, however, exceed the term of office of the appointing board, although the manager can be reappointed. A town manager can be terminated for cause at any time.

The response to the town manager option by Indiana towns appears to be positive. By 1980, approximately twenty-six towns had appointed town managers. Some of the larger towns which had made such appointments included Chesterton, Danville, Lowell, Munster, Plainfield, Porter and Yorktown. Moreover, many towns which have not appointed town managers seem favorable to the idea. In a survey of town board presidents conducted in 1975 and 1976 in towns of 1,000 population and over, seventy-five percent of the responding board presidents, i.e., fifty-seven of seventy-six, indicated that the town manager option was either highly desirable or somewhat desirable. Nearly fifty percent of the same group also favored the appointment of town managers for their towns.[48] Some, however, indicated that they did not have the funds to hire a town manager. Overall, however, it seems apparent that given the opportunity some Indiana towns will use the council-manager approach and that many others seem favorable toward this idea.

Given the traditional nature of politics in Indiana, it is perhaps not surprising that it was not until 1971 that Indiana authorized the use of the council-manager approach for its towns. Actually, however, Indiana was probably one of the earlier states to pass legislation authorizing both the council-manager and commission forms of local government. The council-manager form began in 1908 in Staunton, Virginia, and thirteen years later, in 1921, the Indiana General Assembly enacted legislation which permitted Indiana cities to adopt either the council-manager or commission forms. Michigan City operated under the council-manager plan during the 1920's and in a referendum in 1927, Indianapolis voted to adopt the plan. The council-manager plan never went into effect in Indianapolis, however, because the constitutionality of the enabling legislation was challenged in the courts and in 1929 the Indiana Supreme Court declared the act unconstitutional. The court challenge was not based on the council-manager form but rather on the time period authorized by the act for verifying names on the referendum petition; i.e., the Supreme Court held that the five days permitted by the act was an insufficient period in a city the size of Indianapolis for verifying the names of the twenty percent of the voters which were required on the petition. Nevertheless, the authorization for the council-manager and commission forms ended with the 1929 decision, and attempts to pass constitutional amendments which would permit these forms since that decision have failed.[49] In 1981, an attempt to pass council-manager enabling legislation for cities in the General Assembly also failed. Thus, Indiana seems to be in the somewhat curious position of permitting its towns to adopt a form which it first authorized but has subsequently and steadily denied to its cities. The traditional nature of the Indiana political system, therefore, seems to explain Indiana's approach to its cities (except for a brief period in the 1920's) but may not explain its approach to its towns or generally smaller municipalities.

Despite the past resistance in Indiana, the council-manager form has been quite popular throughout the United States as a whole. By 1981, 2,445 local governments were using the council-manager plan, including more than fifty percent of all municipalities in the 25,000 to 250,000 population range. In many of the states surrounding Indiana the plan has been widely used. In 1981, for example, approximately 187 local governments in Michigan, 107 in Illinois, and 81 in Ohio were operating under the council-manager plan.[50] According to the International City Management Association, the number of municipalities throughout the United States which have adopted the council-manager form has averaged 65 per year since 1945 except in 1973 and 1976 when the unusually high numbers of 159 and 133, respectively, were recorded. Whether the plan will eventually prove to be as popular in Indiana, of course, remains to be seen. Its use in Indiana towns, however, should provide Indiana citizens with an opportunity to evaluate the plan in a way that has not existed in the past. With this new experience, it seems likely that the council-manager form will be extended to Indiana cities and counties as an option in the years ahead.

Special Purpose Units of Government

Special purpose units of government serve a valuable function in Indiana. They fill many gaps between the service delivery roles of general purpose local governments on one hand and the service delivery role of state level agencies on the other hand. Special purpose units of government provide services that, for a variety of reasons, are deemed to be inappropriate for general purpose state or local government to provide.

While there is no exact count of the number of special purpose governments in Indiana, it is safe to say there are hundreds. They exist in all parts of the state and aggregately provide a multitude of different services. One difficulty in counting the number of special purpose units of government is that it is sometimes difficult to determine what is a legitimate special purpose unit of government and what is merely an agency of a general purpose unit of government. Literally thousands of boards, commissions and agencies exist at all levels of Indiana government. Most are arms of the units of government to which they are attached. Many, however, do have a significant degree of independence, and thus, can be considered as special units of government. The basic criteria for determining if an agency is a special purpose unit of government are:

1. The agency exhibits independent governmental powers. Most importantly, it has the independent power to sue and to be sued.
2. The policy makers of the agency are chosen directly (by election) or indirectly (through appointment by elected officials) and the agency has the operating characteristics commonly associated with governmental units. Critical here is whether or not the agency is able to undertake legislative and executive actions that have the effect of law.
3. The agency has the power, independent of any other unit of government, to raise and spend monies restricted only by the procedures established by state statute.[51]

While many agencies exhibit the first two sets of characteristics, it is the third characteristic that disqualifies them as true special purpose units of government. County level park boards in Indiana, for instance, operate with a high degree of autonomy, but because their budgets are part of the overall county budgeting process (e.g., the budgets must be approved by the county commissioners and the funds are actually appropriated by the county council), they are not considered to be special purpose units of government. Local housing authorities, on the other hand, have a highly restricted role to play in terms of legislative functions but determine their own budgets independently of other units of local government and thus can be considered to be special purpose governments.

While individually special purpose units of government provide only one or, at most, a limited number of services, collectively they provide many highly specialized types of services. They come in a variety of shapes and sizes. Some cover a very small geographic area many times consistent with the boundaries of a city, town or county. Others cover whole sections of the state and include all or part of many counties.

Special purpose units of government are usually administered by a board composed of three, five, seven, or nine members. Board members can be either elected or appointed but usually serve for a fixed term. In most cases, members can be removed only by the appointing authority for just cause or, if they are elected, by an impeachment proceeding. If board members are appointed, often the appointing authority is shared between an executive official (mayor, county commissioner, governor) and an appropriate legislative body. In some cases in Indiana at the county level, the circuit court judge will have a role in making these appointments.

The boards of special purpose units of government function then as both the legislative and executive branch of the unit. In almost all cases, however, the board will hire a full-time professional staff headed by a director or supervisor to actually administer the agency.

Most of the special purpose units of government in Indiana do not receive a great deal of publicity and thus are largely unknown to the public as a whole. The reason for the anonymity most of these units experience is that the services they provide are perfunctory and noncontroversial. Such things as sanitary districts, building authorities, or soil conservation districts exist for years with few people other than those directly concerned with their function having any idea of what the unit is doing.[52]

Probably the most widely known special purpose units of government are local school corporations. They began to emerge in their current form in the early 1960's when the state legislature chose to reorganize local school districts. School corporations exhibit all of the characteristics of any governmental unit. They have their own governing body, either elected or appointed (the Board of School Trustees), have the power to set property tax rates, and are given administrative autonomy under state law. The superintendent is the chief administrative official. School corporations are usually organized on a town, city, or township basis, and many townships may be included in the same corporation. It is also common for school corporations to include townships in two or more counties.[53]

While school corporations may be the most common form of special purpose units of government, others are well known at least within particular individual communities. They may not, however, be recognized by the general public as special purpose units of government. For instance, few people recognize that local redevelopment commissions, housing authorities, and most public transportation corporations are in reality special purpose units of government. These agencies, in most cases, operate as if they were agencies within county or city governments.

Like other units of government, all special purpose units are established by the state legislature. In recent years, it appears that the state has come increasingly to depend on them to deal with identified special service delivery needs. In many cases, it is easier to create special districts than to alter existing city, county, or state government.

There are, however, some dangers in the proliferation of special purpose units of government. The existence of too many of these units contributes to decentralized local government. It makes local control difficult and coordinated policy development and implementation next to impossible. It creates a situation where the officials that the public holds accountable for the conduct of government (elected officials) do not have control of government decision-making and thus are virtually powerless to exercise any real authority over some aspects of the process of government. A proliferation of special units of government, each with its own independent taxing authority, can result in very expensive local governments with dubious levels of efficiency. Perhaps, the 1981 home rule legislation giving general purpose units more authority will serve to discourage the creation of new special purpose units of government.

Special purpose government units are here to stay and their numbers are likely to increase. As demands for governmental services (particularly in the environmental and transportation areas) increase, units of this type are the most logical way to deliver needed services. Even with the 1981 home rule legislation, there seems to be little sympathy for the kind of additional massive restructuring of state and general purpose local government that would be required to make special purpose governments unnecessary. They are more important today than most citizens realize, and they are likely to become even more important in the future.[54]

Administration and Politics in Local Government

Local government in Indiana is, of course, more than just structure that delivers services. It is also a process by which disputes are settled, conflict is resolved, and ultimately it is presumed the will of a community's residents is carried out. As recent legislative developments show, both the roles of local government and the processes by which it undertakes these roles are changing. Both facets must be understood if one is to claim broad understanding of Indiana local government.[55]

In 1977–78 the legislature created a "local government study commission" with a mandate to make change recommendations for improving local government in Indiana. In its 1980 and 1981 sessions, the General Assembly also took action which could have far-reaching consequences for local governments—and relieve the legislature of having to deal with so many local concerns each year. It enacted a set of "home rule" laws which will permit virtually every city except Indianapolis and every county except Marion County the option of restructuring its government, within limits, as it pleases. If a local government does not wish to change its organization, it can continue to operate under provisions established by the General Assembly.

The 1981 legislation was a significant step in the direction of local government reform. It did not, however, deal with a number of important areas of concern. For instance, this legislation did not alter the existing methods by which local units of government raise and spend tax monies. Nor did it substantively deal with the question of local intergovernmental relations, e.g., how cities and counties can more efficiently work together. Thus, this legislation fails to confront two significant issues facing both cities and counties—providing for equity in taxing and in delivering public services.[56]

Changing Role of Counties

The decentralized system of county government supported by a strong political party system works against the development of a coordinated county level approach to public policy. Even with the home rule legislation, the constitutional offices are assigned a specific range of administrative responsibilities and are under few obligations to either cooperate with each other, with the county commissioners, or with the county council. Only the commissioners have the capability to develop and implement policy on a county-wide basis, but they lack the resources to do so. Further, the necessity of their sharing power with the other offices, plus the fact that they are themselves a three-headed executive argues against major initiatives.[57] In short, it is difficult at best for county government to do anything other than provide the traditional range of services and carry out the functions mandated by the state, even with home rule.

In the future, however, it is not likely that counties will be able to enjoy the convenience of carrying on business as usual using traditional methods and approaches. The demography of Indiana is changing, and as a result, counties are being asked to undertake new and innovative responsibilities and to do so with greater efficiency and effectiveness than before. Indiana counties, particularly those that encompass urban areas, are likely candidates to experience these changes in the years to come. Ironically, with the least flexible structures of any of the units of local government, counties will most likely be the units that will face the greatest pressures for change.

The forces for change are coming from three directions. One source of this pressure is internal and is a result of the urban sprawl that most Indiana counties are experiencing and will continue to experience: the movement of people from the central cities to the suburbs and beyond. This movement, of course, includes more than just people. It includes whole communities; factories, stores, churches, and offices. In many areas, the most desirable places to which these communities are being relocated are outside of any existing municipalities—unincorporated areas whose only government services are provided by townships and counties. As a consequence, these units rather than cities and towns are being asked to provide a range of services that either they have not previously provided or that were provided at only minimal levels. They are being asked to provide such things as land use planning, strict building code and zoning code enforcement, parks and recreational facilities and services, and professional fire protection. And, they are supposed to provide these services with far greater efficiency than has ever been the case before. Just as important, they are also expected to effectively serve a role as an arbitrator of conflict and to negotiate between the demands of competing interests. These pressures have been directed to both counties and townships, but because the role of township government is so very limited, most of the pressure has focused on counties.[58]

A second set of pressures is coming from the state. These pressures result from the realization that some of the most serious problems facing the residents of Indiana fall in the gap between local authority, particularly cities, on one hand and the general state authority on the other hand. Many problems, such as air and water pollution, transportation needs, and even social services are, at the very least, "area wide" in nature. Even with the home rule legislation, there is little reason to believe that the state legislature will stop mandating counties to undertake new functions. Thus, counties, either alone or in consortium with one another, are being asked to take the lead in dealing with newly identified problems. It is the realization of multi-jurisdictional problems that has prompted the state to allow counties to create such nontraditional entities as multi-county planning bodies, regional transportation boards, and local and regional airport authorities.[59]

The third set of pressures on counties comes from the federal government. In the 1960's and 1970's when increasing amounts of federal funds were made available to counties, they were forced to alter many traditional practices in order to become eligible for federal assistance. The Comprehensive Employment and Training Act of 1974, for instance, requires that participating counties establish professional and merit-based personnel systems, an approach to personnel matters that has largely been alien to most county administrators. Similar federal restrictions are sometimes imposed when counties seek assistance for such things as sewage system improvements, airports, and money from the U.S. Department of Housing and Urban Development for various renewal projects. Even with the reductions in federally funded programs of the 1980's, most of the federal requirements have remained.[60]

The response on the part of counties to these new demands has been inconsistent. The state legislature has, over the last several years, given counties a greater range of powers and greater authority. The limited "home rule" legislation has given counties the power to expand their responsibilities, and counties have been given the opportunity to professionalize their administrative roles by employing a full-time county administrator to undertake all of the powers of the Board of County Commissioners. The majority of counties, however, have not fully adopted these changes. A few counties, such as Marion, St. Joseph, and Lake, have attempted to make alterations that will accommodate the new and changing demands they face. Most counties, especially the smaller ones, however, continue to operate as they did fifty or one hundred years ago.

In the future all Indiana counties will have to respond in some way to the new sets of demands they face. Counties, it appears, will increasingly be asked to behave like cities, to undertake municipal responsibilities as well as maintain their traditional range of responsibilities. In order for them to respond, however, they will need to undergo both structural and procedural changes. It is only when these changes are made that counties will be able to take advantage of the more progressive provisions already accorded to them and to fully and effectively assume the new responsibilities that residents of the state will expect.

City Government in Indiana

One of the interesting contrasts for which local government in Indiana is known is inherent in the politics and administration of Indiana cities. When comparing cities in Indiana to cities in other states, it would appear that in many ways the political systems of Indiana cities are more representative of the type of city government that existed in the latter part of the nineteenth century than they are representative of American cities in the twentieth century.

Cities in Indiana, to some degree at least, escaped the progressive reform movement that swept across the country in the early part of the twentieth century. Thus, Indiana cities feature a strong mayor-council form of government and can be contrasted with cities that feature either a "weak mayor," "commission," or "council manager" form of government. In addition to the organizational differences that each form of city government implies, there are substantial procedural differences as well. In order to understand the Indiana strong mayor plan of city government, it is useful to compare it with some of the governmental plans that exist in other states.[61]

City Executives

A major distinction between many municipal governmental plans is the division between legislative and executive responsibilities. In Indiana cities, the common council serves as the legislative body for the city while executive authority is vested almost exclusively in the mayor. In plans that have been adopted by many states, this clear distinction of authority that Indiana cities exhibit may not exist. In "weak mayor" cities executive responsibility is shared between the council and the mayor, while in commission and council-manager plans a single elected executive is altogether absent; with these plans the "council" or "commission" assumes both legislative and executive responsibilities. In strong mayor plans, executive power is concentrated in a single person who is directly responsible to city residents through the electoral process. The mayor is the actual as well as the symbolic leader of city government. With other plans—"weak mayor," commission, and council-manager—power is distributed among many persons. Even in cases where a municipal manager is responsible for developing an issue agenda, there is no one person who is responsible for all important city functions.[62]

Whether political power ought to be concentrated or dispersed is a debate that has raged for years. There are advantages and disadvantages to both approaches. With power concentrated, there is greater opportunity for it to be abused, but decisions can be effectively made, and it is possible to develop and implement consistent and coordinated policy for all aspects of government. When political power is dispersed, even if administrative responsibilities are centralized under a professional manager (council-manager plan), policy tends to be narrowly rather than broadly defined. Individual programs are likely to be efficiently administered, and the chances of political corruption are reduced, but the ability to resolve political conflicts is also reduced.[63]

City Legislature

The Indiana strong mayor plan also differs from many other systems in that most of the members of city councils are elected from small single member districts while a minority are elected, as is the mayor, on a citywide or "at large" basis. In many cities, particularly those with commission or council-manager plans, all the members of the council (or commission) are elected on an "at large" basis.

The distinction between "at large" as opposed to single member district representation is subtle but important. It directly affects the types of interests that are represented in the city's policy making process. In cities like those in Indiana where the councils are predominately composed of members from individual districts, representation on the council is based geographically. The city is divided into distinct geographic sections. Neighborhood and other locational concerns stemming from different geographic representatives tend to dominate the council deliberations. Most council members tend to be more concerned about the district they represent than for the city as a whole.

In councils that are composed primarily of members elected at large, a different form of representation occurs. Representation tends to be more broadly based and focuses on such interest groups as organized labor, the business community, the board of realtors, or some other important constituencies. Councils tend to be less concerned about geographic areas and more concerned with matters affecting the various interest groups that the individual members represent.[64] There is no council plan that guarantees that council members will act in the best interest of the city as a whole.

Political Parties

A third difference between Indiana cities and many cities elsewhere is the role of political parties in the local government process. In Indiana, political parties play a major role in local politics. Municipal politics is highly partisan. Candidates for city offices run as members of a political party and are nominated in a party primary. This approach is contrasted to the "non-partisan" approach used in some cities. In these cities, candidates for public office supposedly run on their own without party affiliations; if primary elections are held, they are used simply to reduce the number of candidates to a smaller number. The general election is then used as a run-off between the survivors.

At the municipal level political parties represent more than just a way to select public officials. Where they exist, they also play an important role in the process of government. Major distinctions can be seen when cities with partisan election systems are compared with cities of similar size with nonpartisan election systems. Partisan cities generally have higher levels of voter turnout than nonpartisan cities. At the municipal level political parties serve as mediating institutions between the people of the city on one hand and the officials governing the city on the other hand. Since parties have no interest other than winning elections, they seek the broadest possible base and attempt to include within their infrastructure the widest possible range of interest groups. Thus, where a political party has influence in recruiting candidates for public office, it attempts to find people who represent different economic levels, ethnic and racial groups, as well as different special interest groups. Only in a highly homogeneous city is a political party likely to be dominated by any single group. Similarly, when attempting to articulate issues or in offering solutions to various problems, parties will seek not to take stands that would be offensive to anyone. Parties in Indiana do not as a rule attempt to exercise a great deal of influence, at least at the local level, in the policymaking process; but the fact that the decision-makers are all products of a partisan election system means that political party interest is still there. Office holders tend to be broadly rather than narrowly representative of the city and are likely to seek to compromise on difficult issues rather than to take a hard, uncompromising position.

When parties are absent, other groups step in and play the role that parties play in partisan cities. The difference is, however, that while such groups as organized labor, business associations, and others recruit candidates, articulate issues, and attempt to influence the public at large in the same way that parties do, their first responsibility is to protect their own organization. If they win elections, it is their own interests they seek to maintain and enhance. Few cities actually have well-balanced, highly competitive interest groups. It is more likely that few interest groups, even if they do not represent a majority of the population, will dominate the social and economic system. In a nonpartisan city, they are likely to dominate the political system as well; and as a result, city councils tend to reflect a narrow rather than a broad spectrum of the community. Thus, the issues and positions councils promote tend to be those important to the groups from which the council members come.[65]

Patronage

The partisan-nonpartisan dichotomy that separates Indiana cities from most cities in most states is closely related to another set of differences—the existence in Indiana of a patronage or job-oriented political system. Unlike systems in most other states, Indiana has just begun to institute civil service and merit systems in the public employment sector. Indeed, one of the reasons that political parties remain relatively strong in Indiana cities is that they continue to exercise influence in appointing people to various local government jobs. It is for the purpose of securing jobs and other favors that many Indiana residents are attracted to political participation. Conversely, it is through the partisan political activity that the ranks of city employees are filled. In many cities in other states, on the other hand, with the demise of partisanship both the appeal and the mechanism for patronage have been removed. Most of these cities, consequently, have well-developed merit or professional service systems.[66]

Operationally, the differences between patronage and nonpatronage systems is more a matter of style than of substance. There is no evidence to indicate that Indiana cities, for instance, are any better or worse at delivering public services than are cities in Michigan that have highly sophisticated civil service systems. Using another example, Chicago, perhaps the last bastion of a true patronage system, was for years known as "the city that works" while Detroit, with a tradition of civil service, was constantly in financial and service delivery difficulties. What is known is that patronage systems do exhibit a high level of employee turnover, particularly if control of the city administration is subject to frequent changes in party control. Patronage based systems are less expensive and with patronage-oriented systems there is greater chance of corruption than in nonpatronage oriented cities. Patronage cities are less likely to be unionized and more likely than nonpatronage cities to be "responsive" to individual and group demands.[67]

Initiative Referendum and Recall

A fifth major distinction between Indiana cities and cities in many other states is the absence in Indiana of institutionalized provisions for petition, referenda, or recall. These provisions, sometimes referred to as "instruments of direct democracy," were an important part of the early twentieth century reformed movement. In effect, they allow citizens to participate directly in the established governmental processes and to take, in limited ways, policymaking into their own hands. If present, these provisions allow citizens to take up a petition in support or opposition to some legislative issue. If enough signatures are obtained (the requirement varies), the issue is placed on the ballot and in a special or general election citizens vote on it (a referendum). If the measure wins, it becomes law (and policy) without having the council act on it. While in some cities virtually anything can be brought up and decided upon by this method, usually only structural changes in government and major expenditures or tax levels are determined by such a vote. In some places like Michigan, all important taxing and spending measures are determined by this method. The recall provision allows voters via petition and referendum to remove unqualified or unpopular public officials before their terms expire.[68]

In cities where initiative, referendum, and recall exist, there is a tendency for elected officials to actually avoid making controversial decisions. In many cases, they opt for the politically safe way of letting the major decision be made via referendum, rather than undertaking that responsibility themselves. In cases like this, the role of the council in arbitrating conflict is greatly reduced. Major issues are, to be sure, resolved quickly and decisively, but the conflict that generated the question or issue in the first place remains.

In Indiana cities where these processes do not exist, elected officials must make all decisions and must live politically with the results. Thus, there is a premium on a process of resolving the problem rather than deciding the issue. Compromises are sought, and there are attempts made to placate both sides of any question.

The decision-making process takes longer to work itself through than is usually the case in cities where the petition, referendum, and recall provisions exist, and in the end the decision may not be totally satisfactory to either side. The chances are, however, that when a decision is ultimately reached, the conflict that originally stimulated the controversy will be resolved as well.[69]

Conclusion

Indiana cities face the same problems of declining core areas, deteriorating neighborhoods, and difficulties in finding the revenues needed to provide essential services that cities in other states face. These difficulties, however, are not necessarily the result of a particular form of government. These are difficulties inherent in the American urban culture as a whole. Urban problems exist virtually everywhere in the United States. There has been no evidence that Indiana cities are any more or less capable of dealing with them than are cities in most other states.

There is, of course, room for considerable improvement in the process of politics and administration employed by Indiana cities. Cities will face new and changing demands, and they must be in a position to meet these new challenges. The state legislature, in addition to looking at the changing role of counties, will also have to look at the changing role of cities, and the two must not be looked at in isolation.

Problems and Prospects for Local Government

Local government in Indiana, like units of local government elsewhere in the United States, will face an increasing array of challenges in the last two decades of the twentieth century. The social, economic, environmental, and energy problems with which the state and the country as a whole must deal will be most profoundly felt at the local government level. Whether or not local governments will be able to maintain their integrity as political units and their viability as service delivery units are questions that cannot, as yet, be answered. What seems to be apparent, however, at least as far as Indiana local units of government are concerned, is that if the challenges of the 1980's and 1990's are to be met, some specific problem areas must first be resolved.

Indiana residents face an equity problem in terms of their relationships with local units of government. The governmental fragmentation inherent in the system of local government means that different groups of residents do receive different services and the costs of providing these services is unevenly distributed among tax-paying residents. In short, fragmented government means that some residents receive services for which they do not pay while others pay for services they do not receive. The equity question is intensified as a result of the township by township method of property tax assessments and the continued movement of people from central cities to suburban and rural areas.[70]

In order to deal with these as well as other service delivery related problems, the structure of local government in Indiana should continue to be reviewed and revised. Some critics contend that the 1981 home rule legislation did not go far enough. Attention should be given not only to the structure of particular local government units such as was done by the Local Government Study Commission but also on relationships units have with each other as well. Accommodation needs to be reached on which set of taxpayers is expected to pay for which set of services. The assumption that traditional incorporated municipalities represent the primary unit of government for urban areas must be altered. As the 1980 census has shown, in spite of the impending energy crisis the movement of people from the central cities to the suburbs is continuing; and taxing and service inequities between city, suburban, and rural residents are likely to increase rather than decrease.

Altering local government, of course, must be done with care. Factors other than equity are also important; government responsiveness and administrative efficiency are two such factors. Making government more responsive without sacrificing the quality of administration is a problem that decision-makers have attempted to deal with for decades. The conventional wisdom is that the greater access citizens have to their local government, the more responsive government is likely to be to their individual and group demands. The recognized difficulty, however, with too great access to government officials is that it interferes with government efficiency. Obviously, some middle ground should be sought. Government must be responsive, but it must also be able to carry out its responsibilities with a manageable level of outside interference. The evidence from local governments in Indiana seems to show that they do a somewhat better job of providing access and responding to the demands of local citizens than they do in actually delivering the public services for which they are responsible. This relative imbalance, however, should not obscure the fact that both problems need to be addresed simultaneously.[71]

County government in particular is a primary candidate for restructuring. The 1981 home rule legislation stopped short of making truly meaningful changes. Its executive powers and functions probably should be consolidated and placed under the authority of a single administrator. Whether or not such an administrator ought to be elected or appointed is open to debate. The bias here is that any single county executive ought to be elected rather than appointed; such an approach would be in the tradition of Indiana government and politics, and since in the future city and county officials will have to work closely with one another, it makes sense that they operate from a similar base (e.g., as elected officials). Others, of course, may have a different view, but Indiana residents are not likely to support proposals to remove policymakers from the ranks of elected officials.

In order for meaningful change to take place in county government, the State Constitution will need to be altered. The constitutionally established county offices must be reexamined and redefined. Provisions need to be enacted that will either eliminate some of these offices or at least limit their responsibilities and encourage the people who hold these offices to work closely with one another. People who perform essentially perfunctory tasks must somehow be held accountable to county level executive authority. Certainly, a thorough examination needs to be made of the roles and responsibilities of the multitude of independent and quasi-independent boards and commissions. The 1981 legislation did take a step in the right direction here, but more could be done. Perhaps some of these agencies could be eliminated altogether while others could be consolidated and made more responsible to county and city executive authority.

The role of townships, particularly in the sensitive areas of poor relief and property tax assessment, should be further reduced or even eliminated. Having what in effect are two separate public assistance programs is not efficient and contributes to tax and service inequities. The responsibility for providing poor relief probably should rest with the county welfare department. Likewise, property tax assessment should be, at the very least, a county rather than a township responsibility.

Cities and towns should not be immune from further reform efforts. The tendency to give municipal powers to autonomous boards and commissions rather than to elected officials should be re-examined, and some further consolidation of existing powers under the mayor's authority beyond what was provided for in the 1981 legislation should be considered. The greatest need for municipal reorganization is with smaller cities (third class). With cities of this size, it may be wise to go well beyond the current home rule provisions and consider a major restructuring—possibly to consider instituting a council-manager or a mayor-manager form of municipal government. Smaller cities tend to be socially and economically more homogeneous than larger cities but still have a need for full-time professional administrative leadership. In short, small Indiana cities are the types of places that in other states professional city managers have been most successful.[72] They seem to be successful in those Indiana towns where they have been hired.

Implied in any discussion of restructuring of counties, townships, cities, and towns is the need to find new ways in which these entities can work together. Attention needs to be given to the problem of service duplication as well as cooperation in program development and implementation. Some services that are the legitimate concern of both cities and counties could be given over completely to counties, while other services could be delivered contractually between a city and a county. With a contractural arrangement any unit can provide a given service for a number of other units through a negotiated contract.

It will also be important in the future for all Indiana units of local government to improve their service delivery mechanisms. The administration of local government needs to be professionalized, and modern and innovative management techniques need to be introduced. Although it is not the driving political force it once was, patronage does play and will continue to play an important role in local government administration, and its functions need to be considered when attempting to professionalize administrative processes. It probably would not be wise to attempt to eliminate patronage altogether. More important will be the initiation of better management techniques and the establishment of more professional personnel relations. The existence of public employee collective bargaining will need to be recognized as reality, and a workable collective bargaining system will need to be instituted.

As restructuring of local general purpose government takes place, the need for some special purpose units of government will be reduced. The need for some special purpose governments will, of course, remain for the foreseeable future, but the proliferation of such units should be halted. Whenever possible, new functions should be given to the established units of government. Even with the potential for major reorganization in the future, it is not possible or appropriate to give a new function to existing units of local government, then new units of special purpose government should only be created according to a predetermined plan, a plan that incorporates guidelines and consistent procedures for creating such units of government. The major problem with special purpose governments is not that they exist; it is that they exist in so many shapes and sizes that it is difficult for all but the most learned experts to fully understand what they are doing. Thus, a process of reviewing and revising local government must include special purpose governments as well.

Probably the most perplexing set of problems facing all units of local government in Indiana flows from the constraints they face in raising and spending money. Local governments in Indiana, like local governments throughout the county, are facing increasingly serious fiscal problems. Revenues have not kept up with increasing costs, and local government officials do not always have the power to allocate money where it is needed. The problems will be intensified with reductions in federally funded programs. Local governments in Indiana do not have the power to institute new revenue raising schemes on their own. They are locked into the state mandated revenue system which limits the amount of revenue a unit can raise through local property taxes and prescribes in precise terms a formula for distributing state money to the local units. The only other source of money that local governments can get are those funds (which are being reduced) made available by the federal government. Traditionally, these funds came in the form of grants-in-aid, block grants, and General Revenue Sharing. Most of the federal funds, except for General Revenue Sharing, are targeted toward particular kinds of activities. Thus, they cannot be used to finance general government activities. The field of local government finance is complicated. There are no pat answers or easy solutions. Local units of government need to have access to new sources of revenue and must be given greater flexibility in determining how that revenue should be used, but it is not likely that the state will give up its traditional role of controlling local finances. It is the state then that will need to insure that taxing and service delivery equity is increased rather than diminished and that any changes are consistent throughout the state. Local government finance is an area that will demand intensive study and debate before anything near a new solution can be considered.[73]

Summary

Local government in Indiana is a study of contrasts. It may be confusing, but there is a degree of rationality to it. Local government in Indiana mixes tradition embodied in the State Constitution with contemporary responses to modern problems. Cities, towns, counties, townships, and the hundreds of special purpose units of government provide a multitude of services to virtually every citizen of the state.

In spite of the fact that much of the infrastructure of local government is rooted in the State Constitution and is difficult to alter, local government is going through a process of change. The state legislature in the late 1970's wisely created a local government study commission, and this commission made some important recommendations; many of these recommendations were enacted into the 1981 law. Thus, for local government in Indiana the 1980's may be the greatest period of change in the state's history.

For all of the innovations that have occurred and for all the changes that are likely to result from them, more needs to be done. The recommendations of the Local Government Study Commission adopted in the 1981 home rule legislation have only gone part way in solving the problems local units of government in Indiana face. There will, of course, be no final solution. Changing circumstances continually generate new challenges, and new responses will be necesssary.

What can be said for local government in Indiana today is that in the end it does the things that a system of local government is supposed to do: it represents the state at the local level, it delivers local services, and it arbitrates the conflict that arises among the citizens of local communities.

Indiana, at the same time, encompasses some of the most traditional, as well as some of the most progressive, local government characteristics. Indiana is both industrial and agricultural; it is urban and rural with both large cities and small towns. The system of local government must somehow accommodate all of these diverse characteristics and do so with efficiency and responsiveness. There are problems yet to be resolved, but it manages to meet most of these demands with relatively high levels of both efficiency and responsiveness.

The last two decades of the twentieth century will, however, bring new challenges to Indiana local government; and the system of local government that is currently in place may not be adequate to meet these challenges. Changes will be necessary. Both county and city government will need to be restructured, and ways must be found for them to cooperate with each other. In particular, the problems of equitable service delivery, professional administration, governmental responsiveness, and financing local government must be studied and resolved.

Notes

1. "1980 Census of Population and Housing: Advance Reports" (Indiana). Washington, D.C. vs. Department of Commerce, (March, 1980).
2. City of Clinton v. Cedar Rapids and Missouri Railroad Company, 24 Iowa 455, (1868).
3. Blair, George S. *American Local Government*. New York: Harper and Row, (1964) pp 60–64.
4. As will be pointed out, Indiana does now have limited provisions for local government "home rule." To an overwhelming degree, however, local government remains under the direct control of the state, especially in fiscal matters. See "Report from Local Government Study Commission." Indianapolis, Indiana, (1981).
5. Blair, *op. cit.*, pp 18–39.
6. See Bridenbaugh, Carl. *Cities in Revolt: Urban Life in America 1743–1776*. New York: Oxford University Press, (1955).

7. Blair, *op. cit.*, pp 103–145.
8. *Ibid.*, p 10.
9. See Kotler, Milton. *Neighborhood Government: The Local Foundations of Neighborhood Life.* Indianapolis: The Bobbs-Merrill Company, (1969) pp 1–11.
10. Lineberry, Robert, and Sharkansky, Ira. *Urban Politics and Public Policy,* 3rd Ed. New York: Harper & Row, (1978) pp 215–220.
11. Barnhart, John D., and Carmony, Donald F. *Indiana: From Frontier to Commonwealth,* vol. I. New York: Lewis Historical Publishing Company, (1954) p 39. Vincennes was actually governed by a court provided by the state of Virginia of which it considered Vincennes to be a part. Virginia did not cede her claims to the Ohio River territory until 1784.
12. *Ibid.*, pp 81–85.
13. Blair, *op. cit.*, p 37.
14. Quoted from Blair, p 37.
15. *Ibid.*, pp 37–38.
16. Town of Longview v. City of Crawfordsville, 164 Ind. 117.
17. Burns Annotated State Statutes, 1931 revised.
18. The Indiana Supreme Court applied the principles of Dillon's rule to state-local relationships in 1920 in: Central Union Telephone Co., 126 N.E. 628, (1920).
19. Bryce, James. *The American Commonwealth.* New York: World Publications, (1889) p 144.
20. "1980 Census of Population and Housing," (Indiana), *op. cit.*
21. "Report of the Local Government Study Commission," *op. cit.*
22. See Blair, *op. cit.* pp 45–48. He describes typical county government functions.
23. Barnhart, John D., and Carmony, Donald F. *Indiana: From Frontier to Commonwealth,* vol. II. New York: Lewis Historical Publishing Company, (1954) pp 8–10.
24. The duties of six of these offices are described in Article 6 of the Constitution of Indiana, 1851. These six are: auditor, clerk of the circuit court, recorder, coroner, surveyor, and treasurer. The office of sheriff is provided for, but its duties are not mentioned. The duties of prosecuting attorney are discussed in Article 7.
25. Blair, *op. cit.*, pp 45–46.
26. *Here Is Your Indiana Government,* 18th Ed. Indianapolis, Indiana: The Indiana State Chamber of Commerce, (1977), pp 63–75.
27. Owen, C. James, and Hall, Dean K. "Financing Local Government in Indiana." Fort Wayne: Taxpayers Research Association, (1980).
28. *Here Is Your Indiana Government,* (1977), op. cit., pp 76, 79, 81–82.
29. *Civic Cinema 1979.* South Bend, Indiana: South Bend Civic Planning Association, (1979).
30. *Here Is Your Indiana Government,* (1977), op. cit., pp 77–84.
31. *Ibid.*, pp 90–94, and Blair, *op. cit.*, pp 49–50.
32. "1980 Census of Population and Housing," *op. cit.*
33. Blair, op. cit., p 48, and *Here Is Your Indiana Government,* (1977), op. cit., p 90–96.
34. Owen, C. James, and Hall, Dean K., *op. cit.*
35. *U.S. Census Bureau Statistical Abstract of the United States.* Washington, D.C.: U.S. Department of Commerce, (1979). "Advanced Report on the 1980 Census." Washington, D.C.: U.S. Department of Commerce, (1981).
36. *Here Is Your Indiana Government,* 20th Ed. Indianapolis, Indiana: The Indiana State Chamber of Commerce, (1981) pp 102–106, and "Report of the Local Government Study Commission," *op. cit.* Prior to 1981 there were five classes of cities.
37. *Here Is Your Indiana Government,* (1979) pp 95–106.
38. Ibid.
39. "Report of the Local Government Study Commisison," *op. cit.*

40. See Banfield, Edward C., and Wilson, James A. *City Politics*. New York: Vintage Books, (1963). The authors describe various roles played by city government.
41. "Report of the Local Government Study Commission," *op. cit.*, and *Civic Cinema 1979, op. cit.*
42. *Here Is Your Indiana Government,* (1981), *op. cit.*, pp 97–101.
43. "Report of the Local Government Study Commission," *op. cit.*
44. *Ibid.*
45. Harrigan, John J. *Politics and Policy in States and Communities*. Boston: Little, Brown & Co., (1980) pp 32–35.
46. *Here Is Your Indiana Government,* (1981), op. cit., 104–105.
47. IC 1971, 18-3-1. 5-4, as added by Acts 1971, P.L. 257, Vol. 1, p 987.
48. See Rowe, Lloyd A. "Current Use of and Attitudes Toward the Town Manager Plan in Indiana," *Indiana Public Management*. (Winter, 1976) p 10.
49. See Rowe, Lloyd A. "Alternative Forms of Government for Indiana's Cities: Attitudes, History, and Prospects," Indiana University, School of Public and Environmental Affairs *Review* 1, (Fall, 1979), p 118 for a brief history of attempts to pass constitutional amendments authorizing the council-manager form.
50. See *Directory of Recognized Local Governments, 1981*. Washington: International City Management Association, (1981) pp 6, 11, 40–41, 47–49, 58–89, for data on the number of local governments which have adopted the council-manager form.
51. Blair, George C., *op. cit.*, pp 244–260.
52. *Ibid.*
53. *Here Is Your Indiana Government,* (1981) pp 107–110. A number of municipally controlled "school cities" or "school towns" still exist in Indiana. In these cases, the boundaries of the school district are co-existent with the municipal boundaries that existed prior to the school reorganization legislation. They are still special purpose units of government, but they are under the control of municipal authorities.
54. Harrigan, John J., *op. cit.*, pp 28–29.
55. Stedman, Murray S. *Urban Politics,* 2nd Ed. Cambridge, Mass.: Winthrop Publishers, Inc., (1975) pp 71–82.
56. "Report of the Local Government Study Commission," *op. cit.*
57. Most authorities on local government agree that a "single executive" offers the most effective form of administrative leadership. See Harrigan, John J., *op. cit.*, pp 25–35.
58. Goldfield, David, and Bronell, Blake A. *Urban America: From Downtown to No Town.* Boston, Houston: Mifflin Co., (1979), pp 1–22, and Gorham, William, and Glazer, Nathan. *The Urban Predicament.* Washington, D.C.: The Urban Institute, 1976. See the introduction where the authors discuss "demographic and income trends affecting the cities."
59. Berman, David R. *State and Local Politics,* 2nd Ed. Boston: Allyn and Bacon, Inc., (1978) pp 33–66.
60. Harrigan, John J., *op. cit.*, pp 37–56.
61. See Stedman, Murray S. *Urban Politics, op. cit.*, p 64, Berman, David R. *State and Local Politics, op. cit.*, pp 226–244, and Lineberry, Robert, and Fowler, Edmond. "Reformism in Public Policy in American Cities," *American Political Science Review,* (September, 1967) pp 701–716.
62. The distinction between the terms "council" and "commission" can be confusing. Some councils in council-manager plans are called commissions, while some commissions in a commissioner plan are called a council. The term council as it is used here refers to a city's legislature in any plan of government.
63. See Lineberry, Robert, and Fowler, Edmond, *op. cit.*, and Hojnacki, William P. *Kalamazoo, Michigan and South Bend, Indiana: A Comparative Analysis of Policy Outcomes,* unpublished doctoral dissertation, University of Notre Dame, 1977, and Wilson, James A., and Banfield, Edward C. "Public Regardingness as a Value Premise in Voting Behavior," *American Political Science Review,* (December, 1964) pp 876–887.

64. Caraley, Demetrios. *City Governments and Urban Problems: A New Introduction to Urban Politics.* Englewood Cliffs, N.J.: Prentice-Hall, Inc., (1977) pp 199–247.

65. Judd, Dennis R. *The Politics of American Cities.* Boston: Little, Brown and Company, (1979), see Chapters 3 and 4. Also see Alford, Robert R., and Lee, Eugene C. "Voter Turnout in American Cities," *American Political Science Review* LXII, (September, 1968) pp 769–814.

66. See Judd, *Ibid.,* pp 87–116, and Lineberry and Fowler, *op. cit.*

67. Banfield, Edward. *Big City Politics.* New York: Random House, (1965). The author describes politics in Chicago.

68. Blair, George. *American Local Government, op. cit.,* pp 154–157.

69. Hojnacki, William P., *op. cit.*

70. Judd, Dennis R., *op. cit.,* pp. 257–287.

71. Caraley, Demetrios, *op. cit.,* pp 387–397, and Stedman, Murray S., Jr., *op. cit.,* pp 113–127.

72. Bent, Alan E., and Rossum, Ralph A., ed. *Urban Administration: Management Politics and Change.* See Chapters 1 and 2.

73. See Owen, James C., and Hall, Dean R., *op. cit.*

7

The 1970's—A Decade of Local Government Reform

C. James Owen
Indiana-Purdue University at Fort Wayne

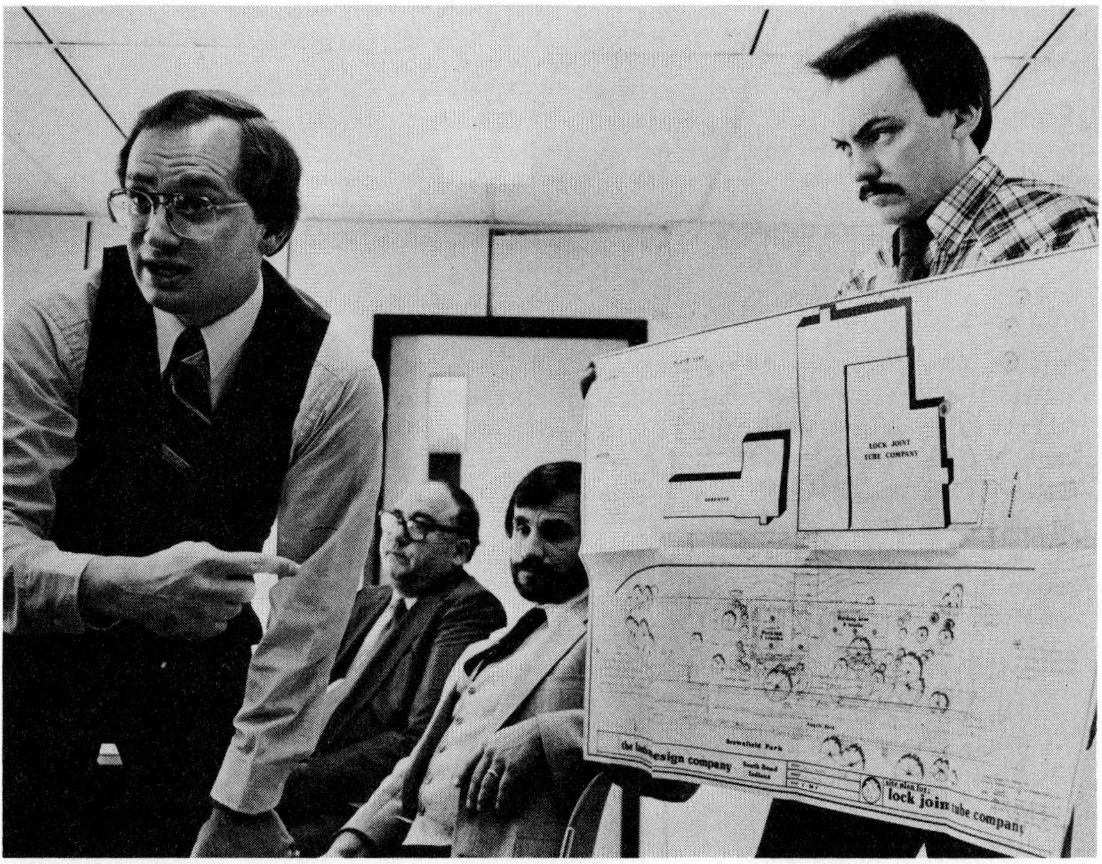

City officials working on a development project.
Courtesy of the South Bend Tribune

The purpose of this chapter is to describe and evaluate the role that the state government has taken in Indiana to assist local governments in their quest to solve urban problems. Indiana is not unlike most of the other 49 states in its governing experience in its cities. There are nineteen first and second class cities and SMSA's in the state. Among the largest of these are Indianapolis, Fort Wayne, Gary, South Bend and Evansville. These cities share with most midwestern and northeastern American cities the general urban problems of population decline, rising crime rates, unemployment, pollution, traffic congestion, and declining revenues. What they share most with other cities, however, is the frustrating inability to respond to their problems in an efficient and effective manner. The existence of urban problems has not been lost on state officials. Indeed, these problems have given rise to three central areas of concern among state law makers as to what can be done about: (1) a lack of an understandable form of local government organization, (2) the minimal distribution of functional and structural authority among local units, and (3) a declining source of local government revenue.

A second purpose of this chapter is to look at the problem of an increased role by the state in the resolution of local problems of governance. The state historically played a preeminent role in establishing local governments. It controlled their ability to exercise authority, and it mandated many functions. In the view of many, the role of the state worked to the detriment of local officials' attempts to manage their own affairs. In the 1970's, the relationship between the states and local units of government, especially cities, began to change. It was a time of transition wherein the state has reversed some of its customary roles with local units, reinforced others, and delegated still others to local officials.

Indiana has not been known for its reform efforts. With the passage of the Unigov law that consolidated the Indianapolis and Marion County governments in 1971, however, this reputation began to change. Since the Indianapolis Unigov experience, other reforms have been introduced; some cities have presented the General Assembly with their own plans for reform, general local government home rule legislation has been passed, local government finance has been restructured, and regional planning agencies have been established in most metropolitan areas.

Political and Social Environment

The state is known for its conservative political and social environment. The two major political parties (Democrat and Republican) are both firmly established and compete vigorously for state and local offices on near even terms. The party leadership is generally expected to oppose governmental changes which they feel might jeopardize their competitive electoral position on their job oriented patronage system. Accordingly, they take a cautious view of most local government reform proposals.

Whichever party has been in control of the state house or the governor's office, Indiana, the home of the American Legion and founding place of the John Birch Society, has traditionally been a conservative state. Paul Friggins' description of the state's capitol city reflects much of the mood of the entire state:

> Indianapolis is a solid conservative community in a historically conservative state. For example, several years ago when the state legislators of Indiana fired a resolution off to Congress urging Indiana senators and representatives "to vote to fetch our county court houses back from Washington," Indiana meant it.[1]

Indiana's conservative mode made it convenient for officials there to defend the *status quo* over the unknown consequences of government reform proposals.

The 1960's: A Decade of Transition

After several decades of timid response to the special needs of cities, the state legislature finally in the 1960's became concerned about urban policy. During this period, urban problems intensified in Indiana and elsewhere, and local governments throughout the nation came under fire for not being responsive to them. Key among the events that prompted a change in attitude among the populace and elected officials were the urban riots during the latter part of the decade which the evening television news brought into every living room. The recognition of the need to reform local government to respond to the specific problems grew. An important factor in getting the state to act on urban matters was the transition that took place in the legislature itself. During the late 1960's and early 1970's, the state legislature was reapportioned and thus the influence of urban legislators was increased while the influence or rural legislators was decreased.[2]

A more subtle recognition of our urban plight was brought about by increased serious study and debate among scholars and community leaders. The National League of Cities, the Advisory Commission on Intergovernmental Relations, the Committee for Economic Development, and the President's Committee on Urban Problems were among numerous national and regional study groups promoting local government reform. Although the merger of governmental functions or areas, through annexation and consolidation, or by the formation of special districts, councils of governments (COG's) or intergovernmental contracts, became the dominant reform wisdom of the time, there was a growing frustration over the inability of local units to adopt these reforms. It was a distillation of these frustrations, nationally, that lead reformers to espouse an increased state involvement in local affairs.

In assessing the course of this change, the authors of a recent publication noted the conditions which add substance to the quest for more state coordination of local affairs.

> We believe the state governments should play a central role in providing leadership, incentives, and technical assistance for improving the productivity of their local governments and further should work toward removing state-imposed impediments to productivity, which in many states are numerous. This does not imply a diminution of local prerogatives; on the contrary, it suggests a need for states to update their traditional responsibility for providing foundations of local government that will permit cities and counties to manage their affairs more efficiently.
>
> To date, the states have had a mixed record of achievement. Outstanding records of progress include Minnesota's creation of the Metropolitan Council of the Twin Cities Area, and Indiana's consolidation of Marion County and Indianapolis into "Unigov,". . . .[3]

It was conditions such as those mentioned in the CED statement that directed government reformers in Indianapolis-Marion County to appeal directly to the Indiana General Assembly for the passage of a unified form of government in 1969. The Unigov experience that we now turn to evoked a heightened interest in local government reform throughout the state and set the pattern for an increased state presence in these activities.

Indianapolis Unigov

Consolidation in Indianapolis was not an entirely unique phenomenon, but the fact that Indianapolis was one of only twelve United States cities to achieve consolidation in the preceding 100 years[4] is notable. What was even more of a singular achievement was that Indianapolis attained consolidation without recourse to a referendum; the change was passed and implemented directly through state legislative action. Thus, it became the only city in this century to effect a consolidation without a direct public vote for approval. Richard G. Lugar, the chief architect of the reform debate and the first Unigov Mayor[5] underscored the significance of the non-referendum issue: "Most Indianapolis watchers are mildly interested in the organization chart but more intensely interested in the question of how it was done."[6]

The Elements of the Reform Debate

Although a great deal can be learned from the Indianapolis experience, the uniqueness of the reform debate makes it highly unlikely that it can be duplicated elsewhere. The political and governmental conditions that were such a vital part of Unigov's passage are very difficult to duplicate. In all there were seven fundamental elements leading to the successful passage of Unigov.

The first such condition was a favorable partisan political setting. Few observers deny that partisan politics were an integral part of the Unigov debate. The political setting which ultimately lead to Unigov's passage first developed in 1966 (three years prior to passage of the bill) when a major reorganization of the Marion County Republican party brought a whole new company of ambitious and farsighted young people into the party and elected many of them to city, county, and state offices in the next two years. Among them was Richard G. Lugar, who became mayor of Indianapolis in a surprise victory over the Democratic incumbent in 1967, making him only the second Republican mayor in forty years. The Marion County Republicans quickly built on this initial achievement, and it was largely through their efforts that the Republican party controlled each level of the state's governmental decision-making process in 1969.

Adroit leadership provided the second critical element of the reform's success. The leadership of the Unigov debate came exclusively from within the ranks of the Republican party. The members of the policy committee who planned and directed the debate were all either Republican party officials, office holders, or appointees. Each one of the Unigov principals demonstrated individual leadership and commitment to the Unigov proposal and risked the loss of his political following by becoming public advocates of Unigov. City council president, Tom Hasbrook, for example, was a most capable exponent of Unigov in the environs of the city's governmental and political circles. Others were similarly effective at the county and state levels.

With so many strong personalities making key contributions to its development, it might appear that the leadership was wholly collective—that there was no leader. But the unquestionable leader, acknowledged by the others, was Mayor Lugar. He was the most recognizable public official in Marion County, and he was the chief spokesman for Unigov in the public forums of debate. With capable assistance from Deputy Mayor John Walls, he provided overall direction and coordination to the policy committees' collective activities. He was, in a word, the glue that held everybody together.

In addition to the commitment, energy and prestige the principals brought to the Unigov debate, they also exhibited great skill in providing keen draftsmanship for the bill and adopting an attitude of compromise on various elements of the reform proposal—two additional decisions that were vital to Unigov's success. As the state capital, Indianapolis has recourse to a number of attorneys with considerable statehouse experience. Two of these, Lewis Bose and Charles Whistler, directing the work of several other attorneys, were able to draft a bill that skirted many political and legal pitfalls while sacrificing only those aspects of the bill that were necessary; compromise was the watchword of the Unigov principals and their attorneys. It was only through a difficult course of compromise and maneuvering that the principals were able to check the opposition of a politically powerful county judge and to reverse the anti-Unigov stance of the editors of the two major Indianapolis newspapers, the *News* and *Star*.

A fifth contributing factor to Unigov's passage was the legal relationship existing at the time between the state and local governments. Indiana was not a home rule state. Thus, in accordance with Dillon's rule, control of local government affairs was still the exclusive jurisdiction of the state government. There was no legal precedent for the establishment, dissolution, or rearrangement of local governmental entities through referendum. It was only reasonable, and perhaps convenient, to assume then, as the Unigov principals did, that in Indiana it is the General Assembly's responsibility to pass on metropolitan consolidations and that a referendum could only be advisory to it.

An additional condition leading to merger—one the principals did not have a hand in—was a series of events that made metropolitan reform a topical issue in 1969. At the time the Unigov debate was initiated in 1968, consolidated government had been a topic of community study and discussion for over 50 years. In the preceding years, no fewer than three separate study commissions had recommended consolidation, and virtually every legislative session in the previous twenty years was presented with a Marion County bill for local government reorganization. Furthermore, as the debate continued, the idea of consolidation finally gained widespread support among the media. In fact, at the same time the Policy Committee was considering the possibility of merger, the *Star* concluded a thirteen part series on local government with a recommendation favoring merger.[7] In a sense, consolidation was an idea whose time had come.

The seventh critical factor in the Unigov debate was the principals' campaign to marshal public support for the bill. Many important bills pass the legislature without such organization, but to introduce a government reorganization bill of such magnitude without demonstrating public support for it would have been a mistake. There were a number of legislators, including the powerful speaker of the house, who were curious as to how much public support the Unigov bill actually had. In order to satisfy this curiosity, the Marion County legislative delegation conducted a vigorous program to educate their fellows on the progress of the public phase of the Unigov debate on a regular basis. A blue ribbon task force of Indianapolis citizens was formed to review the reform proposal. Public hearings were held, a public opinion telephone poll was conducted, a speaker's bureau was started, and a petition was circulated to secure signatures favoring Unigov. All of these activities, orchestrated by the Unigov proponents, were so far superior to anything done by the opponents that legislators from outlying parts of the state were hardly exposed to any arguments that opposed Unigov. As a suburban Indianapolis newspaper summed up the situation: "As so often happens, however, the ungreased wheels of public opinion may have moved too slowly to exert any influence—one way or the other—on the well oiled gears of the Unigov machine."[8]

Whether all of the aforementioned elements of the Unigov debate were imperative to its passage or not cannot be fully determined. It is clear that if anyone of them were missing, the debate would have taken a somewhat different course. A key element, however, was the leadership exercised on behalf of the reform. It was this leadership, after all, that saw the political and governmental circumstances as they were and utilized them to Unigov's best advantages. The draftsmanship, compromise and public support elements were actually strategies adopted and controlled by the leaders. The only element where the leadership was not an incisive agent was the tenor of the reform discussions that determined the positive setting for the Unigov debate. But favorable reform debates of this nature that exist in most large American cities usually crumble under the direction of a less capable leadership.

Unigov is far less a unified government than the term implies. There was considerable opposition raised against the Unigov proposal, and many important compromises were negotiated before final passage was secured.

The Reorganized Government

The term "Unigov" or unified government connotes a governmental arrangement with a far greater degree of consolidation than what actually exists in the Indianapolis-Marion County system of government. The most important aspect of the reform was the establishment of a single county-wide executive and a combined city-county council. The county is now the important political unit. The mayor is the focus of political leadership and responsibility in the county. The city-county council is the singular policy-making body for both the old city of Indianapolis and Marion County. The new mayor and the combined council clearly exercise public authority to a far greater extent than before. Despite these major accomplishments, a number of significant governmental entities such as the schools, the courts, the townships, four excluded municipalities, and several special service districts were omitted from Unigov. Important political offices and administrative functions were integrated to be sure, but at the same time many centers of local autonomy were continued. Unigov is an interesting compromise between unity and plurality.

The consolidation of the mayor's office with the county executive offices was done in an ingenious fashion. Prior to Unigov all counties in Indiana were governed by three constitutionally prescribed commissioners. In order to bypass the trials of a constitutional amendment, the Unigov principals retained the county commission offices in name but stripped them of virtually all of their authority and stopped electing new commissioners; this removed authority is now exercised by the mayor. Those functions retained in the commissioner's office—someone must still sign on county-backed bond issues—are administered by three other county officers serving part-time in an ex-officio capacity: the Auditor, Treasurer, and Assessor.

The mayor is now elected by citizens of the old city of Indianapolis, suburban county residents, as well as citizens of the four excluded municipalities, who also elect their own mayors. This "double vote" was upheld in a 1973 court decision which stated that in voting for the county mayor, residents are voting for their interests as recipients of county services.

Besides merging the city and county executive offices, Unigov also provided for a comprehensive administrative integration of departments, agencies and boards in the mayor's office. The mayor's office is organized into six major departments (see Figure 7.1). The Department of Administration is responsible for the general administrative functions of the consolidated city. These include functions previously performed by the city controller, city and county legal departments, city and county purchasing departments, and centralized data processing center. The department director is a cabinet level officer appointed by the mayor and is accountable directly to him.[9]

The Department of Public Safety is administered by the Director of Public Safety, a mayoral appointee who is assisted by a five-member safety board whose primary function is to advise the director on matters of policy and management. Consolidated in the Department of Public Safety are the old city's fire and police forces, civil defense, weights and measures, and the municipal dog pound.

In terms of the number of governmental units involved, the most significant merger occurred in the Department of Transportation. The new department was given the road and street responsibilities previously exercised by five separate agencies: the County Commission, the County Highway Department, the City Street Department, the Park Board, and the Mass Transportation Agency. DOT's director is appointed by the mayor with council approval and is directly accountable to the mayor.

Before Unigov, there was already a county-wide Department of Parks and Recreation. The chief change was to place the department directly under the mayor in a cabinet position, with the director appointed by him, and with a far less independent board of directors.

Figure 7.1. Unigov organization chart (Consolidated government for Indianapolis—Marion County)

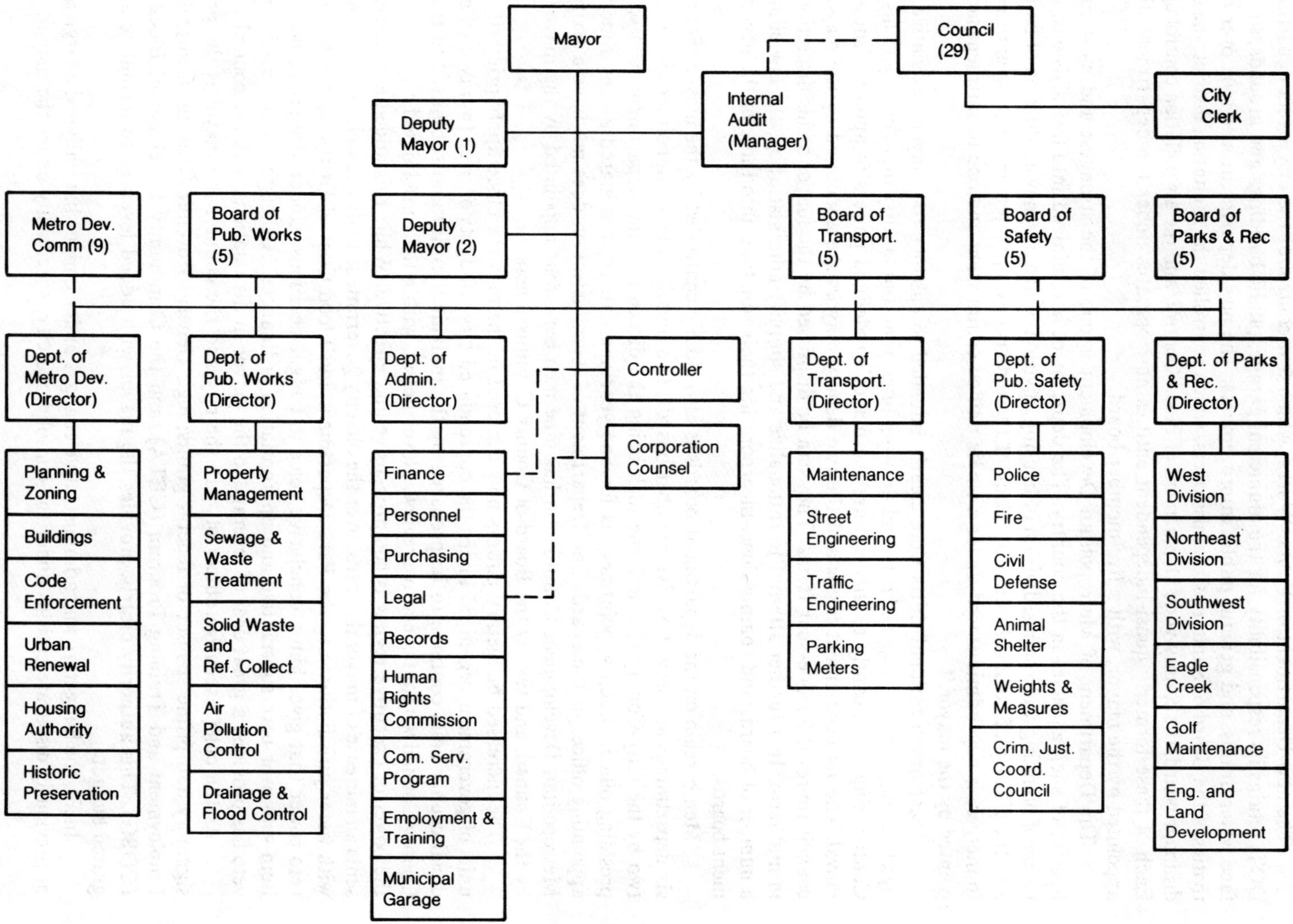

The new Department of Public Works, which lost control of the city street department to DOT, retains its responsibility for the municipal garage, public buildings and grounds, some surface water drains, and general public improvements. The new department also took over the activities of the Board of Sanitary Commissioners, which controlled the sanitation district, the county drainage board, the county-wide Department of Flood Control, and the air pollution control agency. Each of these formerly quasi-independent entities now operates under the department director appointed by the mayor, with a five-member board.

The Department of Metropolitan Development is one of the strongest and most comprehensive of such agencies in the country. The department is organized into five divisions: the division of planning and zoning, division of housing, division of urban renewal, division of buildings, and the division of code enforcement. Each of these divisions, operated as separate entities prior to merger, is now administered under a single unified commission and one department head appointed by the mayor.[10]

These organizational shifts were clearly intended to enhance the mayor's executive power by clarifying areas of responsibility and drawing lines of accountability more closely to his office. Contributing significantly to this end are the mayor's redefined powers of appointment and removal. The six department heads and the two deputy mayors are appointed by the mayor with council approval for one-year terms. They can be dismissed by the mayor at his discretion, even in mid-term. In a further attempt to rationalize and simplify administration, the law eliminated a number of boards and commissions, incorporating their functions into those of the new department boards.

Membership on the department boards is also closely controlled by the mayor. Four of the six departments are served by five-member boards, two members being appointed by the mayor, two by the City-County Council, the fifth being the director of the department who serves as presiding officer. Each appointment is for one year and can be terminated at any time by the appointing officer of the board. The Department of Administration does not have a board. The Metropolitan Development Commission has nine members, four appointed by the mayor, three by the Council, and two by the Board of County Commissioners.

The increased budgetary powers now centered in the mayor's office apply primarily to the units of government organized under the consolidated city. Budgets of over twenty civil and judicial county units continue to be prepared by the individual entity and submitted to the City-County Council without executive review. Nevertheless, within the consolidated city departments the power of executive review is comprehensive and effective. While this added authority represents an increase of mayoral control over the old city government units (as well as over some units with wider jurisdiction; i.e., the Park Department and Flood Control District), it is the mayor's veto power that gives him a conclusive voice in budget decisions. Under Unigov he now has an item veto over both substantive and appropriation ordinances. Although seldom used, the item veto has provided a great deal of leverage to the mayor in his relations with the council.

As the chief executive officer of both the city and the county, the mayor is the principal signatory and prime sponsor of federal grants; e.g., General Revenue Sharing, Comprehensive Employment and Training Program (CETA), and the Community Development Block Grant (CDBG). This authority clearly provides the mayor with added leverage to formulate an integrated budget.

In all, the budgetary and administrative changes under Unigov have aligned a large number of previously disparate entities under the consolidated city, specifically under the mayor.

Despite the substantial administrative changes brought about by the reform, two notable municipal functions, police and fire, were not consolidated under Unigov. These two old line city departments now are organized as special service districts. They are administered by the mayor under the Department of Public Safety but operate with a separate tax base and industrialized policy-making process in council (about which more later). The five service district boundaries are equivalent to the former city limits. Fire service outside of the district is provided by "volunteer" departments in townships, towns, and the excluded cities. Many of these have developed a professional character in recent years, especially since the advent of General Revenue Sharing. Annexation to the fire service district can only be done at the request of a preponderant proportion of taxpayers in the area to be added.

The police service district was initially coterminous with the five service districts. But the police district was expanded in 1970 to take in some areas of the county that contain large industries. These areas are not densely populated but include territory with businesses and industries that have significant assessed property valuation. Outside the police service district, service is provided by the county sheriff, town marshals, and city police forces in the excluded manicipalities. Attempts to consolidate the police and sheriff functions still occur from time to time, but it is doubtful that a merger will occur in the near future. Although the Indianapolis police department has cooperative agreements with the police departments of the excluded cities—a very important one exists with the City of Speedway for the control of traffic on the day that the "Indianapolis 500" race is held—no attempt has been made to merge with any of these departments. There is considerable sentiment in these cities that they already receive police service that is better than that provided by the larger Indianapolis force.[11] It is generally believed that a merger proposal would be greatly opposed by the small cities.

Summary

The unique political and governmental conditions of Indianapolis and Marion County required a reform law tailored especially for local conditions. Unigov does not stand as a model that can be applied in its entirety elsewhere. Interested reformers in other cities will be successful only if they borrow those ideas best suited to the reality of their own situation. What Unigov seems to have done most is to bring national status to Indianapolis and to heighten the reform debate. This is especially true in Indiana where Unigov became an impelling factor in local government reform proposals throughout the ensuring decade.

One of the things that focused attention on Unigov was the fact the General Assembly passed the law without recourse to a public referendum; the first state legislature to do so in the twentieth century. This had the consequence of placing the ultimate burden for local government reform squarely on the General Assembly. Although they quickly tried to lessen the burden by mandating a referendum for Evansville's merger proposal, they had established a precedent for legislative sanctioned municipal reform that would excite reform petitions from local units throughout the 1970's.

Other Urban Reform

From 1905, when the Indiana Municipal code was established, until 1969, comprehensive governmental reform was not widely pursued in Indiana cities. A movement for city manager government ended when Indianapolis' manager system was declared unconstitutional in 1929 and subsequently not tried again. Numerous special service districts were formed during the post World

War II era, always on a piecemeal function-by-function basis. An Interlocal Government Cooperation Act passed in 1957 was seldom used.

Most of the larger cities had made modest attempts at reform prior to Unigov, but activity has increased considerably as a consequence of Indianapolis' success. The typical intercity rivalry for new industries, federal dollars, state programs, or increased population is intensified in Indiana by the widely held belief that Indianapolis consistently benefits more from state legislation than any other city. This attitude was reinforced when Indianapolis gained national prominence in the 1970's. Stimulated by Indianapolis' reorganization, Chambers of Commerce, Leagues of Women Voters, legislative study committees, and other civic groups increased their efforts for reform, and a number of spirited campaigns advanced as far as the legislature. A description and analysis of these events is the subject of the following.

Evansville: Vandigov

A reorganization effort in Evansville-Vanderburgh County was the most notable attempt to duplicate the Unigov performance in Indiana. Originally proposed by Evansville Future Inc., a citizens civic study group, the merger idea received legislative support when the General Assembly authorized a local government study committee in 1969, the same year Unigov was passed.

The study committee's merger proposal was endorsed by Democratic Mayor Frank McDonald and submitted to the 1971 General Assembly. It failed to pass, but a new, more broadly based study committee was authorized to prepare a revised bill which was introduced in 1972. The 1972 bill was drafted by newly elected Republican Mayor Russell Lloyd's City Attorney, John C. Cox, who was a member of both study committees. This bill died in a close vote in house committee where it was felt that the powers of the new chief executive office was too great.

Following this 1972 legislative setback, Mayor Lloyd and attorney Cox sought to achieve a number of functional mergers by means of city and county ordinances that would combine the departments of purchasing, traffic engineering, building control, weights and measures, city and county garages, and property maintenance. Had ordinances merging all six functions passed both the city and county councils, a fairly comprehensive merger of functions would have been obtained. As it happened, however, only purchasing was consolidated, and the reformers turned once again to the Vandigov idea.

The third version of the Vandigov bill was submitted to the 1973 General Assembly; the proposed mayor's powers were lessened and those of the council strengthened, and the length of the bill was reduced from 90 to 40 pages. Thus revised, the bill passed the 1973 General Assembly. Final approval then hinged on the outcome of a referendum, required by the statute, to be held at the general election in November, 1974.

Although the proponents of Vandigov were better organized and better funded than the opponents and enjoyed the support of the Chamber of Commerce, League of Women Voters, the city administration and both major newspapers as well as other media, the proposal lost overwhelmingly by a 36,971 to 13,177 vote. The new government proposal was defeated most conclusively in the areas outside the city where it lost by a 10 to 1 margin, but it also lost in the city, failing to carry in a single ward.

The Vandigov debate was substantially influenced by the Indianapolis experience. Although the merger idea was formulated at least ten years prior to Unigov, the actual merger campaign spanned the five years immediately following Unigov's passage. Many of the Unigov strategies were used. The form of government, with adjustments for the political realities of Evansville-Vanderburgh County, was nearly identical to Unigov. Evansville's campaign to secure citizen support was intensified by the addition of a referendum to be sure, but many of the same techniques were employed. Evansville's lobbying program, closely patterned after Mayor Lugar's, was largely responsible for the bill's passage in the General Assembly. The lesson is clear, however, that while the reform effort benefited from Unigov as a forerunner, it also inherited a share of its legacy. Consolidation opponents across the state, feeling they had been caught unaware in 1969 through the passage of Unigov without a referendum, were now vigilant. They would undoubtedly try to add a referendum requirement to any future consolidation bills. Local officials in Indiana are aware of the fate of referendums generally. Accordingly, other local reform measures have been much less comprehensive than either Unigov or Vandigov.

Less Comprehensive Reform Elsewhere

While the merger debate continued in other Indiana cities, no further city-county consolidation bills have materialized and none are expected. Local governments are presently resigned to seek statewide reforms such as home rule or tax reform and to restrict local reform bills to incremental changes in those areas which are clearly most troublesome.

Only St. Joseph County and South Bend (the St. Joseph county seat) have made substantial changes since Unigov. The new government established in South Bend is largely a realignment of existing governmental entities into a cabinet of six major departments, each one directly responsible to the mayor. South Bend's governmental arrangement follows closely the administrative restructuring which accompanied aspects of Unigov. The mayor's appointment and removal powers were increased; heretofore quasi-independent agencies were made more accountable to department heads and thus to the mayor; and budget lines of control were drawn more closely to the mayor's office. The 1981 home rule statute has now made the South Bend model available to all cities who choose to adopt it. Interestingly, Evansville was the first city to do so.

The St. Joseph County reform bill was two-fold. First, new electoral districts were formed wherein all nine members of the county council and the three county commissioners are elected in single member districts. Second, while the three-member commission was retained, its powers were substantially reduced and transferred to the county council, whose legislative powers were formerly limited to taxation and financial matters. With these changes the county governmental arrangement now more closely resembles an executive-legislative system of checks and balances. The system of electing council members by districts has had the intended result of lessening the traditionally rural dominance of its membership and agenda. The urban interest is now directly represented by three districts in South Bend, one district in the neighboring city of Mishawaka, and a fifth district shared by the two cities. Again, 1981 Home Rule legislation made it possible for all counties to adopt the St. Joseph County model.

The Reform Debates

Although the South Bend-St. Joseph County reform debates were parallel in time and shared overlapping memberships, the city and county each steered separate and decidedly different courses to reform.

The county reform process was more overtly organized, included a considerably greater amount of citizen involvement, and extended over a longer time than did the city's debate.[12] The debate for county reform began with the appointment of a St. Joseph County Government Committee to study the metropolitan problem. The Committee's first completed report, submitted to the 1971 General Assembly session, had, in addition to the above mentioned reforms, a provision to do away with the county commissioners who were to be replaced by a single executive. It was essentially the controversy related to this issue that caused the state legislators to add a referendum requirement to the enabling act. The referendum for adoption held during the 1972 fall general election was defeated by a decisive margin. Shortly after the defeat, a smaller group of the original study committee submitted a new bill to the General Assembly. This bill, which retained the county commissioners' offices, was passed without a referendum requirement and became law by direct state legislative statute action.

The city's reform debate developed in the midst of the Study Committee's deliberations when in 1972 the Democratic candidate for mayor, Jerry Miller (a former county commissioner and study committee member) campaigned on the issue of bringing a cabinet form of administration to the mayor's office. Shortly after Miller's election, the Democratic St. Joseph County legislative delegation presented the cabinet government bill to the General Assembly as a voter approved reform that also had unanimous delegation support. Following its custom of generally acceding to the wishes of a united local delegation, the legislature passed the bill virtually without opposition, 80 to 3 in the House and 39 to 2 in the Senate. Support for the bill was so broad that it was not necessary to remind the Republican legislative majority that it was two St. Joseph County Democrats who provided two critical senate votes for Unigov three years previously.

Unigov's significance to the South Bend-St. Joseph County reforms was mostly indirect. Unified government along the lines of the Indianapolis experience was discussed in the early committee deliberations. But this provided keen opposition among certain local elected officials, and their opposition made Unigov appear to be an unattainable objective. The city and county reformers were impressed by the General Assembly's generosity to Indianapolis, however, and this evoked a kind of optimism that they might be accorded the same treatment—albeit for their own reform plan.

Home Rule

In addition to individual reform efforts in particular cities, through the customary channel of a general state statute devised for a particular place, there has been increased attention in the post-Unigov years to the process of extending more home rule for Indiana cities and towns generally.

Home rule is a comprehensive and complex matter, and much more could be said about its legal, philosophical and political meaning than can be covered in this short space. Charles Adrian's concise definition is most appropriate for the present context:

> The power granted to local units of government to frame, adopt and amend charters for their government and to exercise powers of local self-government, subject to the Constitution and general laws of the state.[13]

Two fundamental questions related to the provision of home rule authority are: (1) Is the grant of home rule authority based on constitutional amendment or on statute authority? and (2) Does the home rule law provide structural or functional authority to local governments, or a combination of both?

Home rule is not a new idea in Indiana. Sixteen resolutions for home rule were presented to the General Assembly in the years 1937 to 1969, and two separate attempts to provide constitutional home rule came close to passage in 1943 and 1953. However, only recently has some measurable success been achieved. This came about initially through the efforts of a Constitutional Revision Commission in the late 1960's which recommended that the General Assembly change course and seek home rule through statute provisions rather than by constitutional amendment.

Constitutional home rule was traditionally preferred over statute home rule because it was thought that it provided more permanence to the law and represented a greater authority that could be more readily upheld by the courts. This approach, however, often proves to be politically unattainable. Although it is more easily adopted, statutory home rule offers no guarantee against future legislative acts that might rescind the granted authority.

Home Rule Reform in Indiana—the 1970's

In the case of Indiana, legislators rightfully felt that they had exhausted attempts to pursue home rule through the state's rigorously prescribed constitutional amendment process.[14] Thus, in effect by default, the General Assembly began to seek statutory home rule as the only practical solution to the home rule dilemma. This, as we shall see, had drawbacks too, but there has been an obvious and ambitious attempt to provide home rule to local governments in the 1970's.

In 1971 a Powers of Cities Act was passed which granted cities enumerated powers in more than fifty areas of municipal authority. Broad residual powers were also granted by the statute, providing cities comprehensive authority to perform all municipal functions not prohibited by the Indiana or United States Constitution or by statute law. The intent of the General Assembly was stated clearly that any questions of the interpretation of the Act "shall be construed liberally in favor of such cities." Similar powers were granted to counties in the Powers of Counties Act in 1975, and to civil towns in 1977. In some ways the 1981 and 1982 legislation was simply an extension of the earlier statutes.

Despite these grants of immediate (the grant of authority is self-executing) comprehensive home rule power, local governments in Indiana had, at least prior to 1981, generally failed to exercise any new functional authority. The reasons for the general failure to implement the older statutes vary, of course, from city to city, but hinge on four fundamental issues: confusing state law, inconsistency in the courts, lack of sufficient local revenue sources, and a reluctance of state agencies to fully subscribe to the principle of home rule.

Confusing State Law

Home rule authority is designed to be exercised within the labyrinth of existent state law. The Indiana code relating to municipalities is voluminous, cumbersome, and in many cases obsolete. Most mayors are admittedly confused as to the scope and magnitude of their authority. They do know that after more than a century of legislation there are few remaining subjects that have not been covered by statute at one time or another, thus seriously restricting the latitude of local officials to act.

Court Inconsistency

Home rule is, in the final analysis, what the courts say it is, and on this the courts have been inconsistent. Diverse and conflicting opinions in different courts in the early 1970's have served to inhibit the exercise of home rule power in most municipalities. It should be added that the state Attorney General's office has been more consistent or clear in its opinions as to the extent of home rule than have the courts.

Local Revenue Sources

One clear aspect of the law governing local government authority is that the state legislature still ranks supreme regarding local taxation and expenditure. This is an obvious practical limitation on the local unit that decides to undertake a new program within legal home rule guidelines but lacks the revenue to fund it.

In 1973 the legislature and the governor passed a property tax relief bill that closely prescribes the amount of revenue local governments can raise through property taxes, the major source of locally derived income for local governments. Although a state reimbursement fund was established to compensate cities for "lost" property tax revenue, no new viable alternatives for new public expenditures have been forthcoming. The vagaries of the property tax freeze bill are discussed in a following section. The point here is that despite its legislation for legal home rule, the General Assembly has in effect gone the other way on the issue of revenue home rule.

State Agencies

The fourth hindrance to the implementation of home rule is the accumulative impact of the regulations issued by state agencies, boards and commissions. Because of the immediacy and ambiguity of rulings by such agencies as the State Board of Health, the Stream Pollution Control Board, the State Highway Commission, Department of Public Welfare, and the State Auditor, local officials are regularly beset by regulations which clearly limit their administration of local affairs. There has been no clear indication that these powerful state agencies are willing to surrender some of their authority to the local units. It would require comprehensive legislation and perhaps a constitutional amendment in order to reduce state agency control over local affairs—assuming, of course, the legislature chose to do so.

The Local Government Study Commission

Because of the constraints that these four conditions placed on local officials, the 1978 General Assembly authorized the formation of a Local Government Study Commission to examine the existing home rule legislation and to make recommendations for its improvement. Following a year-and-a-half study, the Local Government Study Commission presented its first-round home rule legislation to the 1980 General Assembly. The Commission did not recommend a broad or new extension of home rule authority. Satisfied that this had already been accomplished, they concentrated instead on fortifying the intent of the law and simplifying the code so that it will be clear in letter and spirit to administrators and judges alike. The Study Commission researched and sponsored major home rule legislation that was passed in two successive legislative sessions in 1980 and 1981. Under the sunset law limits of its term, the Local Government Study Commission ended its work on June 30, 1981, having completed the most comprehensive home rule legislation in the history of municipal law in the state. The following discussion focuses on the home rule legislation of these two General Assembly sessions.

Home Rule Legislation, 1980

In all, the 1980 General Assembly passed fourteen Commission sponsored bills, each relating in varying degree to home rule or to the Commission itself. Four of these bills constitute the essential elements of the legislative package. The thrust of the legislation is found in House Enrolled Act (HEA) 1001[15] which restates the home rule principle, recodifies the existing home rule law under a new title of the Indiana Code, and includes a list of general powers for local units. Placing the provisions of three separate home rule laws under one title (Indiana Code 36-1-3) and making a general statement of the powers granted to local units will simplify matters for heretofore confused and hesitant mayors and commissioners. The Commission was cautious not to add new authority to the statutes; their singular aim was to make the existing law more usable. The three companion bills to HEA 1001 are also directed toward the same end.

HEA 1002, for example, is a recodification of previously diverse laws concerning the structure of cities, counties, townships, and towns under title 36. The purpose of HEA 1003 is to relocate statutes that do not fit under the newly created local government title to other relevant parts of the code. The last of the four bills, HEA 1004, was used to weed out laws that are obsolete and thereby disruptive to the implementation of home rule. In total the act deleted 96 laws, or parts of laws, dating back to 1852.

The changes made by Local Government Study Commissions' 1980 home rule legislative package were modest. The recodification of the law under one title and the removal of irrelevant statutes responded directly to three of the four major criticisms of previous home rule bills. The powers of local officials were immediately affected by the new code. While their authority was not increased, local administrators were given a clearer understanding of the scope and magnitude of it. The restructured law also gave direction to the courts in terms of establishing greater consistency in their home rule decisions. In this regard, the removal of a large number of obsolete laws will also be of considerable assistance to the courts. The least predictable outcome is the role state administrative agencies will take in accommodating local attempts at home rule. The authority of these agencies has been accumulating for a long time, and the legislation explicitly omits any mention of changing existing relationships between state and local entities. There was no attempt in the legislation to grant additional revenue raising authority to local units.

One of the fundamental conditions tied to the passage of the 1980 legislation was that the effective implementation date be set back sixteen months to September 1, 1981. This delay gave administrators time to familiarize themselves with the new law and allowed for time to amend it if needed. The most significant reason, however, was that it provided the Local Government Study Commission added time to thoroughly research and draft legislation authorizing alternate sources of revenue to local governments and to provide charter making powers. These and other home rule measures were reserved for the second part of the two-phase Study Commission strategy.

Home Rule Legislation—1981

As intended, the Local Government Study Commission presented the second round of its home rule legislative package to the 1981 General Assembly. A large portion of the 1981 home rule legislation was a continuance of the 1980 effort to recodify local government statutes and to weed out "125 years' growth of statutory underbrush in the local government area."[16] As to the provision of new substantive or charter home rule authority, the final results were mixed. Although the Commission failed to secure passage for its charter home rule bill, and a local government revenue bill did not emerge from its own deliberations, numerous, less comprehensive bills (eighteen in all) were passed which did extend additional important powers to local governments.

The intent of the comprehensive home rule bill was to extend the legislative authority of local councils and boards and to streamline the executive branch of local government focusing administrative authority in the executive office of mayors. Specifically, the bill was drafted to provide cities, towns, and counties the authority to adopt a new form of government, such as the council manager for cities and towns, or the single executive to replace the three-member commission form of county government. These measures, which invariably evoke political opposition from incumbent office holders, were accompanied by a provision allowing for the consolidation of local governments through a local option referendum process. The latter provision raised the spectre of Unigov among the state's traditional opponents of consolidated government. Unfortunately for the proponents of charter home rule, the combined opposition of these groups effectively kept the bill penned up in the Cities and Towns Committee in the House where it died.

Timing was also a key element in determining the fate of the bill. The fact that the bill was quite large and was introduced late in the legislative session placed it in an unfavorable position on the legislators' agenda. Legislators were beginning to reach their tolerance level on the number of home rule bills they would consider:

> Some of the members were growing weary of home rule legislation. We had been inundated with home rule legislation in both 1980 and 1981, and many legislators were beginning to feel that we had gone far enough, for awhile, in granting local governments home rule.[17]

The Commission members showed good judgment in tempering their request for charter home rule. For, in so doing, they avoided the growing possibility that they would jeopardize the prospects for passage of their other bills that were already further along in the legislative process. Thus, through their insight and willingness to compromise, the Commission was subsequently able to claim passage for eighteen separate but related home rule bills that, in piecemeal fashion, accomplished much of what they had originally hoped to do.

The basic home rule philosophy and general substance of the 1981 legislation is found in House Enrolled Act 1001. The introduction to this first bill to be in the 1981 session reads as follows:

> The bill broadens the legislative authority and executive flexibility of local, elected officials in several areas, such as administrative structures and appointments.[18]

The resultant changes in the law provided for the "conversion" of 45 state statute provisions to local legislative authorities.[19] Local legislative bodies were also freed in their deliberations from restrictions eminating from existing permissive legislation. Several sections of HEA 1001 (notably sections 22, 23 and 24) are written to provide added appointive powers to mayors, and to give them the initiate ordinance for the creation and reorganization of new departments for council approval.

The mayors' increased appointive powers were particularly significant in that they now have the authority to name the department heads of a number of heretofore quasi-independent agencies, such as the Park Board and Redevelopment Commission. These kinds of appointments added to his reorganization authority (held jointly with council) provided mayors with the option of creating a more unified administration through the adoption of a cabinet form of government.

Mayor Michael D. Vandeveer of the city of Evansville was the first mayor to seize the opportunity provided by the new legislation and submitted a reorganization ordinance to the City Council in June, 1981. Mayor Vandeveer's proposal was specifically based on the 1981 home rule legislation:

> Section 23, IC 36-4-9-4 of House Enrolled Act 1001 states that, "the city legislative body shall, by ordinance passed upon the recommendation of the city executive, establish the executive departments that it considers necessary to efficiently perform the administrative functions required to fulfill the needs of the city's citizens."[20]

The Evansville proposal establishes six major executive departments combining formerly independent entities as divisions in the new departments. The directors of the new departments plus the corporate council and the deputy mayor constitute the mayor's Executive Committee (cabinet). The function of the cabinet is to "serve as the official conduit for policy and decisions from mayor to department heads to divisions."[21] One of the more notable realignments was the incorporation of the economic development and redevelopment functions into the Department of Planning and Development. In addition to unifying these critical functions more closely under the mayor's direction, the proposal was expected to save the city a substantial amount of money. It was projected that $37,804 would be saved through elimination of the merged department's directorships.[22] Through the creation of a secretarial pool, $25,000 would be saved, and $62,000 would be saved through the establishment of a city-wide motor pool.

In sum, Evansville utilized the 1981 Home Rule legislation to unify its governmental structure, create administrative savings, and to balance responsibility with authority in the mayor's office.

Other provisions of the 1981 acts were devoted to revising the state planning and development law and public safety statutes, especially as the latter relates to the establishment and organization of police merit boards. It also allows a mayor to go outside the system to recruit a police or fire chief.

An important Senate act (SEA 461) reduced the number of classes of Indiana cities from five to three by moving all cities previously classified as fourth or fifth class cities (populations of less than 20,000 and more than 1,500) into the third class. This will provide smaller cities with organizational and administrative opportunities not available to them before, and will greatly simplify the state's municipal code.

Before concluding its work and in an admittedly ironic departure from their home rule philosophy, the Local Government Study Commission requested that the General Assembly require that all local governments codify or recodify their ordinances. The Commission was aware of the burden this mandate placed on local governments, but they were aware that the nearly dysfunctional state of local ordinance codes in many cities and towns required codification before they could effectively operate under the new state law. The General Assembly agreed with the Commission's reasoning on this point, and local governments are now in the process of systematically rewriting their ordinances in a code that will reflect the changes of the 1980–1981 home rule legislation.

Conclusion

There is little question that the legislation of the two General Assembly sessions at the beginning of the 1980 decade were successful in granting important new powers to local governments in Indiana. Some critics argue persuasively that more should have been done, and that the Commission should have been extended beyond its sunset limits. But these arguments should not detract from the importance of what was in fact done. Nor should they ignore the political reality of how much could be realistically passed in a heavily burdened legislature.

The intent of the General Assembly to grant significant home rule authority has now been clearly established in a totally new section of the state statutes dealing entirely with local government affairs. Extensive statutory power has been converted to local ordinance authority, and local governments may now exercise extensive local determination in choosing their own form of government. These and the other listed provisions combine to provide extensive home rule powers never before exercised in Indiana.

No doubt the home rule debate will continue throughout the last two decades of this century. The 1982 legislative session debated a number of local government revenue options, and new federalism initiatives will add a new dimension to it. Nevertheless the work of the 1980 and 1981 General Assemblies will stand for many years as the hallmark of a home rule commitment in Indiana.

Local Government Finance

In 1973, five years prior to California's celebrated "Proposition 13," the Indiana General Assembly, at the urging of the Governor,[23] made major statute changes intended to bring property tax relief to local governments. Chief among the legislators' concerns were the regressive effects that property taxes had on citizens with fixed incomes and the rapidly escalating tax rates which continually magnified the problem. These problems were especially acute in cities where property values were declining while service needs were growing. The thrust of the legislators' act was twofold: (1) it provided for specific controls on the property tax, i.e., a property tax freeze, and (2) it made other revenue sources available to local governments.[24]

The Property Tax Freeze

The central feature of the property tax controls was to place restrictions, or to freeze, the amount of revenue which the property tax can raise. The basic implementation guidelines for the freeze were spelled out in the 1973 and 1977 sessions of the General Assembly.

Both of these legislatures placed restrictions on the amount of revenue which the property tax can raise. After 1973, and prior to the action of the 1977 legislature, local units of civil government were required to maintain their tax rate at the 1973 base year level. Local units could raise additional property tax revenue only through new development or a reassessment which would increase the property tax value and the tax levy—the rates remained the same.

The 1977 session of the General Assembly changed the rules. It stated that beginning in 1978, the tax levy of local governments could increase either by the amount which would be raised by the increased assessed valuation or by five percent, whichever was the greater amount. This means that if the assessed valuation of the governmental unit increases by seven percent, the tax levy can increase by seven percent, and the tax rate remains constant. If on the other hand the assessed valuation increases by only three percent and the levy is permitted to increase by five percent, this will cause the final rate to increase. Although these control revisions provided local policy makers with a certain amount of flexibility, the overall impact has been that local governments have been severely restricted in seeking new revenues during the six years of the act. Most increases were tied to new community growth which added to the total assessed value of the taxing district rather than increasing the tax burden on the existent rate payers. Although this benefited heavily taxed home owners, mayors were deeply concerned about declining revenues which could not match spiraling inflationary costs.

To further reduce the property tax burden, the 1973 legislature included a property tax replacement fund provision in the tax freeze bill. Funded by an added two percent on the state sales tax, the state now pays 20 percent of the local rate payers' tax bill. The individual property owner is still presented with a bill for the full tax levy on his property. This bill is then reduced by 20 percent and the owner pays the remainder. The state then reimburses the local taxing unit for the accumulated difference between the amount billed by the taxing district and the amount paid by the aggregate rate payers.

The Local Option Tax

In addition to the property tax controls and relief fund it established, the Indiana General Assembly, for the first time, gave counties the right to enact a local income tax. According to the 1973 act, the proceeds from this tax (at a rate of 1/2 percent, 3/4 percent or 1 percent) is distributed among the governmental units in the county and used either as spending money (in addition to the property tax) or as further property tax relief. Actions of the 1977 Indiana General

Assembly, however, made the local option tax primarily property tax relief and did not permit it to provide additional spending money for governmental units. A 1979 Act reversed this and again permits an increase in local option tax money (over 1978's level, or the first year the option tax is adopted by a new county) to be used as new spending money over and above the property taxes raised under the freeze.

To adopt the local option tax, action has to be taken by the County Council. Once the County Council adopts the tax, the proceeds from that tax are distributed to all units of government within the county. The money allocated to school districts is to be used as property tax relief, while the money going to civil units was originally divided between spending money and tax relief funds. As indicated above, actions by the 1977 and 1979 General Assembly changed the use of these funds but did not alter the method of adoption. Cities or other smaller civil units may not adopt the tax themselves. It must be adopted for all the units within a county by the County Council.

It was expected in 1973 that the urban centers in Indiana would be the first to adopt the optional income tax. After all, it was those centers which were complaining most loudly about a general lack of funds. However, after six years, none of the five largest counties has adopted the tax and only 38 of the remaining 87 counties have adopted it. Since then, one county (Kosciusko) has reversed itself and repealed the local option tax. With only a couple of exceptions, the counties which adopted were mainly rural.

The property tax freeze and the local option tax were clearly landmark decisions in local government finance in the 1970's, but the overall impact of the legislation has met with mixed assessments. The property tax freeze with its companion property tax replacement provision has successfully curtailed a previously escalating property tax burden. The local option income tax, on the other hand, has only been adopted by a few counties, and all of these with rural or semi-rural populations. Thus, the counties with the state's largest cities are still left without a viable alternative revenue source. This was clearly not the intent of the original law.

Another unintended consequence of the law is that there has been a shift of the local finance burden away from the local units to the state and federal governments. Future legislatures will certainly be confronted with the dilemma of adding flexibility to the present law or considering an alternate revenue source.

A second major mission assigned by the state legislature to the Local Government Study Commission was to study and make recommendations on the local finance situation in Indiana. This was, or course, very much in keeping with the Commission's charge to prepare home rule legislation for local units. At this writing, reports are being prepared for the 1983 session of the General Assembly that will cover three areas for improving local finance: (1) an improved administration of the current revenue system; (2) use of alternative sources of revenue; (3) a universal state imposed income tax.

Related concerns for improved local administration are state mandated programs which require local governmental units to provide a new service or to advance the level of an established program. These mandates are especially burdensome among Indiana local units where the state has imposed limits on the supply side of the budget while at the same time mandating services on the expenditure side. It is expected that in the future attempts will be made to have the legislature seriously weigh the financial impact of mandated programs. There may also be an attempt to achieve a consolidation of state payments to local finance officers who now receive periodic payments from over twenty-five separate funding sources. Also in the future it is likely that the state will encourage improved cash management techniques for local units and encourage them to invest idle cash balances. These changes would serve to increase local government revenue without placing an increased tax burden on anyone.

Alternative sources of revenue will also need to be considered in the future. Among the three sources of revenue under consideration the innkeeper tax appears to be the most readily adoptable. Not all counties can benefit from a tax which is heavily dependent on tourist trade, but it does seem likely that more than just the current ten utilizing counties could gain substantial revenue from the innkeeper tax. Two other alternate taxes—the occupational income tax and an employment tax—are not likely to receive extensive support. The occupational income tax, intended to tax non-resident employees in the adopting counties, is currently pending a court decision on its constitutionality. The employment tax which levies a 50 cent monthly tax on employees and employers will not generate enough income at twelve dollars per year for each employee to make the tax feasible.

Two additional alternate taxes are the local or the locally imposed supplemental net tax on corporations. Both of these taxes can be "piggy-backed" on existent state tax programs for administrative savings. A major deterrent to the use of these taxes is the open market system of each county's particular economy. Consumers and businesses required to pay these taxes would simply name their activities to another governmental jurisdiction without the taxes.

Because of the particular difficulties of administering each of the above alternative taxes, other approaches will need to be considered. One approach would be to focus on making recommendations to strengthen the utility of the county adjusted gross income tax (CAGIT). One presently discussed method to do this would be to increase the level of new expenditure revenue obtained from the local option income tax. A second proposal would require a statewide imposition of CAGIT at a one percent rate. This option would provide for more local revenue for new expenditures, but less local revenue autonomy.

Whichever alternative or group of alternatives the state legislature adopts, it seems certain that there will not be a major transfer of fiscal authority from the state to local units of government. This lack of fiscal home rule may limit somewhat the broad use of local autonomy promised by previous home rule law. It is a bit ironic that while the legislature was making grants of extensive functional home rule powers and holds forth the promise of a new charter making home rule, it has at the very same time passed increasingly prescribed tax laws for local units.

Summary

The 1970 decade was an unusually active period for municipal reform in Indiana. There had been stirrings for municipal reforms throughout the previous decades of the century and several serious attempts at it. But these attempts were generally thwarted by the machinations of a highly competitive political and social environment, a highly competitive political party system, and a difficult and lengthy constitutional amendment process. Starting with the Indianapolis-Marion County merger of governments in 1970, however, the quest for municipal reform has decidedly changed to a more active and successful mode.

The Indianapolis Unigov contribution to the change occurred in two ways. First the reform itself projected Indianapolis onto the national scene as Indiana's progressive city, and this in turn evoked a sharpened interest among other Indiana cities to advance their own status. Second, the reform process, which was achieved by direct state action through the General Assembly, projected the state into a more active role in municipal reform than was previously the case.

Despite the success of Indianapolis as the focus of an intensified municipal reform debate, there has not been a trend to duplicate the Unigov arrangement. The overwhelming defeat of the Evansville Vandigov referendum proposal disuaded other cities from seeking comprehensive reforms on a similar scale. Subsequent reforms proposed by individual cities have been small piecemeal proposals that are especially designed for each city. Although measured success was achieved through this process, legislators found it to be a wearisome and protracted procedure. The General Assembly's response has been to pass comprehensive legislation for property tax relief and to provide local government home rule.

Two important omissions from the 1970's home rule legislation seem to be indicative of the course that state and local relations will take for some time to come. While the General Assembly has demonstrated its willingness to grant greater substantive and charter autonomy to local units, it did not provide for the necessary local taxing authority that would be required for an extensive exercise of the new powers. Nor did it make any attempt to lessen the role of state agencies that play an important regulatory and administrative role in local affairs. From this it appears that the state's posture is now one of allowing a certain amount of local autonomy—particularly in the area of structural matters—while retaining the balance of authority at the state level. Until the home rule law is more fully implemented, (it did not go into effect until September, 1981) it is impossible to tell exactly where the dividing point of state and local authority will fall. What is more certain is that the state will continue to play an important and growing role in local government activities.

Notes

1. Friggins, Paul. "Without Federal Aid," *National Civic Review,* Vol. LII, No. 5, (May, 1963) p 247.
2. See Maddox, Russell W., and Fuquay, Robert F. *State and Local Government* (4th ed.). New York: D. Van Nostrand Co., (1981) Chapters 6 and 7.
3. *Improving Productivity in State and Local Government,* New York: Committee for Economic Development, (1976) p 68.
4. "Consolidated City-County Governments in the U.S. . . .," *The American County,* (February, 1972) p 14.
5. Now senior United States Senator from Indiana.
6. Lugar, Richard G. Speech to the Robert A. Taft Institute of Government, Waldorf-Astoria Hotel, New York, May 21, 1970.
7. Data was gathered from *The Indianapolis Star,* March 10 to March 22, 1968.
8. *Northeast Topics.* (February, 1969) p 1.
9. For a detailed description of the departments under Unigov see: *Unigov and You—Cooperative Government in Indianapolis and Marion County,* Judith M. Davis, SPEA, Division of Public Service, Indiana University, Bloomington.
10. The department head chosen by the commission under the original Unigov act was changed to a mayoral appointee in a 1972 amendment.
11. Ostrom, Elinor, Parks, Roger B., and Whitaker, Gordon P. "Do We Really Want to Consolidate Urban Police Forces? A Reappraisal of Some Old Assertions," *Public Administration Review,* Vol. 33, No. 5, (September-October, 1973) pp 423–432.
12. A concise analysis of St. Joseph County's reform debate was completed by Walton R. Collins as an MPA thesis at the School of Public and Environmental Affairs, South Bend, Indiana.
13. Adrian, Charles R. *State and Local Governments.* New York: McGraw-Hill Book Company, (1972) p 117.
14. As has been noted elsewhere, the constitutional amendment procedure in Indiana requires that a proposed amendment be passed in the same form by two successive legislative sessions before it is submitted to a referendum vote and finally to the governor for signature into law.
15. House Enrolled Act No. 1001, Second Regular Session, 101st General Assembly, p 4.
16. *Understanding the New Local Government Law.* Indianapolis, Indiana: Local Government Study Commission, (1981), Appendix V, p 6.

17. Representative Mitchell v. Harper, Member of the House Cities and Towns Committee, personal interview, Fort Wayne, Indiana, March 3, 1982.
18. Understanding the New Law, Appendix V, p 1.
19. HEA 1001, Section 4.
20. "Proposed Reorganization Outline," unpublished photocopy, City of Evansville (Evansville, Indiana), June 1, 1981, p 1.
21. *Ibid.*, Attachment B & C.
22. *Ibid.*
23. Governor Otis Bowen, M.D., a strong proponent of property tax relief, provided strong leadership in getting the 1973 legislation passed. The property tax relief bills are commonly referred to as the "Bowen Tax Package."
24. See Owen, C. James, and Hall, Dean, R. "Financing Local Government in Indiana," Fort Wayne, Indiana: Taxpayers Research Association, (1980) for further explanations of local government finance in Indiana.

8

Indiana in the Eighties: The Politics and Policy of Retrenching and Reneging

Leonard M. Fleck
Indiana University at South Bend
with research assistance from LISA GILMAN

An old industrial plant in Northern Indiana
Courtesy of the South Bend Tribune

Michael Harrington has contended that America is entering a "decade of decision." "For better or for worse, the 1980's will change our lives at least as profoundly as the 1930's."[1] The decisions that we will have to make are not merely political or economic decisions. Rather, they are decisions that are philosophic and moral in character; and hence, they are truly profound decisions that will affect virtually every institution in our society. There is a two-part philosophic question that we are being asked to reconsider. First, what is the legitimate or appropriate domain of government decision making in our society? That is, what sorts of social issues should be thought of as requiring a resolution in terms of public policy as opposed to private social decision making? Second, assuming that a particular issue requires a response in terms of a formal public policy, what level of government should be responsible for articulating that policy?

With respect to this latter question, the working assumption over the past fifty years has been that the major social problems of our society are best resolved through policy initiatives at the federal level. The practical result of this has been that the states in some way have been reduced to administrative units of the federal government. In the minds of conservative political theorists and many state officials, this represents a disturbing and potentially disastrous development within our political system. From their point of view, the political autonomy of the states is being usurped by the federal government, for the individual states are allowed to establish their own policy agendas and chart their own political course only in a rather minimal sense. The Reagan Administration, under the banner of "The New Federalism," has promised to reverse this political trend. More specifically, in the early part of 1982 President Reagan proposed transferring some 43 social programs administered by the federal government to the states. Under his proposal, the states would ultimately have the right to maintain, modify, or abolish those programs as they see fit.

A critical part of the President's proposal is that, over time, virtually all federal support for these programs would be eliminated, and the existing requirements on how the states administer the programs would be significantly altered. This is a serious presidential proposal that will dramatically redirect the policymaking process in this country. Even if it is not completely implemented, it deserves serious critical scrutiny by public policy analysts. In the past policy analysts have focused their attention on public policies and the policymaking process at the federal level. Relatively little attention has been given to the policymaking process at the state level. Under the circumstances, it would be presumptuous to assume that policymaking at the state level is just policymaking at the federal level "writ small." On the contrary, studies that have been done suggest that there are significant differences in the policymaking processes at these two levels, and hence, that the policies that are a product of these processes will be affected in various ways, depending upon whether they are state or federal policies.[2] The details of these differences will be explored below. For now what this proposed shift in policymaking responsibilities clearly warrants is closer analysis of public policy and the policymaking process at the state level. In particular, we shall want to examine what the new federalism means for the public policy agenda in the state of Indiana.

There will be two major parts to this essay. In the first part, we shall examine the larger national framework which shapes in substantial ways policy options within the state of Indiana. For the most part, that larger national framework will be defined in terms of economic problems, for those are clearly the problems that top this nation's policy agenda. They also seem to be the problems that will top the policy agenda of the state of Indiana for the last two decades of this century. Hence, in the second part of this essay we will explore those policies that have been suggested or enacted and that are intended to foster economic development in the State. We shall also want to explore how Indiana's social welfare policy is affected by its economic policies. This will be an especially critical area because of proposed changes at the federal level; specifically, the President's proposal, under the rubric of "The New Federalism," that 43 social programs, now administered by the federal government, be transferred back to state control. The fear is that in states such as Indiana, which are financially hard pressed, many of these social programs will be abandoned in order to make more resources available for economic development. That is, we will be tempted to renege on our commitment to the poor and to those who are in other ways disadvantaged and unable to fend for themselves economically.

An Economic Dilemma for the Eighties: Equity or Prosperity

There is a sense in which economic problems have always been with us—we never have all the resources that we need in order to do all that we would like to do. But there is another sense in which economic problems have not occupied the forefront of our national policy attention in the way they do today since the time of the Great Depression. For most of the past twenty years, economic prosperity has been a presupposition of, not a problem for, the policymaking process in this nation. How else could we have afforded the massive development of federal social welfare programs? How else could we have afforded to debate—seriously—in 1972 the question of whether continued economic growth was really desirable, and whether we would not really be better off in a no-growth economy?[3] How else could we justify imposing a property tax freeze in 1972 in the state of Indiana, given the fiscal strain that cities in Indiana labor under in the 1980's? Obviously, prosperity was our presupposition.

Zero-Sum Economics

By the beginning of the 1970's we believed that we had locked into permanent prosperity. That expectation became part of the American psyche. It had achieved the status of a deeply held religious belief that shaped our whole world view. Thus, the current economic ennui, unaffected by the enthusiasm of the supply-side Gospel revivalists, encourages the deep suspicion in our collective consciousness that God is dead, that the world is absurd, and that someone has robbed the national piggybank, leaving $1 trillion in IOU's. Perhaps all of this could be explained by our collective commitment to the Old Testament belief that salvation is by spending alone. If so, then all those IOU's are as good as grace. Then again, there seems to be a new faith about, a New Testament, according to which salvation is by saving alone. If so, then all those IOU's are as shameful as sin. Hence, we must now make amends for those sins through economic sacrifice.

Some readers might be bothered by the religious analogies. Economics is supposed to be a science. It is supposed to yield knowledge. Yet that is precisely what encouraged the false belief that prosperity had become a permanent feature of the American economy. At best, our knowledge of economics is imperfect, as it must be; for it is a science that is about us and about our values, not about things in the world.[4] If economics were anything other than a very imperfect science, then we would expect economists to be among the shrewdest and richest investors in the world.

What does all this mean so far as our national economic problems are concerned? It means that we must choose among alternative economic policies, and that we must make these choices under conditions of risk and uncertainty. To say that we "must choose" is to say that the God of the economists is dead, that there is no "invisible hand" providentially guiding the decisions of the market. There are only the human, all too human hands of our economic brethren attempting to manipulate the mechanisms of the market.

Ours is a managed economy. The fundamental political significance of this for understanding the economic problems of this decade is something that not enough economists have reflected on. Lester Thurow, the author of *The Zero-Sum Society,* would be one exception to this statement. According to Thurow, our economy contains a substantial zero-sum element. A zero-sum game is any game where the losses exactly equal the winnings. Poker is a zero-sum game. In such a game there are clear winners and clear losers. The losers in poker can accept their fate with some degree of equanimity, for they can reason that they "did not get the cards," or that they played their cards poorly, or that they exercised poor judgment in their betting. They can accept their fate because the rules of poker are fixed, the rules of poker do not favor any one player, and the deck is not rigged. But, as noted earlier, our is a managed economy. It is managed by changing the rules of the game, that is, our economic policies.

The rules of the economic game are always undergoing change in response to events in the world. The purpose of the rule changes is not to augment the economic welfare of any individual in the game but to improve the economic welfare of the nation as a whole. Of course, there is no such thing as "the nation as a whole." There are only individuals and groups of individuals who will benefit from these improvements in economic welfare. During prosperous times, such as the 1960's and early 1970's, it does not matter politically that some groups benefit more than others, for everyone feels better off economically, and hence, satisfaction is fairly widespread. But as our rate of economic growth flattens out, we come closer to being in a zero-sum game. It becomes clear that in order to just maintain our current level of economic welfare we will have to make substantial changes in our economic policies which will have the effect now of creating clear winners and clear losers. Thus, if we believe that inflation is our most serious economic problem, then we adopt monetary policies that will have the effect of raising unemployment. Those groups that were the victims of inflation, e.g., savers and investors, become the beneficiaries of this policy while those groups that were able to protect themselves from inflation, e.g., organized labor with cost-of-living clauses in their contracts, now suffer the losses of that new policy in the form of high unemployment in their ranks and downward pressure on their wage demands, e.g., contract concessions to Ford Motor Company by the UAW in Feburary 1982.

It must be emphasized that it was not logically or economically *necessary* that the reduction of inflation be our prime economic target. We could just as easily and justifiably have chosen to reduce unemployment and adopted a different set of economic policies.[5] That would have produced a different set of winners and losers. The point is that political *choices* are being made here. Winnings and losses are being distributed not by an impersonal economic process, but by the managers/policymakers of our political and economic system. Few people are motivated to accept large economic losses voluntarily for the general welfare. No one is motivated to accept large economic losses when the general welfare can be maintained or enhanced by some means other than one that imposes economic losses on them. Yet, that is the situation in which we find ourselves. We are not without solutions to our economic problems. If anything, we have mutliple solutions, but all of them involve having to allocate losses to various groups, most of whom are at least powerful enough to exercise a veto. According to Thurow, our dilemma is this: our political system is very bad at solving problems that require allocating losses. "When there are large economic losses to be allocated, our political process is paralyzed. And with political paralysis comes economic paralysis."[6] This seems to be precisely where we find ourselves today. A few quick examples will illustrate the point.

Many economists today would contend that America is confronted with a productivity crisis, that that is the real source of our current economic malaise. We are too much a consumption-oriented society. We have failed to make the necessary investments for assuring a prosperous economy in the future. Thus, Americans have an investment level that is less than 10% of the Gross National Product, while the Germans invest at a 15% level and the Japanese at a 20% level. Thurow suggests that if more investment will improve productivity, then we ought to invest another 5% of our GNP, or about $150 billion. But where will that money come from? Would we want a 20% increase in our taxes? That is what that figure represents as a percentage of the federal budget. We could eliminate all welfare payments (AFDC). That would generate 1.2% of the needed 5%.[7] Who will pay the rest? Who will accept those losses in terms of a standard of living for the good of the nation as a whole?

Another example. We all want cheap, plentiful, secure energy. Nuclear energy might be our best source of such energy. But since the Three Mile Island (Pennsylvania) nuclear accident that occurred, there is a widespread perception that nuclear energy is not as safe as it was once thought to be. Consequently, no one wants a nuclear reactor in or near their city, though they do want the benefits of a reactor sited elsewhere. Natural gas is another excellent energy source. It is cheap now because its price is regulated. But an excessively low price discourages new exploration. If natural gas is deregulated, then its price to the consumer will rise substantially. It could mean heating bills of $2,000 per year or more for many consumers. If everyone had to heat their homes, then there might be some rough equity in the distribution of the economic pain. But in fact gas consumers in the Northeast and Midwest sections of the country would bear the brunt of those costs. In the meantime, those companies and their investors would like to increase their profits significantly, and those states that are rich in natural gas, primarily states in the South and West, would see their economies prosper. The cycle would continue in that the industries in these states would, no doubt, become more competitive because their energy costs would be significantly lower; and that in turn would make it even more attractive for energy-intensive industries in the North to consider relocating in the South and West. Such a relocation might make those industries more competitive in the world market, and thereby improve the economic welfare of the nation as a whole. But, why should the North and the Midwest, why should Indiana, bear those economic losses for the good of the nation?

The Reagan Administration in 1982 proposed spending about $1.5 trillion on national defense between 1982 and 1987. That represents annual increases of about 15% in real terms in defense spending. In a zero-sum economy that means that some other set of socio-economic groups will have to sustain losses of an equal magnitude. Since the imposition of losses of that magnitude represents a political impossibility, the Reagan Administration has chosen to accept deficits that will approach $½ trillion during that period. But even that imposes economic losses in a differential way, for deficits of that magnitude tend to push up interest rates, thereby imposing the heaviest costs on certain industries (housing and auto) which are very sensitive to interest rates and which are heavily concentrated in the Northeast and Midwest. Hence, there is both a regional and an industry-specific bias to these economic losses.

To further complicate matters, the decision was made in the late 1940's and early 1950's to encourage the establishment of defense industries in the South and West. This was a deliberate effort on the part of the federal government to contribute to the industrial development of those regional economies. At the time, there was little reason to resist that move since it did not represent a threat to any other regional economies. But clearly that is not the case at present. From the perspective of states in the Northeast and Midwest, the proposed defense budgets represent a pouring of hundreds of billions of tax dollars generated in the Northeast and Midwest into regions of the country that are already prospering, thereby contributing even more to the attractiveness of those regions for further private investment and for the movement of more industry from the Northeast and Midwest.

Why is our political system so poor at allocating economic losses? The first answer that Thurow gives to this question is that the acceptance of economic losses by any particular group is perceived to be voluntary in that alternative policies would allocate losses differently, and the major socioeconomic groups in our society have the power to avoid having to accept those losses voluntarily. Thus, political paralysis produces economic paralysis. But there may be an even deeper form of paralysis that grips our society, moral paralysis. This is suggested by two other answers that Thurow gives to our leading question. Specifically, he says that our government is poor at allocating economic losses because (1) it seems unable to make explicit equity decisions, and (2) because it seems most of the economic actors in our society value economic security over economic prosperity and the risks associated with that.

> With respect to the problem of equity Thurow writes: Since government must alter the distribution of income if it is to solve our economic problems, we have to have a government that is capable of making equity decisions. Whose income ought to go up and whose income ought to go down? To do this, however, we need to know what is equitable. What is a fair or just distribution of economic resources? What is a fair or just procedure for distributing income? Unless we can specify what is equitable, we cannot say whose income ought to go down. Unless we can say whose income ought to go down, we cannot solve our economic problems.[8]

In the past, prosperity had obviated the need for having to make explicit equity decisions. That is, if a policy required that a particular group had to accept a loss, then we could obtain the voluntary acceptance of that loss by subsidizing that group in some other way. But in a zero-sum economic game such subsidies are no longer available; and hence, we are then compelled to convince the members of a group that the losses we would impose upon them are fair or just, which is difficult to do when there is no commonly agreed upon conception of justice in our society. This point is closely tied in with the next; namely, the demand for economic security.

As Thurow observes, in agricultural societies economic destruction was for the most part the result of impersonal, uncontrollable natural forces about which no one could do anything. But "economic destruction in industrial societies is caused by identifiable human actions that can be controlled."[9] Economic progress seems to require that such destruction occur. The pace of technological change is such that old products and processes quickly become outmoded, which generates a high degree of economic insecurity. Government is then seen as a vehicle for guaranteeing economic security. But once someone gets government protection, then that starts a chain of requests for protection that has no natural stopping point. Thus, we start with requests for federal loan guarantees to bail out Lockheed and Chrysler corporations and soon we have potato chip manufacturers, who have lost 19% of their market, demanding that the government legally declare Pringles a non-potato chip. The more that this occurs, the more we get locked into current economic activities; and this "makes it difficult to shift to the new products and processes that are the heart of economic progress." "Economic construction is based on economic destruction."[10] If a society has a shared understanding of, and commitment to, a fundamental set of values, such as a conception of justice, then that provides the foundation for some kind of social trust. Lacking that, the politics of mistrust must prevail, thereby exacerbating our economic problems (a stagnant economy), our political problems (the inability to allocate losses), and our moral problems (the inability to make equity decisions and establish a sense of social trust).

Zero-Sum Politics: The New Federalism

Diffusing the Political Pain

A convenient way to summarize Thurow's analysis of our economic difficulties for the decade is to say that the federal government, the Reagan Administration, is faced with the two-fold task of having to allocate economic losses and of having to allocate those losses equitably. Given the apparent political impossibility of this task, the obvious strategy is to shift responsibility for accomplishing the task to someone else. This might be labelled a "loss diffusion" strategy as opposed to a "loss distribution" strategy. Rather than attempting to distribute losses directly, one diffuses responsibility as widely as possible for the distribution of the losses themselves. The result is that those who are the ultimate bearers of the economic losses will have great difficulty identifying the distributors of the losses, because the lines of diffusion will be unclear, and they will have even greater difficulty bringing significant political pressure to bear upon the loss distributors because they will be so dispersed.

A couple brief examples will illustrate how the lines of loss diffusion can be unclear. First, the President proposes to disperse 43 social welfare programs to the states, with the individual states having the option of picking up the programs. If a state chooses not to accept a particular program, then that might be accomplished by inaction rather than any formal legislative action. Thus, the program dies, but no specific legislator could be identified as a cause of its death. Likewise, many corporations have benefited from the tax reductions of the Reagan Administration. For that they have been asked to assume responsibility in their local communities for the social welfare needs that will no longer be met by the federal government. But their tax reductions are not adequate to meet that need, nor were they given for that exclusive purpose. Hence, as representatives of social welfare agencies approach the heads of corporations for contributions, they can be honestly told that no one corporation can support all the social agencies in town, without anyone having any idea which, if any, social services they choose to support. Thus, responsibility for economic losses is diffused in a politically harmless way.

This same analysis applies to the diffusion of political pressure to the states and to corporations. What is at work here is a political strategy that is the opposite of the strategy that brought into existence the programs of Lyndon Johnson's Great Society. That is, rather than dispersing one's political strength over fifty state legislatures to get civil rights laws passed, one applies all political pressure to one point, Washington, which has the power to bring all the states into line, and which garners most of the media attention anyway, that media attention itself being a potent political tool that is not as readily available at the state level. Thus, President Reagan's strategy seems to be that of dispersing responsibility over the fifty states for many social programs, thereby dispersing the political strength of his opponents as well as the attention of the media. It is also worthy of note that in half the states, including Indiana, being a legislator is a part-time job, which has the effect of dispersing certain sorts of political pressures.

The rhetoric of the new federalism is that government has grown too distant from the people who are most affected by the policies it promulgates, that government must be brought closer to the people in order to be more responsible and more responsive. The reality of the new federalism is that government has become less responsible, less willing to consider the very real equity issues that are part of our current economic difficulties. The rhetoric of the new federalism is that the states must be seen as partners of the federal government in the task of governance. The reality of the new federalism is that the states will remain servants of the federal government, and they will be responsible for administering programs that are judged to be political liabilities by the federal government. Worse, they will be charged with administering those programs without being given the resources needed to carry out the task. Over the long run, however, the states will have to accept the political risks of trying to raise those resources on their own through increased state taxes. These efforts to raise state taxes will likely be hindered by three factors: (1) basic taxpayer resistance to higher taxes during a period of prolonged economic stagnation, (2) state policies that give high priority to economic development which might be undermined by increased taxes, and (3) very strong competition from the federal government for the relatively limited pool of tax dollars.

This last point is especially worthy of being highlighted, for it suggests a fundamental flaw in the new federalism. The federal government is expected to be both a partner of the states and their strongest competitor for limited tax resources. This is a difficult relationship to maintain during a period of prosperity when there are extra dollars to lubricate points of intergovernmental friction. But in a period of retrenchment there are no lubricants to reduce the friction or to induce the unwilling to cooperate. To further complicate matters, there is friction, not just among the various levels of government, but among the states. For the states are competing with one another to develop their own economies, and the perception is that the economic policies of the federal government tend to favor one state or region over another. Hence, why should the Frostbelt states cooperate with federal economic policies that will bring advantages to the Sunbelt?

Our Revolving Economic Problems: Self-Caused Causes

The major economic problem this country faced in the late 1970's was inflation. The inflationary period, however, was accompanied by a slowing of "real" economic growth, a state of affairs some economists termed "stagflation." Most economists agree that the primary cause of stagflation was high interest rates. In the 1980's, it appears that the major economic problem that the country will face is recession. The recession, however, is also being accompanied by continued high interest rates. Ironically, a primary cause of the high interest rates is the government itself. For 1981, the inflation rate, as measured by the Consumer Price Index, was 9.8%. This has encouraged consumption and diminished the incentive for saving since the typical passbook account offers only a 5% rate of interest. This, in turn, has produced a diminished supply of capital for investment purposes, thereby pushing up the cost of borrowing money.

What seems to have compounded this problem, however, are the stratospheric deficits in the federal budget that have been predicted to be between $300 and $500 billion between 1982 and 1985.[11] Since the federal government has the easiest access to the capital markets, high deficits mean the government must borrow money and that level of borrowing by the government puts intense upward pressure on interest rates. In effect, the government competes with the private sector for available money. The net effect of such high interest rates is to discourage significant new private investment in plants and equipment. The rate of return on such investments would have to be several percentage points in excess of the prime rate in order to justify the investment. In a sluggish economy, those sorts of investment opportunities are rare. Yet, failure to generate such investments is part of what contributes to the sluggishness of the economy. That is, this is part of the "productivity crisis" in America today that Reagan's supply-side economic program is supposed to cure.

High interest rates also contribute to a sluggish economy on the demand side by depressing consumer ability to borrow money, especially for two items that are key components of the American economy, housing and autos. Mortgage rates during 1980 and 1981 hovered around 17%, which means that only 5% of American families are able to afford the average priced home in America ($72,000 in 1981). But even then the traditional long-term, fixed rate mortgage was virtually impossible to obtain. In many places the traditional mortgage has been replaced by short-term (3-year) mortgages or variable-rate mortgages. These sorts of mortgages pose real risks for home buyers who might just barely be able to afford the initial monthly mortgage payments. A minor 1–2% rise in the rates might force a family to give up their house at a loss. Further, it is not just the height of the rates that poses a problem but the volatility of the rates. There was as much as a 9% spread (13–22%) during the period from 1980 to 1982 with numerous peaks and valleys. This has a very discouraging effect on virtually all sorts of long-term investments. Yet, it seems that these are precisely the sorts of investments that must provide the foundation for a revitalization of the American economy.

The auto industry has been particularly affected by high interest rates and the stagnant state of the American economy; and, since the rubber, chemical, steel, and aluminum industries are all tied into the auto industry, declining production in the American auto industry has added to the malaise of the economy as a whole.

In the 1970's imported cars succeeded in capturing a significant part of the American auto market, almost 30%. The reasons have to do with poor management and the failure of the American manufacturers to adjust quickly to the consumer demand for smaller, more fuel-efficient cars. Other factors influencing this trend have to do with the self-protective efforts of organized labor. Specifically, labor gained cost-of-living clauses in their contracts that protected union members from having their paychecks eroded by inflation. Some industry analysts contend that the labor agreements helped push up the price of American cars dramatically, thereby making them non-competitive abroad and significantly less competitive at home. It should be noted that the wage-rate for auto workers in Japan is only 55% the American rate.

The result of all this is that the Reagan Administration seems to be trapped in a series of economic dilemmas. As noted earlier, the Reagan Administration has committed itself to a supply-side approach to resolving the long-standing problems of the American economy. The essential idea behind this approach is that if more of our economic resources are devoted to investment in the productive side of the economy and less is spent on the consumption side of the economy, then this will create new jobs, which will then mean that those new jobholders will be able to stimulate the demand side of the economy. The basic assumption behind supply-side economics is that the government is taxing businesses and wealthier individuals, the primary sources of investment capital, at such a high rate that they have little incentive to invest and even less resources to invest. As a result, they either spend their money on luxuries (as a hedge against inflation), or they save (protect) their money by putting it into non-productive, speculative investments, e.g., art, real estate, and U.S. Treasury notes.

In the meantime, what has the government been doing with the hundreds of billions of dollars that it collects annually in taxes? According to supply-side economists, the government has been spending (frittering away) that money on a broad range of social welfare programs, none of which represent productive forms of investment.[12] If so, one solution to our economic problems would be to slash the federal budget drastically. The Reagan Administration has attempted to accomplish this in two ways: through a three-year program of tax reductions for both individuals and corporations, and through reductions or elimination of a broad range of social welfare programs now funded in whole or in part by the federal government.

The tax reductions were intended to stimulate saving for investment purposes. But, in fact, by the beginning of 1982 the rate of saving had actually declined from 6.1% to 5.8%. This may be explained by the fact that the recession has caused the unemployed and workers whose hours have been cut to draw down on their savings. Whatever the precise explanation, the fact is that the investment capital needed to stimulate the economy has not been generated. This has two other adverse effects which tend to compound our economic problems. First, the deeper the recession, the more people who will exercise their claims on various federal and state social welfare programs. Thus, even as the Reagan Administration slashes the benefit levels of various social welfare programs, the cost of these programs increases because so many more people are becoming entitled to those benefits. This contributes to the mounting federal deficit. Second, these same individuals who draw from the various welfare programs are not generating any tax revenues for the government since they are unemployed or underemployed, with the result that federal deficits are driven even higher. Finally, the tax reductions that were supposed to stimulate the economy now represent nothing more than a further drain on federal revenue, thereby escalating deficits even further, thereby pushing interest rates higher, thereby diminishing the incentive of investors in the business community, thereby weakening the economy just a bit more, and so on.

The federal deficit in 1982 was around $1 trillion, which required interest payments of about $100 billion this year or 14% of the federal budget. This may be compared with the deficit in 1972 when interest payments on the federal debt required less than 7% of the federal budget. In this period both the deficit and the federal budget have more than doubled, more as a result of inflation than real economic growth. If interest rates had remained low and stable during that period of time, then interest on that debt would not be contributing to increasing the real, as opposed to inflated, size of the debt; nor would it be putting further upward pressure on interest rates generally, thereby choking off the opportunity for a strong economic recovery.

The reader will recall that what initiated this discussion of our nation's economic problems was the problem of inflation. Only one year ago, as President Reagan took office, he declared that inflation was the number one problem that faced this nation. At that time, hardly a day went by without an editorial or substantial article in the business pages decrying the ravages of inflation on our economy. One year later, inflation is hardly mentioned in newspapers at all. It would be premature to conclude that President Reagan's policies have solved the problem of inflation. A more reasonable judgment would be that they have contained the problem of inflation by creating the problems of recession, unemployment, rising federal deficits, and high interest rates. That, of course, was not the intention of the Reagan Administration. Thus, President Reagan has described the current recession as "an unfortunate occurrence," as if it were just another natural disaster along with mudslides and tornadoes, something for which his Administration is not at all responsible. This strikes many policy analysts as rather disingenuous.

An alternative explanation can be offered that does not require us to analyze motives or intentions behind Reagan's policies, and that, in addition, seems to shed considerable light on the policy dilemmas that we find ourselves faced with this decade. Aaron Wildavsky, in his book *Speaking Truth to Power: The Art and Craft of Policy Analysis,* contends that since the Roosevelt Administration the federal government has sought to be more and more responsive to a broader range of social concerns by developing appropriate policies and programs.[13] Initially, federal policies coming out of the Great Depression of the 1930's were aimed at ameliorating or resolving social problems caused by factors in the world outside the domain of government. Thus, the Social Security program sought to provide minimal income for individuals who retired or who planned to retire whose companies had gone bankrupt, thereby wiping out their pensions. The companies went bankrupt for reasons that had nothing to do with any federal policies. But as policies and programs are put into place, they become part of the world "out there." That is, they begin to generate effects of their own, some of them problematic. As government programs and policies multiply, what Wildavsky calls "policy space" becomes "more densely packed."[14] Policies and programs begin to bump into one another, causing consequences that are unpredictable, but that appear controllable. The control takes the form of new policies, which create an even denser policy space with even more problematic consequences that are more a product of the policies and programs in place than "natural factors" in the world "out there." It is in this sense that policy becomes its own cause.

Currently we index social security payments to the consumer price index in order to protect the elderly from the effects of inflation. This certainly seems fair and reasonable, except that this practice threatens to bankrupt the social security system. In order to prevent that from happening, the social security deduction from the paychecks of current workers has been steadily increasing. This takes away from the consumption abilities of current workers, who are then motivated to save less in order to maintain their standard of living. Their failure to save contributes to the capital shortage problem and helps to push up interest rates, which in turn reduce the level of new investment in industry and weaken the economy in its foundations. In the meantime, the social security income of the elderly increases in real terms since the Consumer Price Index overstates the real effects of inflation on the incomes of the elderly. The chief reason for this overstatement is that currently high costs of housing (tied to high interest rates) are a significant part of the CPI, though in general the elderly have paid off their mortgages, and hence, their housing costs are much lower. This "overpayment" to the elderly contributes in its own way to further elevating the rate of inflation, not in an episodic way, but in a *structural* way. What this example points up is the degree to which policy has really become its own cause.

The New Federalism: Can It Create New Policy Space?

Might it be the case then that the new federalism of the Reagan Administration represents an attempt to create some "new space," less cluttered space at the federal level by shifting policy and program responsibilities to the state and local level? Might this not be a way of bringing government closer to the people and closer to the *real* problems in their world? Might we not discover that many of these problems should never have been part of "public space" in the first place, that they could be better solved in the more spacious domains of the private sector? Certainly these questions are consistent with the rhetoric of the Reagan Administration, but are they consistent with the political and economic realities of the last two decades of twentieth-century America? Just how "spacious" is the private sector of our economy? Just how commodious are the policy regions around state and local government?

It is far from clear that there are vast uncluttered expanses here where creative solutions to our most pressing social and economic problems can be fashioned and deployed. Consider first the private sector of our economy. It seems that the profit motive constricts considerably the size of that domain. There is no profit in meeting the social welfare needs of the poorest people in this nation, unless that profit is artificially provided by the government, e.g., through something like the Medicaid program which allows the so-called "Medicaid mills" to thrive in poorer areas of our major cities. In 1981, the federal government spent on three welfare programs alone (AFDC, Medicaid, and Food Stamps) a total of $36.6 billion dollars. It is difficult to imagine not-for-profit social agencies, which are part of the private sector, being able to generate resources of that magnitude to respond to needs of that magnitude, especially if those agencies had to compete with for-profit enterprises for the use of those dollars.

Another way to put this same point is to say that public goods tend to get "crowded out" of the private sector, the reason being that it is not in the interest of any one individual or corporation to pay for a good that will be freely available to all, e.g., clean air and water, roads, and so on. What is characteristic of our time is that a larger and larger number of goods are coming to be thought of as public goods, i.e., goods that the private sector is either unwilling or unable to produce or protect adequately.

Technological development is a case in point. We might see it as something that belongs in the private sector, but, in fact, the bulk of the most basic kinds of technological research are funded by the federal government through our universities and other research centers. No doubt the nation as a whole is materially better off for having supported such research. Everyone can agree that we would be materially worse off if that research were not funded. Yet, given the size of the investment that is often required, the risk of failure that attends all innovative research, and the length of time necessary for such research to yield productive applications, it is understandable why private interests have no incentive to make these kinds of research investments. Hence, the federal government steps in to provide and protect these goods, thereby cluttering up its policy space.

Is it really necessary that the *federal* government be responsible for these public goods? Could not state government do just as well? Is that not part of what the new federalism is all about? Certainly the states, as sovereign entities, ought to be legitimately concerned with protecting and enhancing a broad range of public goods. But can they, given what is likely to be the economic climate of the 80's and 90's? That is, each state is concerned with its own economic development and economic prosperity, and it sees itself as competing with 49 other states for jobs, new plants, capital investment, and so on. Under these circumstances the states become more like their for-profit corporate brothers and less like political entities that are supposed to be protectors of public goods. To be sure, they have to remain sufficiently concerned about those public goods that are directly beneficial to their own citizens, e.g., roads, primary education, police and fire protection. But they have little reason to be concerned about, or to invest in, public goods that benefit many who are not their citizens or public goods that benefit only their non-productive citizens. Thus, states have little reason to invest in the interstate highway system if traffic is simply passing through the state on the way to commercial centers that will be the prime recipients of the economic benefits of that highway. This is why the federal government pays 90% of the costs of that system. Likewise, there is some indication that states are beginning to disinvest in higher education; for states subsidize 80% of the cost of a university education often only to see their best and their brightest students move elsewhere, thereby providing an economic benefit to some other state. This is especially true for states in the Northeast and Midwest, which have borne the brunt of recent recessions, and which are seeing their university graduates move in droves to the more prosperous states in the South and West. This sort of economic mobility is almost certainly a public good that results in the nation as a whole being materially better off. But why should Indiana pay for "the nation as a whole" being better off?

This same line of reasoning applies to covering the costs of basic technological research and medical research. The states have no more motivation than any private corporation to bear these costs when these benefits are going to be so widely dispersed across the nation. This also holds true with respect to clean air and water and other sorts of environmental concerns. If Indiana, for instance, establishes strict environmental standards, then that improved environmental quality is a public good available to many outside the state of Indiana, though the costs of that improvement will be born only by the citizens of Indiana. Better, the thinking goes, that the citizens of Illinois should have strict environmental standards and pay the costs, including the possible loss of jobs and factories, as corporations consider relocating to states with lax or non-existent environmental standards. During prosperous times, any state can afford to lose a few factories; but during periods of economic stagnation, such losses mean an eroded tax base, increased demands on state welfare programs, increased taxes or increased deficits or both, which can trigger further economic erosion, and so on. If all states are motivated to think this way, then environmental quality as a public good is lost. Consequently, we see the federal government intervening to establish a national environmental policy.

It might appear that the establishment of social welfare programs should be the responsibility of individual states, for the costs and benefits seem to accrue to individuals living in each state. But the matter is not quite that simple. If the states really are competitors in the economic development game, then they have little incentive to put money into social welfare programs. Corporations might invest in an attractive benefit package in order to attract and retain the best employees. But welfare benefits go to those who are the least productive citizens in the state. Far from being a benefit, they represent a drain on the fiscal resources of the state. More than that, they represent a diversion of scarce resources away from programs for economic development within the state. Hence, the states have little motivation to fund social welfare programs adequately. The net result of this is that those who are least well off in any state, those who are most disadvantaged, are the ones who really pay the cost of competition for economic development among the states. This runs contrary to what our intuitions of justice suggest ought to be the case.

There is also a larger public good that would be unprotected if the individual states had sole responsibility for welfare programs. That larger good is the economic welfare of the nation. As things are now, during a recessionary period the demand for welfare assistance increases just as tax revenues are declining. The federal government responds with increased outlays for Food Stamps and AFDC. This has a stabilizing effect on the economy as a whole. It may increase the federal deficit, but this poses no special problems for the federal government. But if these programs belonged exclusively to the states, then the stabilizing effect of these programs on the economy would be lost. For many states, like Indiana, are prohibited by their state constitutions from engaging in deficit spending. Hence, during a recession those states would either have to raise taxes or lower the benefit levels to all. The net result of either course of action would be a worsening of the recession since there would be no infusion of new money into the state economy when it was really needed. If most of the states reacted the same way, the net result would be a worsening of the recession at the national level. Again, that is a public good that no one state will want to protect at its cost.

In fifty states the question will be raised, why should the taxpayers of Indiana (or wherever) protect the nation as a whole from recession? It is precisely this sort of question that results in the federal government having to intervene and design policies and programs that will protect this public good. This does bring about the crowding of policy space remarked upon earlier. But this is because there are so many more public goods that require governmental protection or enhancement. We considered the possibility that state governments, rather than the federal government, might take more responsibility for those public goods, that this would be a way of uncrowding policy space at the federal level, that this was one of the essential purposes of President Reagan's new federalism. However, we have discovered that there is something of an internal contradiction in the new federalism, that states are supposed to act both as a major form of government (and hence be concerned about protecting public goods) and as competitive economic units (which cannot afford to waste scarce resources on public goods that do not contribute to the economic vitality of the state). We shall examine what this means for public policy in the state of Indiana in the next section of this essay.

Indiana: Economic Policy for the 80's

Within the state of Indiana, we cannot influence the rate of inflation, the unemployment rate, interest rates, the size of the federal deficit, the amount of taxes collected by the federal government, the size of the Gross National Product, or the rate of growth of the Gross National Product. Yet all of these things have an impact on Indiana's economy. These impacts, especially the adverse impacts, might be accepted in a spirit of equanimity if it were the case that they were more or less uniformly distributed across the states. But they are not. The national unemployment rate is about 9% at this writing, but the unemployment rate in the state of Indiana is almost 13%. As noted earlier, this is not a product of "market forces" dissociated from political choice. Rather, there is a direct relationship between the Administration's attempts to cope with the problem of inflation through a tight monetary policy and a triggering of higher levels of unemployment. These policies affected the auto and related industries more than others since they are sensitive to the high interest rates brought about by the tight monetary policy. Since these industries are heavily concentrated in the Northeast and Midwest, states in these regions have had to pay the cost in terms of higher unemployment (lower tax revenues, higher welfare costs) for bringing down the rate of inflation in the nation as a whole. This again evokes the question of why any one state or region should have to pay the costs for a benefit that goes to the nation as a whole. If it were possible to point to other policy areas where the trade-off was reversed, then that would take some of the political force out of the question. Unfortunately, it is difficult to identify such counter trade-offs.

Inter-regional Competition: The Frostbelt vs. the Sunbelt

Since the mid-70's, the perception has grown that the economic policies of the federal government strongly favor the Sunbelt states while strongly disfavoring the Frostbelt states. These policies have contributed to a dramatically increased movement of people, industry, and capital from the Frostbelt to the Sunbelt. It would be inaccurate to suggest that the federal government has been exclusively, or even primarily, responsible for these inter-regional economic shifts. For there has been a large number of non-policy factors that has provoked or contributed to this shift. Still, as we shall see, the regionally differentiated effects of these factors have been exacerbated by various federal policies that came about as a response to these factors. Some examples will clarify this point.

The energy crisis of 1973 occasioned by the oil embargo of the OPEC nations has had a markedly adverse effect on the American economy overall. Certainly the rapid surge in oil prices over the past nine years has contributed in a major way to our national economic problems. But the Frostbelt was especially hard hit by the energy crisis and the rise in oil prices because this area of the country is a net importer of energy, especially for heating purposes. The policy of the federal government became that of reducing as quickly as possible our dependence on foreign oil, for we had been importing as much as 50% of our daily needs. The prevailing belief was that the United States had ample supplies of its own oil, but because of federal price controls and other disincentives to new exploration and the use of more expensive extraction techniques, it simply was not economical to develop that oil. Hence, controls were lifted and other incentives were supplied to encourage the development of domestic oil reserves, which for the most part are located in the Sunbelt. From a national perspective this policy has been rather successful, for we have increased our own oil production and reduced to 20% our reliance on foreign oil. From a regional perspective, however, the Frostbelt is paying a heavy price, for it must still import its oil from the Sunbelt. Moreover, a number of states impose a severance tax on oil that is shipped out of state, which serves to increase the transfer of economic resources to the Sunbelt. More specifically, this tax serves as an incentive for energy-intensive industries in the North, which want energy that is both cheaper and more secure, to move their plants to the Sunbelt. Clearly this was not the intent of the federal government when these policies were enacted.

Moving large industrial plants is a rather expensive undertaking. Ordinarily no one economic factor will provide sufficient economic justification for making such a move. Consequently, relatively few major plants that are energy-intensive have moved from the North to the South. Rather, the more typical scenario is that a large firm is ready to expand by opening a new plant.[15] A decision must be made about its location. Cheaper, more secure energy now becomes a critical factor. Cost of labor is also a factor. The Sunbelt offers labor that is substantially less expensive (40–50% in some cases) than labor in the North, for unions have not been as successful in their organizing efforts. Taxes are another factor, especially as they relate to business and industry. Generally, states in the North have chosen to spend more on education and social welfare than states in the South. In part there has been some incentive from the federal government for doing this since many programs in these areas involve matching funds from the federal government. That is, they serve as mechanisms for importing federal revenue into the state. But if the President's new federalism program is enacted, then these states will have to make the very painful choice of either having to reduce their programs or raise taxes substantially. Raising taxes would certainly create serious problems for attracting or retaining business and industry. Again, the new federalism is not intended as a tool for economic development in the Sunbelt, though it seems like it will have that effect.

Another problem further clouds the economic future of the Frostbelt, namely, the aging of the cities and industrial plants of the North. Those plants operated at the peak of their productivity from the 1940's through the 1960's. They are now in need of modernization or replacement. The Reagan Administration passed a policy that was designed to speed up depreciation on plants and equipment, thereby providing a significant tax incentive for investing in new plants and equipment. Unfortunately, this too will have the effect of hastening the flight of people, capital, and industry from the Frostbelt to the Sunbelt. It is not as if this factor by itself is decisive, but in conjunction with all the other factors listed it strongly biases the decision in one direction.

There are other factors that have made these inter-regional economic shifts more problematic. In the five-year period from 1975–79, the Midwest had a negative "balance of payments" with the federal government of $110 billion. That is, they sent that much more money to Washington in taxes than they received back. In that same period of time, the South and West had a positive balance of $100 billion.[16] Much of that money went to support the defense industry, which is predominantly located in the Sunbelt. Seen in that light, Reagan's proposal to increase defense spending from $159 billion in 1981 to $292 billion in 1985 represents another major shift of the North's economic resources to the Sunbelt. This also involves a massive loss of jobs, not just jobs in general, but *manufacturing* jobs. In the three year period from 1977 until 1980, Indiana lost 55,000 manufacturing jobs, Michigan lost 121,000, and Ohio lost 77,000.[17] Many of these jobs were replaced by jobs in the service sector, such as retail clerks, which pay only 1/3 to 1/2 what a job in the manufacturing sector pays. That means that these states experience a real reduction in their standard of living, though this is something that will not be evident from just looking at employment statistics. These problems are further compounded by the Reagan Administration's cut of CETA funds for fiscal 1982 by $4.7 billion, and a further cut of $2 billion for fiscal 1983, since these cuts will have a more adverse economic impact on cities in the North where the rate of unemployment is much higher.

It might seem that if one area of the country is economically stagnant and another area is relatively prosperous, then those who are unemployed will simply move to where the jobs are. This, in fact, is what happens to that segment of the population that is younger, well educated, and equipped with several technical skills. As John Crusoe, the director of placement services at Wayne State University in Detroit, notes, it used to be the case that 90% of their technical graduates went to work in the Detroit area; but in 1981, 85% of their graduates in technical areas took jobs out of state.[18] In constrast to this, those who are unemployed and older or undereducated, or lacking in marketable technical skills, or just plain poor are least able to move to some other part of the country where they might find employment. That means that these individuals become permanent social welfare problems in areas of the country that lack the resources necessary to be adequately responsive to their needs.

It has been pointed out by the members of the President's Commission for a National Agenda for the Eighties that it is inaccurate to say that the Midwest or the Frostbelt is in a period of economic decline; that if we look at the standard indicators of economic performance, what we find is that the population of this region has grown over the past decade, per capita income has increased, the number of jobs has increased, retail sales are up, and so on. Of course, the increases have been modest, especially when they are compared to the rather more substantial increases in all these indicators in the South and West. Still, the Commission concludes that this is just a matter of "regional convergence working within the national economy," that "might be heralded just as accurately as the South 'catching up' as the North 'stagnating' or 'declining'."[19] Yet when this argument is examined more carefully, it can be readily seen that there is something specious about it. If it were the case that these were relatively prosperous times for the nation as a whole, then it would be easier to accept the interpretation that the South was just "catching up" by being rather more efficient in securing the economic gains of prosperity. But if we are caught up in something like a zero-sum economic game, as Thurow contends, then they have won their economic gains at our expense. Moreover, the South has not achieved those gains by virtue of superior entrepreneurial skills, but by virtue of national economic policies that have given them an unfair competitive advantage. Finally, the Frostbelt states could afford to be a bit more sanguine about all this if the belief was that this was just a temporarily aberrant state of economic affairs. Instead, it seems that some rather definite trends are in place that will adversely affect the economic vitality of the North. Let us now consider what all this means for the state of Indiana.

An Interstate Comparison: Texas and Indiana

We may better understand Indiana's economic policy agenda for the 80's if we make some key comparisons of our economy with that of Texas. Between 1970 and 1980 Texas' population grew from 11.2 million to 14.2 million, making it the second fastest growing of the ten most populous states. According to federal estimates, almost half of the state's growth in the seventies came from net migration into Texas of more than a million Americans from other states. Most of these migrants settled in urban areas. Eighty percent of Texans now live in cities. The nation's fifth, seventh, and eleventh largest cities are Houston, Dallas, and San Antonio. The population of Indiana has grown steadily since 1920. In 1980 our population was about 5,400,000, giving us a ranking of twelfth in the nation. That figure represents a population increase from 1970 of about 3%, compared to Texas's 27% increase, California's 18% increase, Florida's 43% increase, and a national average of 11.4%. Thus, we may not have declined in real terms in population, but politically we experienced the real loss of one congressional representative.

In Texas, the population boom has caused a tremendous increase in both the number of people working and looking for work. In the past decade, Texas's labor force grew by over 35%, compared to a national increase of 24%. Despite this growth in the work force, the Texas unemployment rate has remained substantially below the national average. The Texas rate was just over 5% in 1980. In Indiana and Michigan, the unemployment rate is over 12% currently, while the rate in Texas is still below 6%, and the national average is around 9%.

Texas has enjoyed a remarkable period of industrial growth during this past decade. Leading industrial growth in Texas was mining with 96,000 new employees, a 92.7% increase. The manufacturing sector in Texas gained almost 288,000 jobs in the 70's. This was more than any other state. There were also large gains in Texas construction employment, which reflected the demand for new factories, offices, and housing, all part of the booming Texas economy. To be precise, there was a 75.9% increase in construction industry employment during the period in Texas, which compared with a national increase of only 29.4%.[20] The net effect of this growth was a large increase in the number of Texas wage earners. Non-farm employment grew by almost two million persons in the last decade, an increase of 54.6%, or more than twice the national growth rate. This, in turn, produced a significant growth in per capita personal income over the decade.

In 1970, Texans' personal income amounted to $3,507 per capita, 90% of the national average. By 1979 the Texas figure was $8,778 per capita, which was a little over the national average.[21] But simple per capita income figures do not account for variations in living costs around the country.[22]

Figure 8.1. Increase in nonagricultural employment, Texas and U.S., 1970–79* (thousands of workers)

		United States		
Industry	**No. of New Employees****	**Percent Increase**	**No. of New Employees****	**Percent Increase**
Mining	333	+53.5%	96	+92.7%
Construction	1,056	+29.4	181	+75.9
Manufacturing	1,606	+8.3	288	+39.3
Transportation and Public Utilities	638	+14.1	97	+38.3
Wholesale and Retail Trade	5,096	+33.9	519	+60.5
Finance, Insurance and Real Estate	1,318	+36.2	125	+66.2
Services	5,495	+47.6	376	+64.2
Government (civilian)	3,060	+24.4	296	+44.8
Total	18,602	26.2%	1,978	+54.6%

* 1979 U.S. figures are provisional.
**Rounded to nearest thousand.

Source: "Why Texas Is Growing" Austin, Texas: Controller of Public Accounts, May 1981

Figure 8.2. Estimated real after-tax income per capita, 1978 (ranked according to adjusted per capita income)

State	Per Capita Personal Income	Per Capita Taxes*	After-Tax Per Capita Income	Adjusted Per Capita Income**
Illinois	$8,870	$3,012	$5,858	$5,829
California	8,916	3,234	5,6822	5,722
Florida	7,578	2,403	5,175	5,631
TEXAS	**7,746**	**2488**	**5,258**	**5,618**
Michigan	8,487	2,909	5,578	5,567
Ohio	7,857	2,514	5,343	5,402
Oklahoma	7,127	2,210	4,917	5,339
U.S. AVERAGE	7,840	2,676	5,164	5,157
New Jersey	8,775	3,133	5,642	5,157
Pennsylvania	7,744	2,629	5,115	5,125
Louisiana	6,738	2,211	4,527	4,926
Arkansas	6,121	1,858	4,263	4,674
New Mexico	6,599	2,180	4,419	4,637
New York	8,230	3,214	5,016	4,615
Massachusetts	7,926	2,917	5,009	4,402

*Includes federal, state and local taxes.

**After-tax income inflated or deflated by cost-of-living indexes computed for each state from Department of Labor comparative annual family budgets for an intermediate income family of four in selected urban areas. Where no metropolitan index for a state exists, the index for the closest and most comparable state is used.

Source: Computed from U.S. Department of Commerce. "1979 State Per Capita Personal Income," News (May 11, 1980), pp. 4–7 and *Governmental Finances in 1977–78* (Washington, D.C., 1980), p. 90: Tax Foundation, Inc., *Monthly Tax Features,* Vol. 23, No. 2 (February 1979), p. 3; U.S. Department of Labor, Bureau of Labor Statistics, "Autumn 1978 Urban Family Budgets and Comparative Indexes for Selected Urban Areas." *News* (April 29, 1979). Reprinted from "Why Texas Is Growing:" Austin, Texas: Controller of Public Accounts' May, 1981.

The chart above compares 1978 adjusted and unadjusted per capita personal income for the most populous states, Texas's four neighboring states, and the national average. It should be noted that the adjusted per capita income of Texans is substantially above the U.S. average, ranking seventh among all 50 states.

Two other indicators of economic growth in Texas may be cited. The first concerns new construction. At the start of the 1980's, new building permits and contract awards totaled more than $13 billion, ranking Texas second only to California in total construction. The second indicator is new plants. Texas has been a consistent leader in industrial expansion. In a single year, *Industrial Development Magazine* reported, Texas attracted over 200 new industrial facilities. In that year North Carolina, another Sunbelt state, ranked second with 98 facilities. Four hundred new industrial facilities began Texas operations in 1980.[23]

What explains such rapid and sustained economic growth? It is noteworthy that Texas does *not* offer very many financial aid programs or special tax inducements to attract new businesses. Yet most of Texas's growth comes from the creation of new businesses and from business expansion. What Texas does offer are uniformly low taxes. Texas has one of the lowest tax burdens nationally and levies neither personal nor corporate income taxes. In addition, no major state tax was increased during the last eight years of the 70's. Finally, Texas has adopted what it might

Figure 8.3. New industrial plants and expansions in Texas, 1970–79.
Source: "Why Texas Is Growing:" Austin, Texas: Controller of Public Accounts, May, 1981.

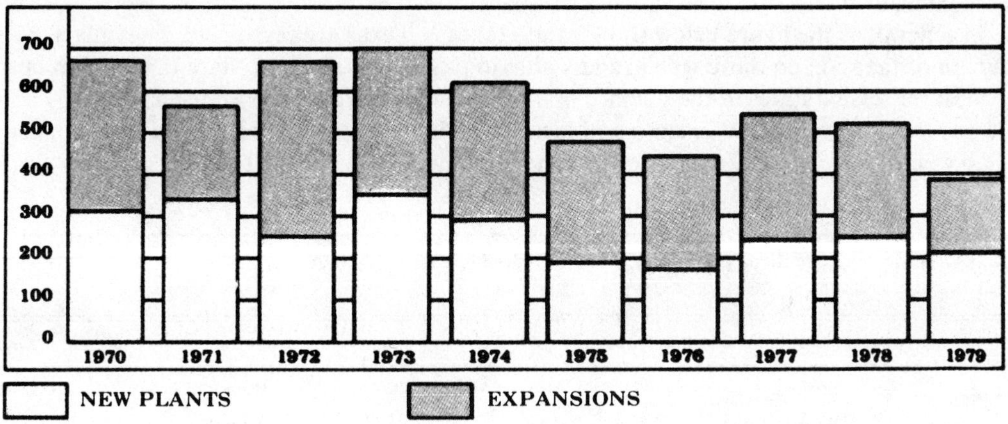

characterize as a prudent, responsible "pay-as-you-go" approach to the financing of state government. Business and government leaders in Texas believe that low tax levels are the most important factor in Texas's favorable business climate and reflect a state government attitude favorable to business growth. For business, low taxes mean lower operating costs and more competitive prices. For individuals, low taxes mean a higher standard of living. Throughout the 1970's, Texans' per capita taxes were significantly lower than the U.S. average, the difference being about $150 per capita by the end of the decade.[24] At the end of the decade, Texas had the lowest per capita tax burden among the major industrial states. Only three states in the union had lower per capita state tax burdens.[25] Indiana ranks 13th among all the states in the union in per capita state tax burdens.

In addition to state taxes, more than 3,600 local governments can collect taxes of their own. Still, Texas has a low tax burden. On a per capita basis, Texans paid $749 state and local taxes in 1979, the most recent year for which data are available. This payment was 80% of the U.S. average of $934. The combined state and local taxes of Texas were lower than all but 11 other states.

The largest source of state tax revenue is the sales tax, which accounts for 39% of the revenue. There is nothing especially remarkable about that. But, the second largest source of state tax revenue is remarkable, namely, its oil and gas severance tax, which accounts for about 25% of state revenue.[26] What that means is that Texas, thanks to its energy-rich status, is able to get energy-poor states (like Indiana) in the North to pay 25% of its state taxes. Knowing that and knowing the rapid rise in energy prices over the past eight years, we should not be so amazed to see that Texas has not raised any major state taxes for the past eight years. That makes being fiscally responsible a rather easy chore. What makes it even easier is that Texas, one of our richer industrial states, has one of the lowest AFDC benefit levels in the union. In fact, despite a rate of inflation that has eroded the value of a dollar by 50% over the past decade, Texas has not seen fit to raise AFDC benefits over the past ten years.[27] It seems that there is something unjust about this state of affairs, yet this may well become the pattern throughout the states as the decade unfolds, especially if Reagan's new federalism is enacted and economic competition among the states is intensified.

In general, as the figure below shows, state taxes in Texas are regressive. They place a heavier burden of taxation on those who are less able to pay. Texas, with its state taxes, is among the three most regressive states in the union. For 1974 a family of four with an income of only $5,000 would pay 9.3% of its income in state and local taxes in Texas, while a family with an income of $50,000 would pay only 3.5% of its income in state and local taxes in Texas.[28]

Figure 8.4. State tax collections per capita, 1979* (ranked lowest to highest)

Rank	State	Amount	Rank	State	Amount
1	New Hampshire	$298	26	Iowa	$ 541
2	South Dakota	356	27	Vermont	543
3	Tennessee	421	28	Oregon	548
•4	Texas	429	29	Connecticut	552
5	Ohio	431	30	Louisiana	556
6	Missouri	446	31	Illinois	563
7	Arkansas	456	—	U.S. Average	570
8	Alabama	464	32	Pennsylvania	578
9	Nebraska	472	33	Rhode Island	579
10	Georgia	478	34	Kentucky	589
11	Florida	484	35	West Virginia	612
12	Virginia	493	36	Arizona	619
•13	Indiana	494	37	Massachusetts	627
14	North Dakota	494	38	Maryland	638
15	Mississippi	497	39	Michigan	654
16	Kansas	501	40	Nevada	659
17	Maine	505	41	New York	662
18	Utah	508	42	New Mexico	681
19	New Jersey	509	43	Wisconsin	691
20	Montana	510	44	Washington	692
21	Idaho	515	45	California	720
22	South Carolina	519	46	Wymoning	762
23	Colorado	520	47	Minnesota	772
24	North Carolina	520	48	Delaware	845
25	Oklahoma	524	49	Hawaii	957
			50	Alaska	2,012

*Includes license fees.

Source: "Why Texas Is Growing." Austin, Texas: Comptroller of Public Accounts, May 1981.

Figure 8.5. Distribution of major state-local tax burdens relative to family income size, 1974 (tax burdens as percentages of income)

State	Income for Family of Four, 1974			
	$5,000	$10,000	$25,000	$50,000
All 50 States (Cities)	11.5	8.9	8.1	7.7
Alabama (Birmingham)	9.8	8.2	7.2	6.4
Arkansas (Little Rock)	8.5	7.0	6/8	7.4
California (Los Angeles)	11.8	8.8	9.1	10.8
Connecticut (Hartford)	18.4	12.3	9.8	7.6
Florida (Jacksonville)	7.5	4.9	3.5	2.6
Idaho (Boise)	9.7	7.8	8.6	9.0
Illinois (Chicago)	14.3	10.7	8.9	7.6
Indiana (Indianapolis)	13.0	9.6	8.1	6.8
Kansas (Wichita)	14.3	10.5	9.3	8.5
Louisiana (New Orleans)	6.1	4.6	3.7	3.6
Maryland (Baltimore)	13.9	12.8	11.9	11.7
Michigan (Detroit)	10.9	8.8	8.6	8.7
Mississippi (Jackson)	6.8	6.6	4.7	4.5
Montana (Billings)	11.2	9.2	8.8	8.8
Nevada (Las Vegas)	8.4	5.5	4.0	3.1
New Jersey (Newark)	20.5	14.4	11.6	9.6
New York (New York City)	11.6	10.6	11.5	15.0
North Dakota (Fargo)	10.1	7.8	8.5	5.5
Oklahoma (Oklahoma City)	9.0	6.4	6.4	6.8
Pennsylvania (Philadelphia)	12.5	11.5	9.9	8.9
Rhode Island (Providence)	14.3	10.5	9.3	8.8
South Carolina (Columbia)	9.1	7.3	7.7	8.0
Tennessee (Memphis)	10.5	7.2	5.2	4.0
Texas (Houston)	9.3	6.1	4.6	3.5
Vermont (Burlington)	11.9	10.4	10.0	11.0
Virginia (Norfold)	10.0	7.9	7.8	7.5
Washington (Seattle)	10.4	6.8	4.7	3.5
West Virginia (Huntington)	7.7	5.6	4.9	5.1
Wisconsin (Milwaukee)	16.3	14.8	14.7	14.6
Wyoming (Cheyenne)	8.8	5.8	4.3	3.3

Source: Stephen E. Lile, "Family Tax Burden Differences among the States," *State Government* 69 (Winter 1976): 16. Adapted from *State and Local Politics,* second edition, by David R. Berman, (Boston: Holland Press, 1978). Reprinted from "Why Texas Is Growing:" Austin, Texas: Controller of Public Accounts, May, 1981.

What this figure clearly implies is that if other states were to abolish their personal and corporate income taxes, then they too would be able to distribute their tax burden in a steeply regressive way. This figure also brings out some of the other implications of the new federalism. For if 43 programs are transferred from the federal government to the states, and if the states must eventually finance those programs, then those costs will be borne for the most part by the lower income groups, while the bulk of the benefits from tax reductions at the federal level will go to those in upper income groups, since the federal tax system is progressive.

As noted earlier, Texas is by far the most important energy producing state in the nation. Though both oil and gas production have declined in recent years, Texas remains a national leader in both. The state accounts for about a third of domestic oil and gas production. Texas leads the

Figure 8.6. Per capita general expenditures by state governments, 1979*

Rank	State	Amount	Rank	State	Amount
1	Alaska	$2,875	26	Idaho	851
2	Hawaii	1,520	—	U.S. AVERAGE	827
3	Delaware	1,125	27	Pennsylvania	819
4	Wyoming	1,075	28	Arizona	811
5	Minnesota	1,051	29	South Dakota	810
6	New Mexico	1,038	30	New Jersey	788
7	Vermont	1,037	31	North Carolina	785
8	New York	1,006	32	Colorado	782
9	North Dakota	987	33	Mississippi	782
10	California	967	34	Alabama	780
11	Rhode Island	965	35	Illinois	779
12	Montana	951	36	Connecticut	773
13	Washington	947	37	Virginia	764
14	Wisconsin	945	38	South Carolina	752
15	West Virginia	935	39	Oklahoma	735
16	Nevada	922	40	Arkansas	718
17	Oregon	912	41	Georgia	712
18	Michigan	910	42	Nebraska	706
19	Massachusetts	908	43	Kansas	695
20	Utah	905	44	Ohio	668
21	Maryland	902	45	New Hampshire	662
22	Louisiana	894	46	Tennessee	653
23	Maine	865	47	Indiana	647
24	Iowa	857	48	Florida	621
25	Kentucky	857	49	TEXAS	620
			50	Missouri	565

*Rounded to nearest whole dollar.

Source: "Why Texas Is Growing:" Austin, Texas: Controller of Public Accounts. May, 1981.

nation in proven reserves of natural gas and is second only to Alaska in proven oil reserves. Texas also has abundant reserves of recoverable lignite coal estimated at more than 12 billion tons. Tax collections have been growing at a rate of 10% per year over the last decade in Texas. Yet there has been no state tax increase since 1971.[29] Texas also maintains firm control over state spending, as can be seen below in a comparison of per capita spending for the fifty states. Texas ranks 49th and spends only $620 per capita. Indiana is 47th and spends just $647 per capita.[30]

Education is the largest area of state spending, accounting for about 50% of the state budget. This is followed by welfare, at about 17% of the state budget, and highway maintenance and construction, at about 15.5% of the state budget.[31]

When we turn to Indiana, we find that its tax structure was revised in 1973 to encourage the growth of private enterprise and to balance the tax burden between citizens and business and industry. The new tax structure, which put a ceiling on property taxes, is intended to provide lower operating costs for Hoosier industry and business. The 1973 tax laws provided for:

—at least a 20% reduction in property taxes,
—frozen property tax rates or levies at 1972 levels,
—the phase-out of the corporate gross income tax,
—an increase of the sales tax rate from 2 to 4%, with the increase earmarked for property tax relief at the local level,
—exemption of groceries and prescription drugs from the sales tax,
—an increase in corporate adjusted gross income tax from 2 to 3%,
—the establishment of a corporate supplemental income tax,
—the adoption of an optional local individual income tax of ¼% by counties.

For the decade between 1967 and 1977, only two states exhibited a smaller rate of growth in per capita state and local taxes than Indiana. In 1979, the major source of state government tax revenue was sales and gross tax receipts, which comprised 65.9% of the total state government tax revenue, while individual income tax accounted for 22.2% and corporate net income tax for 4.8%. In per capita taxes in 1977, Indiana ranked 21st and Texas ranked 17th. In taxes per $1,000 personal income, Indiana ranked 6th and Texas ranked a very close 7th. Since 1977, Indiana has improved its ranking on this latter item. It now has the lowest personal tax bill of the 48 contiguous states, just $88 per $1,000 of personal income. This compares to the national average of $112 and Michigan's rate of $115.

It seems that in all these respects Indiana compares rather favorably with Texas. Yet we are far from enjoying the level of economic growth with which Texas has been blessed over the past decade. Why? A major reason must be that Indiana has abundant supplies of coal that, unfortunately, produces unacceptable quantities of environmental pollutants when burned. We already noted that oil prices have been decontrolled, which produced windfall profits for states like Texas. Now natural gas prices are in the process of being decontrolled over a five-year period, which will produce another windfall for both Texas and Louisiana, as well as other Sunbelt states. But there are other reasons, besides energy, for Indiana's less than vibrant economic performance.

Alexander Grant and Company has been doing a study for each of the past three years of the industrial climate of the 48 contiguous states. Figure 8.7 displays the results of that study.[32]

What that map shows is that Indiana ranks 25th among the states for its industrial climate while Texas ranks second. What accounts for those differences, given relatively light tax burdens in each state? Two significant factors stand out. First, Indiana "was 45th in a key measure of productivity—a comparison of value added by manufacturing employees per dollar of production payroll."[33] The simple interpretation of that is that industrial workers are overpaid for the work they produce. A more careful interpretation would raise the possibility that workers are using machinery that is older and less than adequately efficient. In either case, it seems that there is little that the state can do to rectify this situation. Thus, even though Indiana's National ranking overall is 25th, thereby making it the most attractive of the Great Lakes states, its ranking of 45th on manufacturing productivity will not make it very attractive to manufacturers anywhere.

A second significant factor that the Grant study isolated was that Indiana ranked 47th in the growth of state and local government debt in comparison with revenue growth. Indiana's per capita debt is relatively low, but it is growing as municipalities struggle to cope with the property

Figure 8.7. Map, state ranks and regional averages
Source: South Bend Tribune, Jan. 31, 1982.

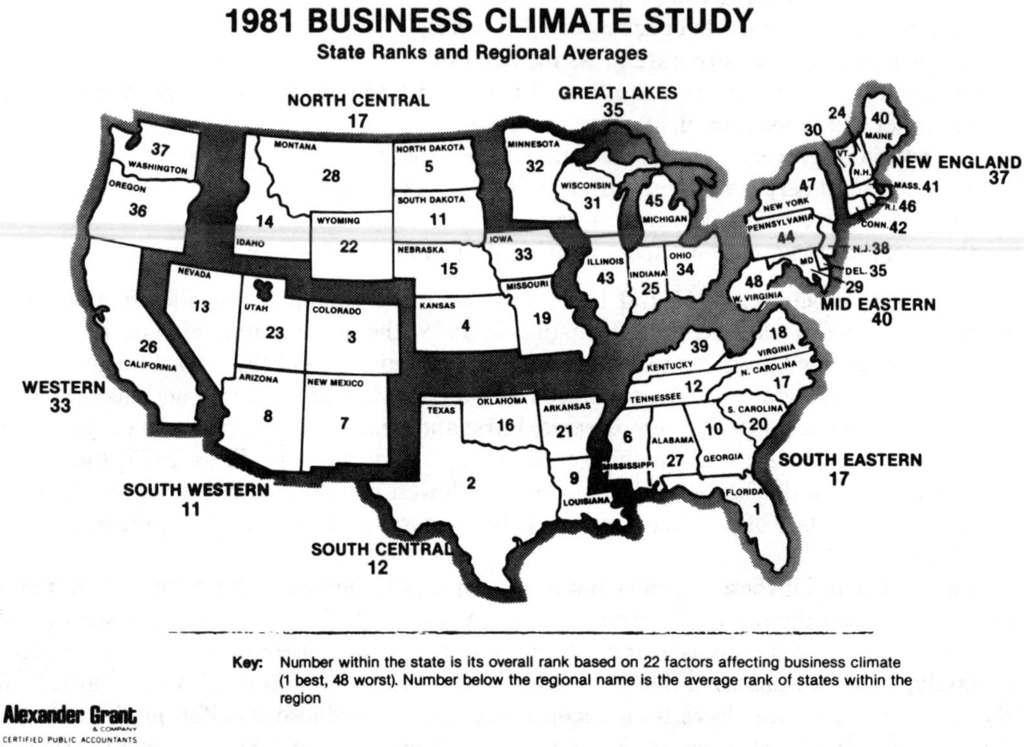

tax freeze in creative ways. That is, cities are using their bonding authority to fund what are really supposed to be operating expenses, such as purchasing new police and fire equipment. The situation in brief is this. Cities in Indiana have been allowed to increase their operating budget by no more than 5% per year since the property tax freeze went into effect. This has been well below the actual rate of inflation during that time. For a while this did not make much of a practical difference because cities had access to a broad range of federal programs that helped in various ways to cover the shortfall, though that is not what those programs were designed to do. But gradually it became more difficult to cover that shortfall other than by laying off people, cutting services, and skimping on maintenance. The most serious blow, however, was the first round of Reagan cutbacks in 1981. These were especially hard on cities in Indiana which, it must be remembered, do not have the power to raise taxes on their own, as do cities in Texas. This imposes a kind of fiscal responsibility on all, but it may turn out to be a rather short-sighted form of fiscal responsibility that undermines any long-term opportunities for economic development in the state. That is, cities are being forced to borrow money at very high interest rates, which in itself is not a fiscally prudent thing to do, judging at least from the current behavior of the business community. But worse than that, cities are being forced to let their infrastructure deteriorate; their streets, parks, sewers, water systems, housing, and so on. If that is allowed to go too far, that will certainly result in Indiana being a significantly less attractive place for industry to locate in, no matter what our tax rate is.

Economic Development: Indiana's Policy Agenda for the 80's

Like Texas, and virtually all other states, Indiana has a variety of program mechanisms designed to attract business to the state or help businesses form and expand within the state. One such tool is Local Development Companies (LDC). LDC's are made up of community-minded citizens who are organized for the purpose of stimulating local economic growth and revitalization. LDC's are eligible for assistance from a variety of federal and state financing and technical assistance programs. For example, the Small Business Administration (SBA) is authorized to make loans and loan guarantees up to $500,000 for each business that is to be provided assistance. Loans may be used to assist small businesses in acquiring, constructing, modernizing or expanding their plants, and purchasing land, equipment, and machinery. The LDC is required to provide from its own sources at least 10% of the cost of a project. Loans that are made to LDC's are made at 2% above the prime rate. In the current economic climate of very high interest rates, these loans are just not very attractive since a project would have to generate a return on investment of over 20% per year, which would be very difficult for a marginal business enterprise to generate.

Another tool of economic development is Economic Development Commissions (EDC). EDC's are established by a city, town, or county and provide up to 100% financing of fixed assets and pollution control facilities by the sale of tax-exempt bonds, commonly known as industrial revenue bonds. These bonds are a combination of corporate bonds and municipal revenue bonds. They offer the advantage of long-term financing while providing the lower cost, tax-free interest rate enjoyed by local units of government. Several other financing means are available: Federal Community Development Funds and Historic Preservation Funds. There used to be, until the first year of the Reagan Administration, Economic Development Administration Grants and Urban Development Action Grants. It now seems that these programs will be phased out along with the Economic Development Administration. We should also mention the Farmers Home Administration program which provides loan guarantees for business and industrial development purposes in predominantly rural areas.

There is no easy way to assess the effectiveness of these various programs. But there is clearly one factor that detracts considerably from the potential effectiveness of these programs and other efforts at economic development in Indiana. That factor is the property tax freeze. Local governments have little incentive for engaging in vigorous efforts at economic development. In particular, they will be very hesitant to invest their scarce tax dollars in economic development since they receive virtually none of the benefit that might be generated by that development. That is, a successful development project in the downtown area may increase the property tax base. That may provide a little bit of further property tax relief for all property owners, but it will not directly add anything to the city's operating revenues. The state as a whole may be better off, especially if the project generates more sales tax revenue or other tax revenue. But then we are back to our old question: why should any one city want to pay for a benefit that goes to the state as a whole?

According to one study, the ten most important industrial incentives are the following: tax exemption or moratorium on land improvements; tax exemption or moratorium on capital improvements; tax exemptions on manufacturer's inventories; corporate income tax exemption; industrial bond financing; tax exemption or moratorium on equipment and machinery; accelerated depreciation; sales/use exemption on new equipment; state-supported training of industrial employees; tax exemption on raw materials used in manufacturing.[34] Texas offers most of these incentives to its industry; Indiana offers only a few of them. Yet, if we were to look at the financial assistance packages overall that are offered by Texas and Indiana, we would find that they are rather comparable. We would then expect that Indiana and Texas should be fairly well matched as economic competitors. But this is far from being the case, as we recall the major successes of Texas in attracting and creating industry. As the 1979 COSMA study showed, Texas was able to win 243,000 manufacturing jobs in the ten-year period from 1968–78 while Indiana was able to win less than 10% of that figure in that same time period, about 21,000 manufacturing jobs.[35] The simplest explanation for this is that success breeds success. That is, it is easier, all other things being equal, for an industry to move to a booming area and to do well than to move to an area in industrial decline and do well. In a declining area, there are just not as many spontaneous opportunities to make a profit. It is more difficult to put together the critical mass needed for rapid economic development.

It would be dishonest to leave the impression that all is coming up roses in Texas. There are major problems that are part of rapid economic development. Inflation is one of them. Currently the cost of living in Texas's major cities is below the national average. But that can change rather quickly as housing shortages develop. Likewise, a rapid influx of strangers into a state generates a high level of social *anomie:* isolation, alienation, rootlessness, distrust, all of which shows up in crime statistics, violent crimes in particular. Thus, the most violent cities in the United States today are not New York, Chicago, or Detroit but Houston, Dallas, Phoenix, and Miami—all cities of the Sunbelt. Finally, while energy is a critical factor in virtually all industrial processes, it is clear that water is the second most critical factor in many industrial processes. The North is blessed with abundant supplies of fresh water, which is why industry was initially so heavily concentrated in the North. In the final analysis that may be what anchors remaining industry to the Frostbelt and provides the natural resources for some level of industrial revitalization. A prolonged drought in north Texas during 1980 vividly reminded residents there of the limited resiliency of nature. There is only a certain level of water that is annually available in the area. That water can only support a certain population level, a certain level of industrial activity, and a certain level of agriculture. It is predictable that as those limits are reached, there will be conflict as choices have to be made among greener golf courses, juicier fruit, and more intense industrial development.

In the meantime, Indiana is continuing to develop new policies for the economic revitalization of the state. In 1980, there was a downward adjustment in the personal income tax rate from 2.0% to 1.9%. It was also decided that the intangibles tax should be phased out over a fifteen-year period. A new act provides for property tax reductions for resource recovery systems. Also, property will be exempted from sales and use tax when it is delivered to a person in Indiana for the sole purpose of processing it in some way and then it is subsequently shipped out of state. Also, there has been some expansion of property tax abatement. New legislation allows for a ten-year partial property tax abatement in designated areas in all Indiana cities and towns for the renovation or construction of facilities.

In 1981, Lieutenant Governor John Mutz proposed an economic revitalization package. Several significant policies were part of that package. The Senate Enrolled Act 250 established the Industrial Training Program, the chief purpose of which was to provide assistance to new or expanding industries for the training, retraining, or upgrading of the skills of potential employees. A fund will be established that will be used exclusively for industrial prospects that will locate new or expanded facilities in Indiana.[36] The House Enrolled Act 1640 creates the Industrial Sewer Set-Aside Fund to provide grants or loans to municipalities or counties for the engineering and construction of sewer lines to new and expanding industry.[37] The House Enrolled Act 1767 creates the Industrial Highway Set-Aside Fund to provide loans and grants to local governments to build or improve access roads to new or expanding industrial facilities.[38] The House Enrolled Act 1284 creates the Corporation for Innovation Development. A tax credit is provided for private investment in the Corporation. With these funds, the Corporation will: (a) invest in newly established Small Business Investment Companies, (b) provide equity and loan financing to established industries which may be slightly larger than those eligible for financing from SBIC's, (c) make direct investments in new business, providing "seed capital" to entrepreneurs who are just beginning production and marketing activities.[39] The House Enrolled Act 1817 amends the current ten-year property tax deduction for the rehabilitation or redevelopment of real property in urban development areas to include a five-year property tax deduction for owners of new manufacturing equipment in urban development areas.[40] Senate Enrolled Act 172 creates the Commission on Enterprise Zones whose purpose is to explore the development of business and industry in depressed areas of Indiana through relaxed governmental controls in these parts.[41]

It would take us too far afield to comment on each of the proposals in the Orr/Mutz Economic Development Package. Consequently, some general observations will have to suffice. First, it seems from our analysis that state economic development policies can only be effective within a somewhat circumscribed area. The economies of all the states are caught up in the swirl of larger national and international economic currents. Over these, the states have no control and probably very little protective ability. The Midwest cannot economically dissociate itself from the distress in the auto industry. Likewise, the random dispersal of natural resources, such as water and energy, can have significant consequences for economies, yet hardly be amenable to the ministrations of economic policies.

Secondly, we must pay heed to what some policy analysts have dubbed "the tiptoe effect" as that might be exemplified in state efforts at economic development.[42] This is a phenomenon that we are all familiar with in ordinary life. A crowd of people are standing on the sidelines watching a football game. Someone in the second row decides that he would like a slightly better view, and so he stands on his tiptoes. If the person in the third row wants to maintain the quality of vision he originally had, then he will have to stand on his tiptoes, i.e., pay a certain price in discomfort just to maintain the comfortable view he had before. This goes on until virtually the whole crowd is on its tiptoes, all uncomfortable, and almost no one any better off than he was originally. This is what economists call "defensive expenditures." The fifty states can easily put themselves in this predicament in their efforts at economic development. That is, one state offers tax or other incentives in order to induce industries to move to the state. It quickly becomes clear that other states will have to match those incentives or risk losing the industry they already have. Perhaps they have already lost some and must now entice some industries from other states. The logical conclusion of the process is to take states to the point where they have nothing more that they can offer. At that point the economic pain borne by each of the states is rather intense, yet they will be no better off in terms of their level of economic development than they were at the beginning of this process. Everyone will be running harder just to stay in place. This could be written off as an interesting aberrant political phenomenon, except for the fact that real resources, scarce resources, are being used to bring about this state of affairs.

Thirdly, it is far from clear that state-offered tax inducements play a major role in the locational decisions of industry. There are several reasons for this. First, state and local taxes are not a major business cost. Roger Vaughan cites a study by the Federal Reserve Bank of Boston that found "that the average U.S. business paid 4.4.% of its income to state and local governments."[43] Second, firms that have plants in many states are able to spread their taxable income among those states with the result that tax differences among the states are of negligible significance so far as the total profit picture for the company is concerned.[44] Third, what does seem to count most in corporate locational decisions are more traditional business criteria: quality of the work force, labor costs, transportation, closeness to markets and suppliers, urban support facilities (sewers, water, streets, power, and so on), and quality of community life. If this is so, then this suggests that cities and states that give large tax breaks to induce a firm to open a new plant in their location may win an economic battle but lose the economic development war. That is, they may erode their tax resources to such an extent that they will be unable to maintain adequately their infrastructures with the result that their long-run economic development potential will be seriously undermined. Vaughan, for example, cites the case of St. Louis, which has exempted over $1 billion worth of real estate, half the city's property tax base.[45] What this third point also implies is that tax inducements are superfluous for many companies that are moving or opening a new plant, but they will certainly take whatever they can get. Again, Vaughan cites the case of a bicarbonate plant that received a 12-year property tax break for moving to Seneca County, Ohio. The controller was quoted as saying, "The tax abatement was a nice kicker on the end, but we chose Ohio mainly because of its strategic location and market growth."[46]

There are other cautions that must be noted with respect to tax incentives. Chief among these is the issue of equity or fairness. Generally, it is much more difficult for firms that are already within a state to get the same sort of tax breaks as firms that are considering moving to a state. In some cases, this results in tax burdens being shifted to those companies and individuals who are already rooted in the state. In effect, some companies will be subsidizing their business competitors. This is clearly unfair. But it may also prove to be counter-productive if it generates a sufficient level of dissatisfaction in the local business community.

A second caution with respect to tax incentives is its effect on adjacent states. Though we have talked much about the economic competition between the Frostbelt and the Sunbelt, the fact is that there can be little direct rivalry between Texas and Indiana. The results of recent research show that the most intense economic rivalry occurs among states that are adjacent to one another. In the case of Indiana, we see our chief economic competitor as Michigan. More candidly, we see Michigan as our most vulnerable economic competitor because their business climate rating is so much worse than our own. Hence, there may be a real opportunity there to lure industry from Michigan to Indiana. But if we do this by means of tax incentives or other state-funded inducements, then we may all be worse off rather than better off. This is, between the two states there is no net increase in the number of jobs. There is just a shifting of jobs from one locale to another. That hardly deserves to be called economic development. Futhermore, when the two states are taken together, there will be a net decrease in their tax resources, the resources that they both need to carry on the business of state government and to meet the needs of their citizens. Again, that state of affairs hardly seems worthy of being called economic development.

This brings us to our fourth general observation about state policies with respect to economic development; namely, that some rather careful thinking needs to be done about policy priorities within the state. State political leaders regularly declare that economic development is their number one policy priority. Certainly there is nothing intrinsically wrong with this choice. Economic development is a public good, and thus, a legitimate activity for state governments. More precisely, we should say that economic development is a legitimate state function when a *public* good is protected or produced, and when circumstances are such that the private sector cannot be relied upon to produce or protect that good. Still, government is not a business enterprise. Its task includes protecting and producing a broad range of public goods, including a large number of social welfare goods which may not simply be ignored for the sake of making more resources available for economic development. An example of this sort of problem may be culled from the 1982 session of the Indiana legislature. The federal government reduced by 35% Title XX funds to the state of Indiana. Those funds, made available as the twentieth amendment to the Social Security Act, support a broad range of social welfare programs that serve people who could be described from an economist's point of view as our "least productive" citizens. Since Title XX requires matching funds from the state, several legislators proposed that the state should match the reductions by the federal government and reduce the state commitment to the program by 35% as well. If that kind of decision is what follows from making economic development our number one policy priority, then we ought to reconsider whether economic development is really a worthy objective of state policy.

Fifth, there is some reason to be hopeful about the ultimate utility of state-based approaches to economic development. It seems that federal approaches to economic development are almost of necessity misdirected and inefficient. That is, in the interest of uniformity across regions and across states shot-gun policies are adopted by the federal government, e.g., broad tax incentives, easier access to capital, public works programs. No doubt this achieves some economic benefits, but this is an inefficient way to do it. If possible, a more precise targeting of economic development policies would be desirable. The individual states would seem to be well suited to carry out this role. In this regard, the new federalism shows some real promise. But in order for this to work, some misguided state economic development policies of the past must be given up. One, in particular, is the practice of "smoke-stack chasing," trying to lure factories from other states to locate in our state. Substantial research shows that this is one of the most inefficient approaches to state economic development. There are just not that many footloose factories around, especially large factories that employ 1,000 or more people. Moreover, this is not genuine job creation; this is just job relocation. What current research shows is that genuine job creation occurs for the most part in small firms that employ fewer than 20 people. Over 66% of all new jobs in the United States are created by such firms.[47] Furthermore, young firms (less than four years old) create more than 80% of the replacement jobs in the United States.[48] Also, there are large regional differences worth noting. Virtually all net new jobs in the Northeast are created by small businesses, compared to 66% in the Midwest and 54% in the South.[49] Small businesses share a number of critical features in common. They are notoriously risky affairs. Half will not survive their first year of operation. Only 20% will see their fifth birthday. Yet they are the chief source of America's economic vitality. What are the critical needs they share in common? They need equity capital (as opposed to debt capital) and managerial/technical assistance. Here in Indiana, the creation of the Corporation for Innovation Development in 1981 to provide venture capital for just such small businesses seems most opportune. The value of this approach to economic development is that it can break us out of a zero-sum economic game. That is, we can all be better off because the jobs that are created in Indiana by this mechanism take nothing away from Michigan or any other state. This approach to economic development allows for thousands of little economic experiments that do not necessarily conflict with one another and that are appropriate to the particular circumstances of a given locale. It is just this sort of diversity that cannot be easily and efficiently supported at the federal level. As Neal Pierce observes, "A state government is in a much better position than the federal government to have a thorough grasp of the economics and special conditions of any area of its state and to provide on-going, special assistance."[50]

The sixth and concluding point has to do with the plight of cities under state economic development policies in the era of the new federalism. Over the past three decades, cities in the United States have sought and received direct financial assistance from the federal government.

This was something that they had to do because most states were dominated by rural state legislators who were less than sympathetic to the needs of their cities. The federal government could not afford to be deaf to the pleas of the cities because it was clear that cities were critical to the economic life of the nation as a whole. Initially, the problems of our cities were growing pains. We were rapidly becoming an urbanized society. Currently, the major problems of cities, especially older industrial cities in the Northeast and Midwest, have to do with aging and contraction. The urban areas in which they are located may be growing, but the cities themselves are being economically strangled by their suburbs. Our cities have become havens for the nation's poor. Between 1962 and 1978, 56% of all new manufacturing jobs were established outside metropolitan areas.[51] The number of poor central city blacks has grown dramatically, from 3.1 million in 1969 to 4.3 million in 1977.[52] "For every household with incomes exceeding $15,000 which entered central cities between March 1975 and March 1978, three households left. Between 1970 and 1978, this net outmigration resulted in a loss of nearly $65 billion in disposable personal income to the nation's cities."[53]

The preceding statistics came from one of the reports of The President's Commission for a National Agenda for the Eighties. Their report recognized that federal urban policy could no longer afford to bypass and ignore the states. Yet at the same time, they realized that "only a very few states currently are willing or politically disposed to assume significantly greater responsibilities for cities in their jurisdictions, despite their increased capability to do so."[54] The Commission recommended that the states work vigorously to modernize the structures, revenue sources, and the service responsibilities of local government in urban areas. More specifically, the Commission recommended that the states "should allow, and indeed encourage, the revision of local government fiscal bases. . . . They could establish systems of statewide revenue sharing and categorical assistance to distressed localities and encourage metropolitan tax-base sharing where annexation is no longer feasible or desirable."[55] The report of the Commission was issued in January of 1981, just prior to President Reagan taking office. A key assumption of the Commission report is that the states are in fact financially able to assist their cities. The current recession and cutbacks in many federal programs that directly or indirectly aided states call this assumption into question. In addition, cities and states are in competition for a relatively limited pool of tax resources. Legislators in Indiana seem to have recognized this because Indiana cities do not have the power to raise taxes of their own. This is rather ironic in that the thrust of the new federalism is that governmental power should devolve to that level of government that is closest to the problem and the people who must deal with that problem.

A further irony, as noted above, is that cities in Indiana have little incentive for engaging in their own serious efforts at economic development because of the state freeze on the property tax levy. That freeze means that cities realize little additional revenue from successful efforts at economic development, and hence, are no better able to deal with their social and economic problems. Worse than that, cities may incur real costs in preparing a site for new economic development (demolishing old buildings, installing new sewer and water lines), and those costs will have to be covered from either current revenue or the sale of bonds. In either case, those costs will not be covered by any of the future economic benefits of the development itself. Certainly any new jobs that are created are a benefit to the community in that they reduce the level of joblessness, increase the level of local economic activity (GNP), decrease demands on the social welfare system, and increase the level of income taxes. But it is the state whose revenues increase from the income tax and the decreased demand on the social welfare system. The city only bears the *costs* of these improvements.

The President's Commission also recommended metropolitan tax-base sharing as a way of alleviating the fiscal problems of our cities. Clearly, that proposal has the virtue of equity on its side, for then the widely distributed benefits of urban government would more nearly be paid for by all the recipients of those benefits. But just as clearly, the proposal is politically unfeasible in that suburban residents could almost certainly bring sufficient pressure to bear to prevent a proposal like that from being enacted. The Commission's third proposal, statewide revenue sharing, is as politically unfeasible as the prior proposal. The federal government has cut grants in aid to the states by $3.5 billion in 1982 and has proposed further reductions of $9.8 billion for 1983. Under those constricting economic circumstances, it is difficult to conceive of any state wanting to share a portion of its revenues with its cities. Yet, if there is any group that will bear a disproportionate share of the costs of President Reagan's tax reductions and his new federalism program, it will be the poor, both the working poor and the non-working poor. For the most part, they tend to be concentrated in central cities, which only adds to the fiscal burdens of these cities. If programs that provide direct aid to these individuals are going to be reduced, then it would seem appropriate that state-based efforts at economic development be more precisely targeted at these distressed cities. But the Indiana program for economic development seems to fail to target aid in this way. Rather, the aid simply follows and reinforces the locational decisions made by individual companies. Consequently, if companies see suburban locations as being more economically desirable (lower taxes, less crime, more space, less traffic congestion), then the state will do nothing by way of providing incentives for a different locational decision, thereby reinforcing the forces of economic decline that already grip a number of our central cities.

In conclusion, it may be the case that cities have to accept some degree of retrenchment with respect to their level of economic welfare. Cities do not bleed and cities feel no pain. But people do. People who are unable to provide for themselves have a moral right to a minimally decent standard of living. This is a philosophically arguable claim, though as a nation we have made this commitment to the poor for the past fifty years. Perhaps as a nation we are making some new choices and new commitments. Perhaps that is what the new federalism is all about. If so, then let us say it plainly. Let us not use the rhetoric of retrenchment to mask the realities of reneging.

Notes

1. See *Decade of Decision: The Crisis of the American System.* New York: Simon and Schuster, (1980), p 11. Harrington, it should be recalled, is the author of *The Other America: Poverty in the United States* (1962) which focused the attention of President Kennedy on poverty in America, and provided both the intellectual underpinnings and moral urgency for Lyndon Johnson's War on Poverty program.
2. The classic discussion of policymaking at the state level is Thomas Dye's work *Politics, Economics, and the Public: Policy Outcomes in the American States.* Chicago: Rand-McNally, (1966). Dye's study focuses in particular on the effects of political and socio-economic variables on state policies.
3. The growth/no-growth debate is nicely summarized in a collection of essays titled *The No-Growth Society,* edited by Mancur Olson and Hans Landsberg. New York: W. W. Norton and Co., (1974).
4. I commend to the reader's attention a book by Victor Fuchs, *Who Shall Live? Health, Economics, and Social Choice.* New York: Basic Books, (1974). Fuchs is an economist writing about the economics of health care policy. But he is especially sensitive to the ways in which our basic value commitments shape our economic choices. According to Fuchs, economics "can explain how market prices are determined, but not how basic values are formed; it can tell us the consequences of various alternatives, but it cannot make the choice for us. These limitations will be with us always, for economics can never replace morals or ethics." p 29.

5. Michael Harrington, a writer and policy analyst from the political left, has taken precisely this position in *Decade of Decision, op. cit.* He argues there that unemployment in our nation has more serious social, political, and economic consequences, and hence, that our public policies ought to be geared primarily to solving that problem rather than the problem of inflation. See especially chapters 2 and 3.
6. Thurow, Lester C. *The Zero-Sum Society: Distribution and the Possibilities for Economic Change.* New York: Penguin Books, (1981), p 12.
7. *Ibid.*, p 10–11.
8. *Ibid.*, p 17.
9. *Ibid.*, p 20.
10. *Ibid.*, p 22.
11. One economist, the former executive director for budget at the Office of Management and Budget, has argued incisively that if President Reagan's 1983 budget proposals are accepted, the four-year cumulative deficit will reach $550 billion—and that involves granting a number of improbable assumptions, without which the deficit soars to $650 billion. See "The Budget of Oz," by William Cutter, *The New Republic* (March 24, 1982), pp 14–18.
12. This is a claim in obvious need of critical scrutiny. What precisely counts as a "productive" investment? Does a government funded nutritional program directed to helping the infants of poor mothers represent a productive investment or just plain collective consumption? Keep in mind that there is substantial scientific evidence that poor nutrition during pregnancy and the first two years of life diminishes neural connections in the brain, which is correlated with diminished intellectual potential.
13. See Aaron Wildavsky, *Speaking Truth to Power: The Art and Craft of Policy Analysis.* Boston: Little, Brown and Co., (1979), especially chapter four, "Policy as Its Own Cause."
14. *Ibid.*, p 64.
15. See in particular the work of Daivd Birch of Massachusetts Institute of Technology. "Generating New Jobs: Are Government Incentives Effective?" in *Expanding the Opportunity to Produce,* edited by Robert Friedman and William Schweke, Washington, D.C.: The Corporation for Enterprise Development, (1981), pp 10–16.
16. Flint, Jerry. "Trouble in the Heartland," *Forbes.* (March 16, 1981), p 123.
17. Leliaert, Ray M. "Indiana's Industry Climate Best in Great Lakes Area," *South Bend Tribune.* (Jan. 31, 1982), p 1. This article is a report on a recent study by Alexander Grant and Company of the business climate of each state in the union.
18. Peterson, Iver. "Midwest Losing Technical and Industrial Talent as Jobs Go to Other Areas," *Chicago Tribune.* (May 16, 1981), Section 2, p 1.
19. *Urban America in the Eighties: Perspectives and Prospects,* a panel report from The President's Commission for a National Agenda for the Eighties, written by Donald Hicks. Washington, D.C.: United States Government Printing Office, (1980), p 27.
20. *Why Texas Is Growing,* Comptroller of Public Accounts. (1981), p 4.
21. *Ibid.*, p 5.
22. *Ibid.*, p 6.
23. *Ibid.*, p 7.
24. *Ibid.*, p 15.
25. *Ibid.*, p 16.
26. *Ibid.*, p 19.
27. The Editors. "Reagan's Article of Confederation," *The New Republic.* (February 10, 1982), p 6.
28. Lile, Stephen E. "Family Tax Burden Differences Among the States," *State Government.* 69, (Winter, 1976), p 16.
29. *Business Regulations and Services in Texas.* Texas Industrial Commission, (1981), p 21.
30. *Ibid.*, p 21.
31. *Ibid.*, p 23.

32. Leliaert, Ray. *op. cit.*, p 1.
33. *Ibid.*, p 1.
34. "The Fifty Legislative Climates," *Industrial Development.* (January/February, 1980), p 3.
35. *Ibid.*, p 4.
36. *Orr/Mutz Economic Development Package,* Indiana General Assembly, (1981), p 3.
37. *Ibid.*, p 4.
38. *Ibid.*, p 5.
39. *Ibid.*, pp 9–12.
40. *Ibid.*, pp 16–18.
41. *Ibid.*, p 39. I wish to say a special word of thanks to Lisa Gilman of Indiana University, who did most of the comparative research on the industrial climates of Texas and Indiana.
42. Hirsch, Fred. *Social Limits to Growth.* Cambridge, Mass.: Harvard University Press, (1978), especially Chapter One.
43. Vaughan, Roger J. "State Tax Incentives: How Effective Are They?" in *Expanding the Opportunity to Produce, op. cit.*, p 261. A more complete discussion of this issue may be found in Vaughan's book *State Taxation and Economic Development.* Washington, D.C.: Council of State Planning Agencies, (1979).
44. *Ibid.*, p 261.
45. *Ibid.*, p 262.
46. *Ibid.*, p 261.
47. Birch, David. "Generating New Jobs: Are Government Incentives Effective?" *op. cit.*, p 12.
48. *Ibid.*, p 12.
49. *Ibid.*, p 12.
50. Peirce, Neal R. "Local Private-Public Enterprise," in *Expanding the Opportunity to Produce, op. cit.*, p 170.
51. Hicks, Donald. *Urban America in the Eighties. op. cit.*, p 18.
52. *Ibid.*, p 18.
53. *Ibid.*, p 30.
54. *Ibid.*, p 66.
55. *Ibid.*, p 66.